D1528310

Smokejumpers of the Civilian
Public Service in World War II

ALSO BY ROBERT C. COTTRELL

Blackball, the Black Sox, and the Babe:
Baseball's Crucial 1920 Season
(McFarland, 2002)

Smokejumpers of the Civilian Public Service in World War II

Conscientious Objectors as Firefighters for the National Forest Service

ROBERT C. COTTRELL

McFarland & Company, Inc., Publishers
Jefferson, North Carolina, and London

363.379
C85N

LIBRARY OF CONGRESS CATALOGUING-IN-PUBLICATION DATA

Cottrell, Robert C., 1950–
Smokejumpers of the Civilian Public Service in World War II :
conscientious objectors as firefighters for the National Forest Service /
Robert C. Cottrell.
p.   cm.
Includes bibliographical references and index.

ISBN-13: 978-0-7864-2533-4
ISBN-10: 0-7864-2533-4 (softcover : 50# alkaline paper) ∞

1. Smokejumpers—West (U.S.)—Biography.   2. Smokejumping—
West (U.S.)—History.   3. World War, 1939–1945—Conscientious
objectors—United States.   4. Civilian Public Service—History.
I. Title
SD421.24C68 2006
363.37'9—dc22   2006020497

British Library cataloguing data are available

On the cover: Byrn Hammarstrom (left), Phil Stanley, and
Gordon Ratigan (courtesy Phil Stanley).

Manufactured in the United States of America

McFarland & Company, Inc., Publishers
Box 611, Jefferson, North Carolina 28640
www.mcfarlandpub.com

To my wife, Sue,
my daughter, Jordan,
and my mother, Sylvia

Table of Contents

Preface

Studs Terkel referred to it as the Good War. In many ways, the label fit perfectly. On the one hand, World War II proved to be humankind's most horrific conflagration with 50 to 80 million fatalities and wholesale devastation wreaked on the continents of Europe and Asia, and considerable damage inflicted on northern Africa too. At the same time, the defeated combatants— militarist Japan, fascist Italy, and Nazi Germany — appeared particularly dastardly. Japan, goaded by young military officers, began encroaching on Manchuria and northern China as early as 1931 before engaging in a frontal assault on the Chinese mainland half a dozen years later. Italy, led by the strutting Benito Mussolini and his *facisti* followers, rained bombs on Haile Selaisse's Ethiopia in the middle of the decade. Germany, rearmed by Adolf Hitler and his Nazi henchmen in violation of the Treaty of Versailles, enveloped Austria and Czechoslovakia before initiating its blitzkrieg assaults throughout western Europe in the final months of 1939.

All the while, the belief by Hitler and German Nazis in Aryan supremacy and dictatorship led to their dehumanizing of various groups, including Jews, Slavs, homosexuals, and gypsies, as well as their targeting of political and religious dissidents. Indeed, first political and economic rights were abridged, with the Nazis resorting to racial epithets and the meting out of violence against foes and supposedly lesser sorts. Concentration camps housed some of those marked by the Nazis; one early victim was the 1935 Nobel Peace Prize recipient, the left-wing editor and pacifist Carl von Ossietzky. After the war began in earnest, Hitler resorted to his so-called Final Solution, a systematic determination to eradicate those he considered sub-species, particularly European Jews. By war's end, some 6 million Jews, two-thirds of those who resided in Europe, had been slaughtered *en masse* in ditches, fields, vans operating as mobile gas chambers, and death camps.

Millions of others, viewed as less than pure and treated as less than human by the Nazis, were also annihilated.

The United States, like other Western powers, reacted slowly to the right-wing aggressor states during the 1930s. However, the Japanese attack on Pearl Harbor on December 7, 1941, terminated the disputes that had raged in the United States between isolationists and proponents of a determined stand against the Axis powers. After the Japanese assault, the war proved enormously popular in the United States; polls indicated near universal support for American participation in the Grand Alliance that temporarily joined together parliamentary, imperialistic England; communist Russia; and capitalistic, democratic America. Support for the war effort in the United States undoubtedly was enhanced by the improved economic circumstances that followed the lengthy economic depression of the previous decade. The popular media extolled those who served in the U.S. armed forces, making icons of military leaders like generals George Marshall, George Patton, Douglas MacArthur, and Dwight David Eisenhower. Many of the major leagues' finest left the playing diamond for military barracks or even battlefields in Europe or Asia; in their barracks could be found pin-ups of Bette Grable and other American beauties, while the radio airwaves carried Kate Smith's *God Bless America* and the Andrews Sisters' *Boogie Woogie Bugle Boy of Company B*. Along with baseball greats Hank Greenberg, Ted Williams, Bob Feller, Joe DiMaggio, and Stan Musial, some of Hollywood's biggest male stars, including Jimmy Stewart and Clark Gable, received greatly reduced paychecks from Uncle Sam. Back home, the economy hummed along, thanks to the profusion of military contracts, with unemployment approaching zero percent, inflation remaining in check because of wage-and-price controls, and savings mounting in bank accounts, in a fashion never before experienced in the United States.

Both the nature of the Axis states and the strike against American soil ensured that little opposition to the war existed on the home front. This was hardly in keeping with past wars that Americans had fought. The War for Independence had, of course, pitted cousin against cousin, figuratively but sometimes literally as well. A large portion of the American colonial population failed to support the Revolution, with approximately 100,000 Loyalists absconding for Canada or England. During the War of 1812, a group of Young Federalists, angered about the supposed Anglophobic nature of James Madison's administration and embargoed trade, discussed the possibility of secession. The Mexican-American War produced critics like Henry David Thoreau, who wrote his classic essay on civil disobedience, and Abraham Lincoln, then a little-known congressman from Illinois. The American Civil War proved to be this nation's bloodiest, as 620,000 lost their lives in the struggle for the nation's soul; as the war wound on, so too did resistance to it, as exemplified by draft riots that erupted in New York City. The Spanish-American War produced a large number of naysayers, including ex-presidents Benjamin Harrison and Grover Cleveland, industrialist Andrew Carnegie, 1896 Democratic Party presidential nominee William Jennings Bryan, and the country's greatest writer, Samuel Clemens, whose pseudonym was, of course, Mark Twain.

World War I witnessed considerable repression in the United States, a reaction, to some extent, against the opposition to the administration policies of Woodrow Wilson expressed by socialists, Wobblies, and pacifists. Socialist Party leader Eugene V. Debs, much beloved by many Americans, suffered incarceration following his conviction for having violated the 1917 Espionage Act; that measure prohibited "false statements" that impeded conscription or encouraged insubordination in the American military, and refused to allow purportedly treasonous materials to be mailed by the U.S. Post Office. Big Bill Haywood, the legendary head of the Industrial Workers of the World, received a prison sentence of his own, along with many of his fellow Wobblies, for also having run afoul of the Espionage Act. Boston Brahmin Roger Nash Baldwin, later director of the American Civil Liberties Union, served 10 months in jail for refusing to adhere to provisions of the Selective Service Act. In addition, the U.S. Post Office declined to deliver various journals and pamphlets, including the *Masses* and the *Liberator*, produced by the Lyrical Left, the group of cultural radicals that had thrived in various intellectual circles during the prewar period. President Wilson condemned those he referred to as hyphenated Americans, while vigilantes engaged in a crusade to ensure the maintenance of 100 percent Americanism.

World War II, by contrast, resulted in little overt opposition in the United States but rather a kind of era of good feelings in the midst of that terrible conflagration. The mounting battlefield successes, the seemingly righteous nature of the fight against the Axis states, and the generally prosperous economic times in America ensured steadfast support for the Allied cause. Opposition also remained muted because the wholesale violations of civil liberties that occurred during World War I were not repeated, with the exception of the particularly egregious treatment afforded Japanese-Americans and Japanese aliens.

Problems, of course, continued to exist. Racism, pure and simple, helped lead to the internment of some 120,000 Japanese-Americans and Japanese aliens in centers that some referred to as concentration camps. Racial tensions occasionally spilled over in other ways, as when Mexican-American zoot-suiters in Los Angeles were roughed up, and during a deadly race riot that erupted in Detroit, resulting in the death of 43 African-Americans. But notwithstanding the terrible and contradictory nature of such events, unfolding as they did in the midst of the fight against fascism, America generally prospered during the war. After a series of setbacks in the Pacific in early 1942, the tide turned and victory there seemed inevitable. With the German defeat on the Eastern front, victory in Europe also appeared increasingly likely. Heart-wrenching developments, ranging from the Bataan death march to D-Day, still lay ahead, but so too did reports of the recapture of one Asian island or nation after another, along with triumphs in northern Africa, eastern Europe, France, and, eventually, Germany itself. The battlefield successes, along with the perceived loathsome nature of the foes the United States was pitted against, ensured that support for the war effort remained strong.

In the United States, small bands of Trotskyists, native fascists, and conscientious objectors did refuse to support the war effort. The Trots, considering themselves, like their recently martyred namesake, Leon Trotsky, the true heirs to Lenin's mantle, envisioned a revolutionary day that had little chance of coming to pass in the United States. Native fascists, including remnants of the Silver Shirts, German American Bundists, and would-be American Nazis, fantasized about a very different kind of future, in the manner of few of their countrymen. Neither the Trots nor the American fascists were well-regarded. Prior to the U.S. entrance into the war, the federal government went after a group of Minneapolis Trots for prosecution under the 1940 Smith Act, which made it illegal to "advocate, abet, advise, or teach the duty, necessity, desirability, or propriety of overthrowing or destroying any government in the United States by force or violence." Prosecutors, relying on speech and publications alone, attained convictions against 18 defendants. Beginning in early 1942, the U.S. government, wielding the twin clubs of the Espionage and the Smith acts, went after homegrown fascists. The most celebrated case, *United States* v. *McWilliams*, involved charges that the defendants had conspired with Hitler's regime to damage American military morale, but ended with a mistrial following the death of the presiding judge. An appellate court tossed out the case, declaring that the defendants had been denied a speedy trial.

No conspiracy trial was undertaken against pacifists, who possessed an alternative vision of their own, which again was shared by only a small number of Americans. They foresaw a world without war and remained steadfast in their determination to bring that about, even if social ostracism and imprisonment came their way, the latter fate shared by over 5,000 conscientious objectors. In contrast to Great Britain, which warded off a potentially catastrophic assault by the German *Luftwaffe*, the United States accorded conscientious objector status only to individuals whose religious beliefs prevented them from taking part in the war effort, not those who sought exemption based on moral or political grounds alone. The Selective Training and Service Act of 1940 did allow for the assignment of individuals who "by reason of religious training and belief" remained "conscientiously opposed to participation in war in any form" to "work of national importance under civilian direction." From 1940 through 1947, 72,354 Americans were officially recognized as conscientious objectors. Civilian Public Service camps were set up, under the tutelage of the National Service Board for Religious Objectors (NSBRO), which the Historic Peace Churches established. The Quakers, the Mennonites, and the Brethren shared administration of the camps with the Selective Service System.

The establishment of CPS camps pleased most pacifists, but not all. Moreover, some came to view the camps as too tied to the U.S. government and military. Among those who ended up behind bars were absolute resisters who refused to have anything to do with the U.S. Armed Forces and the Selective Service System. Some who served time during the war, like David Dellinger and James Peck, believed in radical pacifism, which they envisioned being used to bring about sweeping social and economic transformations. Their displeasure with prison rules led to hunger strikes and other forms of nonviolent resistance, the kind that would increasingly be employed by various political and social groups in the United States in the decades ahead. Civil rights, antiwar, New Left, antinuclear, and anti-abortion groups were among those that would resort to such tactics.

By contrast, another group of conscientious objectors agreed to the rules devised by General Lewis Hersey of the Selective Service, in conjunction with the peace churches. That enabled some 12,000 pacifists to participate in CPS camps that performed useful functions on the home front during World War II. CPS participants effectively received no pay for their work, with their own families and churches covering expenses. The work that CPS participants engaged in was sometimes dangerous and enabled the young men to demonstrate that they were "not the yellowbellies" many considered them to be. Some volunteered for important medical experiments. Others toiled in mental hospitals and schools. CPS men engaged in agricultural and construction enterprises. Among the hardiest operated at the behest of the U.S. Forest Service, whose operations had been decimated due to the manpower needs of the American armed forces.

This is the story of CPS smokejumpers who battled against the elements, including dangerous winds, searing heat, and devastating fires, from 1943 until 1945. There were fewer than 300 World War II conscientious objectors who served their country as smokejumpers, operating out of CPS bases in Montana, Idaho, and Oregon. But that small band of brothers helped to keep alive Forest Service operations in the Pacific Northwest and thus sustained a recently established program to fight potentially crippling fires. When the war wound to a close, CPS smokejumpers, like millions of World War II combat soldiers, were "ushered out" of wartime service. Similar to many returning GIs, some encountered difficulties in adjusting to civilian life. Nevertheless, in the fashion of numerous of their generational cohorts, the one-time CPS smokejumpers often went on to make other remarkable contributions to their communities, their nation, and the world at large. All too infrequently recognized for their wartime performance, CPS smokejumpers—many of whom came to revere their temporarily adopted state of Montana—were nevertheless members of the recently proclaimed "greatest generation" of Americans.

This book features this one group of CPS men who opted for an alternative to war or a different way to fight. In his fine study, *Fire in America: A Cultural History of Wildland and Rural Fire*, Stephen J. Pyne points to the importance of William James's essay, "On the Moral Equivalent of War," which first appeared in August 1910 when fires raged throughout the western sector of the United States. James, in the fashion of Theodore Roosevelt, appeared to have heralded the notion of "the strenuous life." Also in the manner of the former president, James contended that "martial values" possessed permanent worth. Such qualities, the philosopher insisted, could be replicated through struggles exemplifying "hardihood." Firefighting, in Pyne's estimation, offered the possibility of an alternative means to attaining that strenuous life so celebrated by both James and Roosevelt. Moreover, the conservation movement, guided by Pinchot, was very much in vogue during the opening stages of the 20th century. Thus, "in fire control the young crusaders who staffed the Forest Service discovered a suitable arena for the conduct of the strenuous life," Pyne asserts.[1]

My study of CPS smokejumpers underscores that very determination. However, I offer no pretense of covering the complete story of the CPS, delivering only passing references to other contributions made as America went to war. After all, CPS volunteers served with the Soil Conservation Service, the National Park Service, the General Hospital Service, state mental hospitals, the Bureau of Reclamation, the General Land Office, the Dairy Farm Project, the Coast and Geodetic Survey, the Fish and Wildlife Service, and the Office of the Surgeon General. The story of those CPS men remains to be fully told, with the rich repository at the Swarthmore College Peace Collection awaiting.

I chose to concentrate on the smokejumpers for a variety of reasons. I have long been interested in the history of conscientious objectors in the

United States, and particularly during World War II, when the cause seemed so right and necessary to virtually all Americans. The smokejumpers I encountered proved to be a lively and interesting lot, ready and willing to share stories of their time in CPS, working for the U.S. Forest Service. Roy Wenger, who directed the smokejumpers camp in Missoula, Montana, proved especially helpful, along with his wife Lillian. I conducted a pair of daylong interviews with Roy, whose memory proved astonishingly vivid, notwithstanding that he had already reached his 10th decade of existence and was approximately 60 years removed from his CPS experiences. Those interviews took place at the Wenger home in Missoula, while many additional interviews resulted from the 2002 gathering of CPS smokejumpers in Hungry Horse, Montana. Like Wenger, the other CPS men proved informative and readily accessible, similarly able to recapture a number of the most important memories from their time working with the Forest Service.

Chuck Sheley, the managing editor of *Smokejumper*, put out by the National Smokejumper Association, first broached the idea for this project several years ago. A former smokejumper, Chuck proved unfailingly supportive and encouraging, helping to connect me with individuals, obtaining photographs, and even reading through the manuscript to cull out errors involving technical matters pertaining to smokejumping. My colleague and friend, Dale Steiner, first introduced me to Chuck. Archivists at the University of Montana were helpful, allowing for the release of materials from the Smokejumper Oral History Project Interviews.

As always, I am most appreciative of the support and love that flow from my wife, Sue, and my daughter, Jordan.

Conscientious Objection

The foremost historian of pacifism, Peter Brock, indicates that the tradition of antimilitarism began in the early Christian Church. Indeed, until the Roman Emperor Constantine gave his blessing to Christianity during the fourth century of the Common Era, a pacifist stance prevailed inside the church of Jesus's followers. Particularly key were Jesus's purported admonitions as recorded by St. Matthew in the New Testament. Matthew challenged the Old Testament directive to return "an eye for an eye and a tooth for a tooth." In the Gospel according to Matthew, by contrast, one is urged to turn the other cheek after being struck. Jesus instructed those who had been wronged to "Love your enemies, bless them that curse you, do good to them that hate you, and pray for them which despitefully use you and persecute you." In this opening chapter to the New Testament, Jesus went still further, insisting that the poor were "blessed ... in spirit: for theirs is the kingdom of heaven." Also, "blessed are the meek," who "shall inherit the earth." And strikingly, Jesus declared, "Blessed are the peacemakers: for they shall be called the children of God."[1]

Once Christianity became the state religion throughout the Roman Empire, however, antimilitarism weakened and justifications for Christian support of war emerged. Decades following Constantine's conversion to the faith, St. Augustine of Hippo (354–430) devised the theory of "just war." Augustine wrote, "If the Christian Religion forbade war altogether, those who sought salutary advice in the Gospel would rather have been counselled to cast aside their arms, and to give up soldiering altogether." Rather, war could be necessary, Augustine continued, to recover goods, restore order, and reestablish justice. In referring to the "pagans" whom the Knights Templar were to battle against during the Crusades, St. Bernard of Clairvaux (1090–1153) expanded on Augustine's tenets: "It now seems better to destroy them than that the rod of sinners be lifted over the lot of the just, and the righteous perhaps put forth their hands unto iniquity." In *Summa Theologica*, St. Thomas Aquinas (1225–1274) further refined the notion of the "just war," declaring that it must be waged by legitimate authority in a just cause conducted with good intentions. Later, Francisco de Vitoria (1485–1546) and Francisco Suarez (1548–1617) underscored the importance of proportionality, referring to a proper balance between the good to be attained and the evil to be overcome.

During the same period when the doctrine of "just war" was being refined, sectarian pacifism began to emerge. The Cathars, Waldenses, Lollards, and Czech Brethren all contested the Roman Catholic Church's perception that antimilitarism was utopian. Writing from Prague in 1420, Petr Chelcicky favored "a return to primitive Christianity" rooted in Jesus's "Law of Love." Chelcicky associated war with the Antichrist, while holding aloft the vision of Christian pacifism. His exhortations provided the seeds for the Unity of Czech Brethren, which, in keeping with Chelcicky, viewed war as a necessary byproduct of organized government. In the midst of the religious battles during the initial stages of the Protestant Reformation in the 16th century, the Brethren relinquished their strict condemnation against the taking up of arms in a righteous cause.[2]

New religious groups cropped up, favoring the practice of nonresistance. These included the Anabaptists in Switzerland and southern Germany, where the Protestant Reformation had earlier begun. The Schleitheim Confession of February 24, 1527, reported, "Worldlings are armed with steel and iron, but the Christians are armed with the armor of God, with truth, righteousness, peace, faith, salvation and the Word of God." The Mennonites, who developed from a schism among the Anabaptists, also subscribed to the Schleitheim Confession and its condemnation of war and implicit support for conscientious objection. During the mid-point of the 17th century, the Quaker movement sprang out of the radical wing of Puritanism, with its leader, George Fox, urging that the Holy Spirit or Inner Light within each individual be rekindled. Gradually but quickly, pacifism became a major component of the Society of Friends, with Fox proclaiming, "The postures of war I never learned"; referring to military service, he asserted, "I was dead to it ... where envy and hatred are, there is confusion." Within the first decade of the movement's founding, Fox went still further, stating in 1657, "For all dwelling in the Light, that comes from Jesus, it leads out of wars, leads out of strife, leads out of the occasions of wars, and leads out of the earth up to God."[3]

A more secularized version of pacifism could be found in the British colonies on the North American mainland, with the British Quakers the first of the religious pacifist sects that emigrated in considerable numbers to the New World. The various colonies treated pacifists, Quakers or not, in their midst in contrasting fashion. Other than in Rhode Island and in Pennsylvania, founded by the Quaker William Penn, colonial governments relied on conscription to ensure that local militia forces were adequate to do battle against Native Americans and hostile Europeans. Rhode Island afforded full exemptions to the Friends, but other colonies required military service, payment of a fine for refusal to serve, or the hiring of another individual to fill one's spot in the militia. Actual punishment often varied widely, depending on the community in question or the timing of one's disinclination to bear arms. But property could be confiscated or prison might await those who proved reluctant to join the ranks of the colonial militia.[4]

In the opening stages of the 18th century, Dunkers and Inspirationists, situated on the radical spectrum of German Pietism, also migrated across the Atlantic, bringing their shared antipathy to military service. While the Quakers sought to change the world, the Pietists, in the fashion of the Mennonites, were first desirous of saving their own members and carving out a separate place untainted by involvement with the outside world. The Pietists referred to themselves as the "Brethren," while German-speaking Moravians hearkened back to the long-suppressed Unity of Brethren. They too objected to participating in military enterprises but, like the Quakers, confronted difficulties in adhering to their pacifist beliefs as they continued to participate in the larger society. During the American Revolution, some pacifists suffered the indignity of being forced into military service. When the War of 1812 broke out, local authorities moved to confiscate property held by various pacifists.

In the early decades of the 19th century, peace movements, along with iconic figures, appeared on both sides of the Atlantic. In America, William Lloyd Garrison and many of his compatriots in the abolitionist movement championed nonresistance, while Henry David Thoreau, one of the New England transcendentalists, wrote about and briefly practiced civil disobedience due to his opposition to the Mexican-American War. During the Civil War, many members of the Amish, Church of the Brethren, Mennonite church, and Society of Friends remained determinedly opposed to participating in martial conflicts. Conscription measures in the North allowed for alternative service or the payment of a substitute. Some, such as the Quakers and the Brethren in Christ adhered to an absolutist position, enduring property confiscation and imprisonment as a consequence. At the midpoint of the war, due to lobbying efforts by Mennonites, Brethren, and Quakers, the southern states allowed for a commutation fee to be paid in lieu of military service. Nevertheless, noncombatants suffered many privations, including physical and emotional abuse, with some perishing because of ill-treatment at the hands of the Union or Confederate armies.

In the latter stages of the 19th century, the Russian count Leo Tolstoy increasingly championed nonviolence. The former general and author of the sweeping epic *War and Peace* came to view the Sermon on the Mount as a spiritual touchstone. The gospels, Tolstoy insisted, required peace and an adherence to nonviolence:

> We forget that Christ could not imagine people believing in his teaching of humility, love, and human brotherhood, quietly and deliberately organizing murder of their fellow men. Christ could not imagine that, and therefore could not forbid Christians to go to war, any more than a father, when giving his son instructions to live honestly, to wrong no one, and to give to others, could bid him abstain from highway robbery.[5]

Tolstoyism influenced a small, but influential group of Americans as the 19th century gave way to the 20th. Among the best-known antimilitarists were the novelist William Dean Howells, the social worker Jane Addams, and three-time Democratic Party presidential nominee William Jennings Bryan. However, an absolute adherence to pacifism largely remained the purview of the peace churches. For some, like Oswald Garrison Villard, longtime editor of *The Nation* magazine, ethical and humanitarian impulses, rather than religious concerns, compelled the adoption of an antiwar perspective. Following that same tact were various ministers and others associated with the Social Gospel movement of the late 19th century and the early 20th, who generally focused on domestic ills, rather than those involving other nation-states. Nevertheless, a number of those who subscribed to Social Gospel tenets came to view war with abhorrence, particularly after the United States became involved in World War I.

Organizations like the American branch of the Fellowship of Reconciliation (FOR) and the American Union Against Militarism (AUAM) challenged President Woodrow Wilson's preparedness program and the martial spirit that seemingly imperiled democratic principles. It was left to Roger Nash Baldwin and a small group of well-heeled reformers to create the AUAM's National Civil Liberties Bureau (NCLB), which sought to ameliorate the plight endured by many opponents of war, who were handed lengthy prison sentences, condemned as cowards, and sometimes physically abused by prison officials. Imprisoned for having violated the Selective Service Act himself, Baldwin and the NCLB represented the type of secular pacifism that WWI helped to spawn in the United States.[6] Notwithstanding their efforts, however, only members of established peace churches received the option of completing noncombatant alternative service. Others proved less fortunate, including members of religious groups outside the peace churches, political opponents of American involvement in WWI, and absolute resisters. Forcible inductions into the military occurred, as did court-martialing, and placement in military camps and prisons. Approximately 500 men were court-martialed, with 17 facing death sentences, later commuted, and another 142 life sentences, all eventually reduced.

The inter-war period saw former ministers like A. J. Muste and Norman Thomas become heavily involved in the peace movement that focused on matters ranging from disarmament in the international arena to the cropping up of Reserve Officers' Training Corps programs at American institutions of higher learning. In 1923, the War Resisters League (WRL) emerged to provide support for conscientious objectors whose worldview was not shaped by standard religious beliefs. A small but growing number of Americans, including Baldwin, Addams, Kirby Page, and Richard Gregg, celebrated the practice of *Satyagrapha* or the campaign of nonviolent resistance employed by Mahatma Gandhi in his effort to rid India of British imperial rule. In 1933, the Catholic Worker movement appeared in the United States, condemning social injustice, demanding social action, and preaching the gospel of radical nonviolence. Protestant clergy joined the ranks of both the FOR and the WRL; particularly represented in those organizations were members of Methodist, Baptist, Episcopalian, Lutheran, Disciples of Christ, Unitarian, and Universalist churches. Like their British counterparts, college and university students took the so-called Oxford Pledge, refusing to go to war under any circumstance.

When the drumbeats of war sounded once again, the Reverend John Haynes Holmes continued to insist on the need for a pacifist stance, pointing to the thousands of students who had opposed war altogether until the latter stages of the 1930s. With the Nazi blitzkrieg throughout much of Western Europe, the German invasion of Russia, and the Japanese attack on Pearl Harbor, however, few remained willing to adhere to such a stolidly antiwar perspective. Even the peace churches witnessed young men determining that service to country overrode the nonviolent tenets they had grown up with. Prior to the advent of World War II, approximately 400,000 Americans were members of Mennonite, Friends, and Brethren churches. Their antiwar perspective received sustenance from the peace churches' own traditions as well as from the action organizations long associated with those churches: the Mennonite Central Committee, the American Friends Service Committee, and the Brethren Service Committee. However, the unfolding of international events proved wrenching for many associated with the peace churches.

The Japanese attack on Pearl Harbor, of course, led most Americans to lend their support to the ensuing declaration of war against Japan. That, in turn, soon led Germany to come to Japan's defense, which resulted in the United States becoming involved in a two-front conflict. At the national level, the peace churches remained avowedly pacifistic. The Brethren affirmed their continued belief that violence was antithetical to the spirit of Jesus Christ. The Friends followed the lead of the Quaker historian Rufus Jones in eloquently stating that in the midst of wartime, some must remain determined to support peace and love, rather than violence. But it was the Mennonites who remained truest to their peace heritage. The Mennonite Brethren Church of North America continued to support nonresistance, while 60 percent of draft eligible men opted for conscientious objector status.

Even before the United States became a combatant, the federal government, for better or worse, turned to the peace churches to help avoid some of the egregious problems that had occurred a generation earlier when America entered the war in Europe. The Roosevelt administration called on the Mennonites, Friends, and Brethren to provide financial and administrative support for the operating of the Civilian Public Service camps. Other peace groups, including the Fellowship of Reconciliation and the War Resisters League, were involved with the operations of the National Service Board for Religious Objectors that helped to run the CPS sites. But the Selective Service System, headed by Lewis Hersey, oversaw the entire program, much to the chagrin of the peace churches, which had envisioned civilian control. Moreover, the program as established, like the Selective Service Act itself, failed to provide for secular conscientious objection, although some non-religiously driven individuals slipped by into the camps. There were no provisions for absolute conscientious objectors, who were generally compelled to enter federal penitentiaries. In addition, there was no clear definition of what "work of national importance" entailed, which dismayed many of the men who joined CPS.

Hersey's own stance regarding conscientious objectors proved decidedly mixed. In one sense, he came to appreciate them, and termed CPS an "experiment in democracy to find out whether our democracy is big enough to preserve minority rights in a time of national emergency." At the same time, he admitted, "The CO, by my theory, is best handled if no one hears of him." The frustrations many CPS men experienced proved hardly surprising, if one considers the general perspective of Selective Service officials. As one declared early in the war,

> The program is not carried out for the education of an individual, to train groups for foreign service or future activities in the postwar period, or for the furtherance of any particular movement. Assignees can no more expect choice of location or job than can men in the service. From the time an assignee reports to camp until he is finally released he is under the control of the Director of the Selective Service.

He ceases to be a free agent and is accountable for all of his time, in camp and out, 24 hours a day. His movements, actions and conduct are subject to control and regulation.

He ceases to have certain rights and is granted privileges. These privileges can be restricted or withdrawn without his consent as punishment, during emergency, or as a matter of policy.[7]

CHAPTER 1

The Reunion

"Them sons-of-bitches," he said, opening with his first subject, "was Mennonites and wouldn't fight in the last war — said they wasn't afraid to work or die for their country but wouldn't kill anybody, so somebody, maybe for this somebody's idea of a joke, had sent them to the Smokejumpers. It turned out them sons-of-bitches was farm boys and, what's more, didn't believe in using machines no way — working was just for their hands and their horses, and them sons-of-bitches took them shovels and saws and Pulaskis and put a hump in their backs and never straightened up until morning when they had a fire-line around the whole damn fire. Them sons-of-bitches was the world's champion firefighters."— Hal Samsel, quoted in Norman Maclean's classic work *Young Men and Fire.*[1]

Some 120 people, from brand new infants to a pair of nonagenarians, gathered during the third week of July 2002 in the small Montana community of Hungry Horse, for the seventh reunion of CPS 103, the group of smokejumpers who operated during World War II under the auspices of the Civilian Public Service and the U.S. Forest Service. Hungry Horse is located approximately 20 miles northeast of Kalispell, on the edge of the Glacier National Park. The scenic North Fork Flathead River weaves through the town of 900, and continues northward into British Columbia. Washington state's border is situated less than 100 miles to the west. A shorter distance to the east can be found the Blackfeet National Reservation, which covers some 1.5 million acres and is home to 10,000 Native Americans, while the Flathead Indian Reservation is south of Kalispell, on the other side of Flathead Lake. Fifteen miles east of the reservation, the expedition headed by Meriwether Lewis and William Clark made its most northerly push in July 1806. No larger natural body of fresh water can be found west of the Mississippi River than Flathead Lake, formed by glaciers long ago. Fly fishers, rafters, kayakers, and sailors delight in Flathead Lake's panoramic beauty.

The village of Hungry Horse just skirts the southernmost reaches of Flathead National Forest, which flits along the Rocky Mountains for over

130 miles. Breathtaking ridges and mountains reaching to 9,300 feet are found in the forest, whose main rivers are part of the National Wild and Scenic River system. Over 3,000 miles of streams and numerous lakes are contained within Flathead National Forest, which holds almost half of America's national forest land. The forest boasts the renowned Bob Marshall Wilderness complex, including the Bob Marshall, Great Bear, and Scapegoat wilderness domains. The Bob Marshall Wilderness, referred to as the "Bob," hugs the Continental Divide. In wintertime, black bears, grizzlies, bighorn sheep, and elk mainly populate this terrain, although scores of outfitting and guide services operate in the vicinity. The immensely popular 15,000-acre Jewel Basin, revered by hikers, is located just south of Hungry Horse, which boasts an elevation of just over 3,000 feet and contains one of the world's great concrete dams. Southeast of Flathead Lake is Seely Lake, a recreation spot, with an elevation over 4,000 feet and a year-round population of less than 1,000. A favorite of fishermen, swimmers, boaters, backpackers, and horseback riders, Seely Lake also contains three Forest Service campgrounds. In the winter, snow is often quite heavy, but groomed trails await cross-country skiers, ice fishermen, and dog sledders.

About 30 miles southeast of Seely Lake is Missoula, a city of 43,000, with an elevation over 3,200 feet. Coursing through Missoula is the Clark Fork River, which was named for William Clark and runs into the Columbia River. The valley where Missoula, ringed by mountains, is located, was joined to Glacial Lake Missoula back in prehistoric times. Missoula is located at the mouth of Hellgate Canyon, along the route where Salish Indians went to scout out the buffalo of the Great Plains. Lewis and Clark undertook a similar passage through the canyon, while the Blackfoot and Salish frequently battled there. One of the region's first lumber mills appeared in Missoula, as would the University of Montana. Significantly, so did a research station that focuses on forest fire research, Region 1 headquarters of the U.S. Forest Service, and the Region 1 training center for smokejumpers.

This western stretch of Montana is familiar to many of those who gathered in Hungry Horse in midsummer 2002 for the reunion of CPS 103. Of the CPS smokejumpers—approximately 240 altogether—just over one-third of those men were still living by that summer. Nevertheless, drawn by a sense of camaraderie, history, and, perhaps, their own mortality, over 50 CPS men, along with wives, children, grandchildren, and even great-grandchildren, showed up in Hungry Horse. Over the course of several days, they swapped stories as combat veterans might, telling tales of derring-do involving firefighting operations, filing for conscientious objector status, and wrestling with families, friends, community members, and, at times, their own misgivings and uncertainties, alike.

CPS-103 The July 2004 reunion at Hungry Horse, Montana (courtesy National Smokejumper Assn.). *Front row* (seated on ground): Chuck Sheley, Roman Cwak, Laurence Morgan, Ernie Tanner, Julie Tanner, Lillian Wenger. *Second row:* Clarence Tieszen, Oliver Petty, Ruby Berg, Lewis Berg, Fred Runger, Ray Funk, Betty Funk, Roy Wenger, Tedford Lewis, Margaret Lewis, Geraldine Braden, Ruth Kauffman, Betty Flaharty. *Standing* (first row): Connie Petty, Barb Landis, Bob Searles, Phyllis Painter, Rosa Stone, Norman Kauffman, Margaret Kauffman, Mary Miller, Lee Miller, Thelma Weber, Bill Weber, David Kauffman, Dick Flaharty. *Standing* (back row): Dale Landis, Bob Painter, Weir Stone, Naomi Wollman, Willis Wollman, Walt Reimer, Clara Reimer, Wilmer Carlsen, Ellis Roberts. Attending but not pictured: John Ainsworth, Phil Stanley, Sylvia Stanley, Warren Shaw, Kassandra Shaw.

The comparison with combat vets is not as farfetched as it might appear to be, at first glance. For these are men of the Greatest Generation, who grew up in the era of the Great Depression and fascist aggression, and were present when their nation fought in World War II, involvement that was supported by virtually all their countrymen. Unlike just over 5,000 absolute resisters who refused to have anything to do with the Selective Service System, CPS smoke-jumpers opted for alternative service. Determined to demonstrate that they were not "yellowbellies," they registered for the draft, filed as conscientious objectors, and joined the ranks of the Civilian Public Service.

Most were religiously motivated and many, but certainly not all who showed up in Hungry Horse, came from the traditional peace churches. At least a pair, however, considered themselves to be agnostics but, like their brethren, were determined not to participate in the war effort, either as combatants or non-combatants. But all desired to perform useful functions during the war years, as indeed they generally would throughout the duration of their lives. They sought, in their own fashion, to serve while remaining true to themselves, to their inner voices. That caused conflicts for some, as did the hostility directed at them by others. While most possessed strongly supportive families, not all did with at least one derided as "a coward" by his own mother and others criticized in a similar manner by erstwhile friends, acquaintances, and much of the general public. Interestingly enough, little hostility came their way from soldiers, either those about to head off into combat or those who had already returned from the battlefields of Europe and Asia.

There were other obstacles along the way, including bureaucratic mazes that annoyed or infuriated them. Due to the deadening sense that much of CPS work was "make-work," some considered walking out of the camps and joining the ranks of absolute resisters. Those who gathered in Hungry Horse, of course, had opted not to do so, but had soldiered ahead, in a manner of speaking, in their determined efforts to make a difference and to contribute to the national community in their own fashion. Eventually, that won them grudging admiration from many they came into contact with but not all were won over. Consequently, six decades after their formative World War II–era experiences, many exhibited emotional bruises or wounds that had failed to completely heal.

Now, they came together, holding a series of sessions at the Glacier Mountain Bible Camp in Hungry Horse. After lunch on July 16, a bull session in a large, lecture-styled room was initiated by 90-year-old Earl Cooley, who in 1940 helped to kick off the smokejumper program. Although no conscientious objector himself, Cooley referred on this occasion, as he did so frequently, to the CPS men as "the best fire-fighting crew we had and have ever had since." Then, looking around the room at the aging group gathered, Cooley joked, "They don't look like it now." At present, Cooley declared, the Forest Service could call on 300 smokejumpers, 30 of whom were women. He told the story of one report involving a smokejumper who landed in a big spruce tree but soon fell to his death. "Well," Cooley continued dryly, "here's the carcass right here." Cooley was asked what he had considered when initially informed that he was going to be working with conscientious objectors. "My first thought was I'd better go to the army," acknowledged Cooley, who had already been operating as a smokejumper foreman and a forester. But he recognized that there was nobody else to do the job and soon came to believe that CPS volunteers, who received a monthly stipend of only $5, were as "good as anybody."[2]

A series of smokejumpers followed Cooley to the front of the room, exchanging one tale after another. Alan Inglis remembered one fellow landing astride barbed wire, where he inadvertently began bobbing up and down. He also recalled ending up safely positioned in a large tree, while a compatriot rammed into a small one but broke his ankle and chipped his hip. "We carried him out of there," Inglis reported. "That was hard work." Calvin Hilty called his fellow smokejumpers "a cocky bunch of fellows." He also referred to the so-called "wafflebottoms from the Forest Service"— those who remained safely at ranger stations while others were exposed to the risk of fighting forest fires.[3]

Lee Hebel spoke of a fire along the Montana-Idaho border that smokejumpers battled for seven days: "We fought and fought, many hours, many days." Gregg Phifer talked about the landing of a couple of Japanese balloon bombs. Earl Kenagy remembered the crowning out of a fire along the Canadian border, which resulted in a CPS jumper exclaiming on the radio, "This fire is huge." The Triple-Nickles, a group of African American army paratroopers, were sent in to help dampen the fire. Some 97 paratroopers landed, but the CPS group put out the fire. Nevertheless, the Forest Service issued a report indicating that the COs "had nothing to do" with quashing the fire, which purportedly would have gone out on its own.[4]

Following dinner that evening, another session was held, titled "Been There, Done That." Bob Marshall spoke of finishing college, marrying, and working with the American Friends Service Committee (AFSC) in Philadelphia through a self-help cooperative endeavor that rehabilitated slum projects. After managing the enterprise for 14 years, he moved to Visalia, California. There, he participated in a similar effort sponsored by the AFSC, which led to the creation of the Self-Help Corporation that obtained government funds from the Office of Economic Opportunity. Much of the work involved providing homes for farm worker families in the San Joaquin Valley.[5]

Norman Moody, who was making his first appearance at a smokejumper reunion, declared that after the war he had resided in a series of alternative communities. Later, he had linked up with AFSC in an agricultural project in Israel that was supported by the Israeli government and Arab villages. All in all, Moody stated, "I've been enjoying life." Al Inglis informed the audience that he had learned to fly in order to minister to a series of small communities in North Dakota. But after a spell, he stopped preaching via the sky, reasoning that "the Lord was on my side but not for too long." Inglis left the ministry during the Vietnam War, when he engaged in draft counseling. He too asserted, "All I can say is I'm enjoying life."[6]

Lee Hebel spoke of growing up in north central Pennsylvania during the Depression years. "Times were rough then. But they were rough for our neighbors and friends too." While in the CPS, he signed up to smokejump. Hebel indicated something that many of the attendees at the conference attested to: "I guess it was to prove to myself that I could do it." Although he had one brother serving in the United States Army and another in the Navy during the war, their relations remained good. After completing ministerial training, Hebel served as a congregational minister for nearly four decades. Following open-heart surgery at the age of 65, he heeded the advice of physicians and retired. He still served part-time on Sundays and remained politically active as a peace proponent and an opponent of acid rain. As for his fellow smokejumpers, Hebel declared, "This is the only group that I've been associated with, including clergy, that does not use vulgarity. And I don't see smoking." Then, referring to both himself and his wife, Hebel said, "We're better people because of you."[7]

Dale Landis disclosed that he had been involved with Project Vote Smart, a non-partisan organization that had been founded by Barry Goldwater, Newt Gingrich, and Jimmy Carter, among others. Joe Coffin reflected on the frustrations he had encountered in a CPS camp where only makeshift work was available. He had seriously considered walking out, an action, he recognized, that could land him in jail. Soon, however, a Dr. Conway came to the camp, seeking 25 men to run a mental hospital in Medical Lake, Washington. Coffin not only volunteered for the work but was selected to direct the project. Consequently, he determined "to stick it out in CPS a little bit longer." Following CPS, he completed his education and taught auto shop in the public school system in Montebello. Soon, however, he decided to try to make something out of scrap tires, calling the substance Duraboard. Now, he told those gathered, "This is a place I've felt comfortable with" since his first days with CPS.[8]

Over the course of the next two days, additional "Been There, Done That" encounters took place. So too did panels on such topics as "The Relevance of Nonviolent Armies," "Wounded Knee and First Nations," and "The Economics and Politics of Peace." Reports on "The Progress of the Forest Service Museum" and "The Smokejumper Association" also were presented. Along the way, various participants joined in brief worship and inspiration sessions. But perhaps most significant of all, old friends came together once again, some of whom had not seen one another for decades and others who had attended every reunion to date.

The CPS smokejumpers who showed up at Hungry Horse exchanged stories and exhibited the kind of camaraderie that combat veterans display. That should hardly be surprising even though this was a group of anti-warriors, who had refused to take up arms against their fellow men even in the midst of the most popular war in American history. Choosing to link up with their fellows as brothers might is a common experience for many soldiers, particularly those who serve in combat. Indeed, this is a design of the United States armed forces, which strives from basic training onward to emphasize group solidarity and to cultivate a belief in the need to watch the backs of those in your squad.

Like those in combat, CPS smokejumpers had bonded into a tightly knit unit. They had done so during the war, undoubtedly out of necessity, as soldiers do. They had to endure their own version of basic training in the CPS and then more extensive training as smokejumpers. All along, they appreciated the need to link together to ward off threats to life and forest-land alike. But CPS men also established threads that wove them together due to conviction. In a world that was literally at war, these veterans of peace operations made a conscious decision to say no to all that, to insist that men should not take up arms against their fellow men. Religious and moral principles generally drove them to that determination, which set them apart from the vast bulk of their countrymen. No matter the invectives and ridicule that came their way, they remained true to their principles. For most, that enabled them to adhere to the teachings and the very life of the figure they considered the Prince of Peace. Uniting them was the recognition that their fellow smokejumpers endured similar abuse, possessed a comparable moral perspective, and volunteered to place themselves at considerable risk, in order to aid their country.

Over half a century later, CPS veterans continued to view their fellow smokejumpers as brothers who had waged their own version of the good fight, the fight for peace. Most had remained actively engaged in peace campaigns of one sort or another, as well as additional crusades intended to ameliorate the plight of the poor, racial minorities, and the disfranchised. In fact, many had devoted their very lives to such efforts, although that continued to cost them a good deal along the way. None, however, appeared embittered by the sacrifices they had evidently made and many expressed appreciation for the friendships they had carved out, the battles they had fought, and the lives they had led. They had operated, consciously or not, in the manner Dr. Martin Luther King Jr. had extolled, striving for "a sense of somebodiness" that would enable them to remain true to their principles and the higher spirit they — or, at least most of them — hearkened to in a steadfast manner.

As of midsummer 2002, the men of CPS 103 remained a determined lot, with little pessimism, anger, or frustration involving personal traumas endured or world events witnessed. Given their advancing age, they

Smokejumper Exhibit at Evergreen Aviation Museum, McMinnville, Oregon (courtesy National Smokejumper Assn.).

also were an all-too-rapidly dwindling band of brothers who had long ago made their mark in a manner that few others have dared to. Their legacy for the nation, however, remained in question, as the history of the CPS smokejumpers threatened to pass from the historical record. This was unfortunate for the story of these courageous men of conviction can possibly offer instructive lessons for their troubled nation as they continued marching through the winters of their lives.

CHAPTER 2

The Originator
PHILIP B. STANLEY

Smokejumping, Mono Forest engineer Ray Brieding told the upstart young conscientious objector at Camp Antelope in California, afforded a new method to fight forest fires. Brieding also indicated that the U.S. Forest Service, due to the mass exodus of its personnel to the armed forces, was experiencing a manpower shortage. Twenty-three-year-old Philip B. Stanley thought about his able-bodied wartime compatriots in the Civilian Public Service who might be able to assist the Forest Service. In the process, those kindred souls, who had declined to participate in the military campaigns their country was now conducting overseas, could serve America in their own fashion. All in all, Stanley reasoned that smokejumping "might be a good project for CPS." Stanley was driven, in part, by a determination to demonstrate that he and his fellow conscientious objectors were "not yellowbellies." Furthermore, Stanley believed that existing programs for conscientious objectors were largely "worthless. Rather than work of national importance, we called most projects 'work of national impotence,'" he offered.[1]

After being hounded by Stanley, Brieding finally relented and passed on the names of some individuals he might seek out. Subsequently, Stanley, a Quaker, initiated "a two-pronged letter-writing campaign," designed to entice willing CPS men into the smokejumping realm. He proceeded to draft a note to Axel Lindh, director of the station at Region 1 Fire Control in Missoula, Montana. Stanley also wrote to the National Service Board for Religious Objectors, located in Washington, D.C.; his brother Jim was working in the nation's capital for NSBRO and serving as an editor for the *Reporter*. Phil suggested that Jim contact the service committees to discover if the Forest Service might be interested in employing CPS volunteers.[2]

In his letter to Lindh, dated October 12, 1942, Stanley declared,

It occurred to me some three months ago that you might need men for your parachute fire-fighting corps, either for experimental purposes or to do the actual fire fighting....

You have probably heard a great deal of CPS both pro and con, but a few pertinent facts might be welcome. We are all drafted men, pretty well fit physically, self-supporting, and have had a moderate amount of fire fighting (mostly in the East). The fires we have been on were probably nothing like ones that require parachute tactics and we would probably need more training both physically and tactically....

If there is the slightest possibility of your being able to use us, we would appreciate more information concerning requirements, the type of forests adaptable to this technique, location of the training school, and any details that you consider useful. Of course, if you can use us, the project will have to be okayed by Selective Service and the Friends' Service Committee in Philadelphia....

We are all very anxious to get into this type of fire fighting, and I think it is safe to say that our enthusiasm has passed the fascination stage. So we would greatly appreciate a favorable answer.[3]

Considerable interest was expressed in the proposal, with Lindh writing back to Stanley, "So far as the Forest Service officials here in this region are concerned, we will be mighty glad to recruit parachute fighting candidates from the Civilian Public Service camps." Earlier efforts involving parachuting firefighters had been undertaken but had ground to a halt after the war began. Indeed, the U.S. Forest Service initially turned to aircraft back in 1917, to scout out wild land fires in California. The next decade saw efforts to employ water and foam against such blazes, along with parachutes that sported large cans, paper bags, or wooden beer kegs. By 1934, discussion took place about the possibility of parachuting in firefighters to battle fires in the American wilderness. The next year, the Forest Service conducted the Aerial Fire Control Experimental Project in California, attempting to put out fires with water and chemicals. By the end of the 1930s, the project had been relocated to Winthrop, Washington, and focused on parachute jumping. Scores of experimental jumps were undertaken into forestland in northern Washington. During the summer of 1940, the Forest Service Smokejumper Project began in earnest, with half a dozen smokejumpers stationed in Winthrop and another seven placed at Idaho's Moose Creek Ranger Station. The initial operational jump occurred in mid–July 1940, when a pair of smokejumpers from Moose Creek landed in Idaho's Nez Perce National Forest. Several additional jumps unfolded before the 1940 fire season came to a close.[4]

During the summer of 1940, Montana witnessed smokejumper training, while by 1941, a larger program cropped up in Missoula, where Johnson's Flying Service operated; that business enterprise provided planes and pilots for the smokejumpers. By the following summer, the U.S. entrance

Byrn Hammarstrom (left), Phil Stanley, Gordon Ratigan (courtesy Phil Stanley).

into World War II resulted in a manpower shortage. Few of the men hired to jump that season had any experience battling forest fires. The next year, the situation was graver still, with only a handful of jumpers to be found. Not surprisingly then, plans to put Stanley's idea into operation quickly bore fruit, although Lewis Hershey, director of the Selective Service, wanted to avoid publicizing the program. Hershey was determined to prevent any evangelizing or proselytizing related to conscientious objection.

Nevertheless, executive camp directors from CPS agencies who met on February 12, 1943, discussed how the plan might be implemented. They agreed that an initial batch of 60 CPS smokejumpers would be chosen, with the number to be increased should necessary equipment and financial support become available. On March 8, the NSBRO Board of Directors approved the idea of a "parachute fire fighting unit." Shortly thereafter, Albert Gaeddert, regional director of Mennonite CPS camps, and Missoula Forest Service operatives agreed how the unit would be administered. Moreover, in addition to the first smokejumpers, a director, an assistant, a nurse, half a dozen cooks, and several assistants were to be selected. The Forest Service promised to provide food and lodging for the firefighters, and to house the director, his wife, and a nurse. The director was to be granted access to side camps, which would receive needed foodstuffs and sleeping supplies.[5]

CPS turned to the camps recently abandoned by the Civilian Conservation Corps, a Depression-era program initiated by Franklin D. Roosevelt to put young men aged 18–25 to work in reclamation programs, soil erosion projects, and the like. The CCC was obviously intended to reduce the ranks of the unemployed and to put some money into the hands of their families, for the bulk of their paychecks was directly sent back home, not retained by the young men who were situated in far-flung camps in the countryside. Another important purpose was served by the CCC operations. These young men were taken off the streets of big cities and small towns alike, ensuring that they could not become foot soldiers for the kinds of mass movements of both the far right and the far left then flourishing on the European continent.

The NSBRO singled out 118 men from a pool of 300 applicants, and forwarded that list to the Forest Service. On April 19, the Forest Service chose the 60 men who would become the initial CPS smokejumpers, attempting to choose an equal number from the Brethren, the Friends, and Mennonites. Gaeddert and Roy Wenger, who directed the Missoula camp, helped to make the selections, along with Earl Cooley, one of the first Forest Service smokejumpers. Five men were drawn from the peace churches to participate in an intensive two-week training course in repairing and packing parachutes conducted at Camp Paxson. The site of a scout camp located three miles northwest of Seeley Lake and approximately 60 miles northeast of Missoula, Camp Paxson had been used by the New Deal–sponsored Works Progress Administration and the CCC during the latter stages of the Great Depression. By mid–May, the other successful applicants, many not long removed from American fields or classrooms, arrived at the Seeley Lake Ranger station in Missoula, determined to undergo rigger school and jump training. Although in good physical shape, they required extensive schooling in the art of firefighting. Within a year, the number of participants had doubled and eventually reached 220 by war's end.[6]

* * * * *

On October 8, 1871, two catastrophic infernos raced across the upper midwestern sector of the United States, wreaking tremendous havoc. Best remembered is the fire that tore through Chicago's business district, leaving in its wake 300 fatalities, 90,000 homeless, and $200 million of property damage. Less well known is the even deadlier Peshtigo Fire north of

Green Bay that took over 2,000 lives and eventually scorched more than 3.5 million acres in Wisconsin and Michigan. That fire and lesser blazes eventually resulted in a rethinking of the federal government's largely *laissez-faire* notions regarding fire suppression. Encouraging the reformulation of such perspectives was the U.S. government's growing determination to ensure, as President Abraham Lincoln had earlier proclaimed, that certain lands would "be held for public use, resort, and recreation," while remaining "inalienable for all time."

In the 1880s, Secretary of the Interior Henry M. Teller, at Congress's behest, turned to the U.S. Army to safeguard Yellowstone National Park. The Army now took on the task previously assigned to park administrators: "to protect the forests from fire and ax." This attempt to control fires on wild lands in the United States was unique, historian Stephen J. Pyne indicates. In the process, the Army established federal fire protection and developed mechanisms to manage wild, forested landscapes. These included the setting up of organized campgrounds, heightened patrolling along well-trodden paths, and the expulsion of visitors who failed to put out campfires.[7]

Through 1916, the Army administered national parks, which tourists could frequent as "pleasuring grounds." After 1897, the Interior Department's General Land Office (GLO), on the other hand, watched over federal reserves—first established in 1891—but which long lacked adequate resources for staffing and enforcement. Nevertheless, the department insisted, "The first duty of forest officers is to protect the forest against fires." The initial foresters toiled under the auspices of the Bureau of Forestry, a branch of the Department of Agriculture. Beginning in 1902, the GLO worked diligently to control fires, but three years later, the Transfer Act placed the Forest Service in charge of administering vast tracts of federal land. Many techniques for controlling fires in forested areas, however, remained unsophisticated. President Theodore Roosevelt, advised by Pennsylvania Governor Gifford Pinchot, established the U.S. Forest Service in 1905. Roosevelt placed forest reserves under the jurisdiction of the Department of Agriculture. A series of cataclysmic fires in 1910, including those that burned some 3 million acres in Idaho and Montana, resulted in efforts to reshape firefighting policies.[8]

As millions of acres of land burned in national forests in 1910, taking the lives of 79 firefighters, the Forest Service confronted the issue of how to grapple with this incendiary reality, triggered by natural causes, particularly lightning. The expansion of federal reserves helped create the dilemma of fires raging out of control in wilderness lands. In 1910, the Forest Service determined to tackle the problem more directly. Regular Army troops were among the thousands of men who fought the forest fires, while a man like Ranger Edward Pulaski, who helped to shield his crew as a fire exploded near the Coeur d'Alene River, became a celebrated figure. Firefighters directly battled against wildfires, calling on axes, buckets full of water, and burlap sacks to halt the spread of deadly fires.[9]

In 1911, Congress passed the Weeks Act, which authorized the Forest Service to purchase lands for national forests and to work cooperatively with states to suppress fires on watersheds. Increasingly, the Forest Service spearheaded efforts to control fires in the Pacific Northwest and, in the process, helped to devise national policy. As Pyne records, the Forest Service called on firefighters to protect large sections of the American West. To bring about fire control, the Forest Service opted to open up and settle territories under its jurisdiction. Increasingly, "systematic fire protection" in California, the home of great stretches of national forests, provided a model for the rest of the nation. Shortly following the end of World War I, the Forest Service and the Army Air Service conducted aerial fire reconnaissance in the state. During the summer of 1919, a pilot from the U.S. Army and an observer from the Forest Service joined patrols over California and Oregon. One observer indicated, "No event in American conservation since the Ballinger-Pinchot controversy (referring to the firing of Pinchot by Secretary of the Interior Richard A. Ballinger in 1909) stimulated as much public interest as the aerial forest patrols of 1919." The decade of the 1920s resulted in foresters urging that soldiers be stationed in national forests when fire season approached.[10]

Through the New Deal programs of Franklin Delano Roosevelt, an even greater amount of acreage came under the tutelage of the Forest Service. At the same time, the ability to ensure fire control became more difficult still, with marginal farmland resettled and cutover woods, confiscated grounds, and poor quality grassland incorporated into national forests. Still, the new administration provided more material resources and manpower — available through the Civilian Conservation Corps (CCC) and Works Progress Administration — to bring about fire control. Now, thousands of civilians participated in firefighting campaigns. Those efforts received further support from a building program involving roads, trails, telephone lines, lookout posts, and guard stations. The CCC offered Roosevelt's "Tree Army," which attempted to battle forest fires; altogether, 29 men gave their lives during the CCC's nine-year long campaign.[11]

By the 1930s, the Northwest stood as a testing ground for firefighting, with the CCC proving instrumental in that regard. After dealing with a series of small blazes out west, CCC units wrestled with the Tillamook Burn, a 300,000-acre fire that, for nearly two decades, burned on and off across lands controlled by the Oregon Department of Forestry. The Forest

Service's Evan Kelley, who was stationed in Missoula, Montana, dismissed the suggestion that men be parachuted in to fight forest fires: "The best information I can get from experienced fliers is that all parachute jumpers are more or less crazy — just a little bit unbalanced, otherwise they wouldn't be engaged in such a hazardous undertaking."[12]

Nevertheless, as the decade closed, two types of operations came to supplant labor-intensive efforts by the CCC or other firefighting campaigns. The loss of 15 firefighters to Wyoming's Blackwater fire in 1937 provided added impetus for greater professionalization of firefighting. The Siskiyou National Forest in Oregon witnessed the appearance of the 40-man crew, while the Chelan National Forest in Washington saw smokejumpers undertake initial tests in late 1939. Guided by Frank Derry, smokejumpers operating for the Eagle Parachute Company, based in Lancaster, Pennsylvania, conducted nearly 60 live jumps. The following year found operational tests planned and a pair of bases set up in Winthrop, Washington, and Missoula. Following a plane crash in the Bitterroot National Forest, a team from Missoula undertook a rescue operation.[13]

During the summer of 1940, smokejumpers made nine jumps, resulting in a determination to place 26 men at a training site in Missoula; the crew could operate over an expansive area. That June, a small group of Army officers checked out that station. But within two years, after the United States' entrance into World War II, only a handful of experienced jumpers showed up in Missoula. The next year the same number of smokejumpers appeared, leading to the decision to solicit manpower from CPS camps.[14]

* * * * *

The man who helped plant the seed for CPS smokejumpers, like many of his compatriots, came from a religiously oriented home and a well-educated family. Phil Stanley, in fact, was born in the Ho Nan Province of Kiafeng, China, shortly following the end of World War I, on April 19, 1919. His Quaker parents, Rupert H. and Helen McCorckle Stanley, were themselves byproducts of the American heartland, growing up in the small community of Monmouth near Indianapolis, Indiana. Both were college graduates— Rupert had gone to Inham College, a Quaker school in Richmond, Indiana, while Helen had attended Monmouth College — who were determined to engage in missionary work overseas. Along with 64 other Americans, they boarded the Manchurian Railroad for China, where Rupert served as a YMCA secretary. In China, Rupert called on techniques familiar to the Society of Friends to "reach out for people that are worse off than we are." The Stanleys' three sons were born in China, where, by the mid–1920s, warlords, Chiang Kai-shek's Nationalist forces, and the communists battled for supremacy. While the Stanleys appeared to benefit from the white-skinned privilege common to foreigners of that generation, soldiers sometimes proved ready to target young white children who played in the fields. At an early age, Phil and his brothers witnessed destruction and death, including the shooting or beheading of captured forces. For all three, such experiences helped to shape a lasting aversion to violence.[15]

In 1927, at the height of sectarian struggles in China, the YMCA opted to send the Stanleys home, due to concerns about their safety. The years away from America, along with their extensive travel, made the Stanleys stand apart from their countrymen at that point. The children, in fact, experienced ridicule at the hands of their fellow students, who, lacking sensibilities about other peoples and nations, viewed Phil and his two brothers as somewhat alien. Ridden mercilessly, the boys learned to tolerate it. Following an abbreviated return to Indianapolis, Rupert and Helen taught religion and history at Westtown School, a prestigious Quaker school outside Philadelphia. Then, a move ensued to New York City, where Rupert attended the Union Theological Seminary and Helen studied religious education pertaining to children at nearby Columbia University in Morningside Heights; eventually, Rupert attained a D.D., while Helen earned her M.A. Phil's older brothers Jim and Rupert remained behind at Westtown, where they completed their high school education. Afterward, Jim enrolled at Oberlin and Rupert at Earlham. In the meantime, Phil became a student at Fieldstone, a private school established by Felix Adler, the famed social worker, and run by the Society for Ethical Culture. Tuition at the school, located at 63rd and Central Park West, ran $750 a year during the period when the Great Depression crippled the American economy, but Phil received a scholarship and his father contributed $75 annually. Also helping out was the $37.50 Stanley received from the Blood Donors Betterment Association every six weeks for 500 cc of his own blood.[16]

At the age of thirteen, Stanley experienced the loss of his forty-three-year-old mother, who was felled by a cerebral hemorrhage. Within two years, his father had remarried and Stanley was attending high school at 242nd Street in the Bronx. After completing his studies there, Stanley served as a strikebreaker, which enabled him to save $500. That sum virtually covered his first year's expenses at Oberlin College. Within a short while, however, Oberlin president Herbert W. Smith called Stanley, who appeared to be lacking direction and encountering financial difficulties, down to his office and declared, "Phil, you have one of the highest I.Q.s to ever hit this school. What's the trouble?" Stanley withdrew from Oberlin at the end of his sophomore year.[17]

Since he was 12 years old, Stanley had been enamored with photography. Consequently, he was delighted to obtain a job in a darkroom in Buffalo, developing and printing photographs. Eventually, he landed a job as a photofinisher in Camden, an urban area located near Philadelphia. He also worked as a photographer, mostly involving aerial shots. However, in 1942, the Selective Service called on Stanley, who had been residing with his brother Jim, then in Civilian Public Service. Just a few months earlier, Jim had been drafted and sent off to Patapsco, Maryland. Stanley soon joined him there, while Rupert, who had been denied classification as a conscientious objector, instead received a 4F label tagging him as unfit for military service. As matters turned out, Rupert served with the Friends Ambulance Corps for a couple of years of service in northeastern China. Stanley sought to join his brother there, but was denied the opportunity by General Lewis Hershey, director of the U.S. Selective Service, who did not want American conscientious objectors representing their country overseas.[18]

The decision to file for conscientious objector status made by all three Stanley brothers, with their lengthy family roots in the Society of Friends, was more unusual than might be expected. Lawrence S. Wittner reports that only one in four draft-eligible Quakers sought 1-O classification. Even for many young men raised in the peace churches, the pressure of opposing a popular war often proved too difficult to surmount.[19]

In a curious twist of fate, conscientious objectors like Phil Stanley had to contend with military bureaucracy throughout World War II. Each individual had to make a choice whether to accede to such demands or to adopt a "purist" position that usually resulted in a prison sentence. More than 5,000 men proved unwilling to participate in the operations of the Selective Service in any fashion, receiving jail sentences instead. Many, like Stanley, chose to make the necessary compromises. He sought to remain true to the dictates of his conscience while avoiding legal entanglements that could scar him for life. At the same time, he possessed "a lot of self-doubt regarding [his] own beliefs." As for his parents, they knew little about their sons' determination to file as conscientious objectors until that had already taken place.[20]

During his yearlong stay at Patapsco, Stanley worked in a tree nursery, where he dug up trees and transplanted them. He volunteered for a transfer to a new camp located close to the Nevada border in Coleville, California, which was supposed to be involved with fighting fires and maintaining trails. However, as matters turned out, the CPS men mainly cleared trails at the behest of the U.S. Forest Service. While promised that they would be engaged in "work of national importance," Stanley and many of his cohorts came to believe they were reduced to makeshift assignments of "national impotence."[21]

After being transferred to Colville, Stanley learned about the U.S. Forest Service's manpower dilemma. Recognizing that many of his fellow conscientious objectors were demoralized, feeling like rejects in the midst of a popular war, Stanley saw an opportunity for the CPS cadre to prove something to themselves and to others. Stanley and the other CPS men appreciated "the chance to show our grit." Moreover, once in Missoula, CPS volunteers felt like a new world had been opened up to them. The people of the community appeared "very accepting of us," as Stanley later recalled. At the same time, the CPS men believed they "were contributing something of value to the nation."[22]

On May 15, 1943, Stanley was one of a small band of CPS men sent to Missoula to receive training as parachute riggers. Frank Derry taught them how to painstakingly pack silk parachutes and how to repair the chutes if the need arose. The parachutes had to remain in pristine shape, which required constant attention to them. Within two weeks, the first large batch of smokejumpers arrived for jump training. All, other than the supervisors from the Forest Service, were assigned to the CPS. The conscientious objectors, including Stanley, were well aware of how popular World War II was among the American public. At the same time, CPS volunteers were cognizant of how "very unpopular" they were. There remained a feeling on the part of many CPS men, who were "very defensive," of the need "to prove ourselves," as Stanley recalled. "We had to prove we weren't yellow. We weren't scared. We wanted to do something that was important besides clearing trails. I think it's very basic. Very simple. We had to prove our manhood." Stanley admitted, "We wanted to be able to do something that would get people's attention.... Prove that we could do something valuable. Contribute to the welfare of the country that wasn't destructive, or that involved maiming and killing. I think it was all of that."[23]

The training, which continued for several weeks during a rainy season, was rigorous, involving calisthenics, general physical conditioning, and learning how to jump from planes. Stanley came to believe that the Forest Service was determined "to get you so stiff from physical conditioning that you couldn't even wiggle, and by then you were ready to jump." Relying on a pair of planes, a Travelair and a Trimotor, the men were instructed how to place their feet on the step before jumping out. They were taught how to let themselves down from trees if a hang up occurred. Then, they were schooled in fighting fires, learning, for example, how to dig fire lines.[24]

Before his first practice jump, Stanley felt "scared to death." Nevertheless, he later reflected that because of the extensive training the smokejumpers received, "We would have jumped no matter what." For Stanley, jumping induced "an extreme feeling of terror," but also "exhilaration" once he leapt from the plane. "Everything is so quiet and serene, and you know you've done it. You've been wondering all this time whether you could or not, and you've finally done it. What a feeling of relief." The next jumps were perhaps still more difficult, for by that point he thought to himself, "What the devil am I doing up here?" After all, "I proved I can do it. Why practice?" In addition to wrestling with his emotions, Stanley had another problem to overcome. Due to his height — he was then 6'2" tall — it was difficult easing out of the Trimotor, which had a very small door. Stanley remembered: "I would invariably hook the top of my backpack on the top of the door of the [Trimotor] and go spinning head over heels, which didn't make for a good opening position." On one occasion, he decided to roll out of the plane, but as he did so, the ripcord on the reserve chute was inadvertently pulled, with the canopy remaining in its pack. Worried about getting all tangled up, Stanley "quickly slapped an arm down over (the canopy) to keep it from falling." He then grabbed as much of the silk parachute as he could and tossed it out, watching the air take hold of it. That made the canopy "completely unmanageable. You ... have two chutes sticking out at a 90-degree angle; one catches the wind like a sail, and you just go with it. You ... can't manage them at all. But it was sure fun."[25]

His first real fire jump, when he worked on a crew with Dave Flaccus and Lyle Zimmerman, took place in Idaho. After landing, they worked a full day on the fire, building a narrow fire line to hold it in place. At that point, smokechasers, who arrived on foot, came to relieve them. The men then hiked to the Ranger Station in Pierce, Idaho, where they encountered a ranger who was displeased with Stanley's apparel. Stanley sported denim work clothes that he had helped to stitch together, to the ranger's chagrin. The ranger evidently relayed that information to Fire Control at Region 1 headquarters, leading to the granting of a clothing allowance. Another jump occurred in Oregon where Stanley and his crew had to contend with trees that rose approximately 150 feet in the air. Still relying on an Eagle parachute, which he could easily maneuver, Stanley coursed his way to the ground. Others proved less fortunate, ending up in the tops of the trees, and having to climb down through the branches.[26]

Among his most memorable encounters was the Jungle Creek Fire that broke out on September 14, 1943. As the 1943 fire season began, the Forest Service boasted only a handful of experienced jumpers. Their age or various physical ailments had precluded them from military service, but they now performed the vital role of instructing the new crop of smokejumpers who included Stanley among their midst. Harry Burks awakened Stanley near midnight, informing him that early the next morning eight smoke-jumpers were going to battle a fire near McCall, Idaho. The plane that was going to transport the men, however, was experiencing engine trouble. Nev-ertheless, Vic Carter, Art Cochran, and Stanley prepared to depart, while another smokejumper, Al Cramer, was sent to retrieve an emergency para-chute. By two A.M., Stanley got his chute and other equipment ready. He went back to bed, while Vic and Art shot a game of pool. At five in the morn-ing on Tuesday, they headed for Hale Field, where they placed their equip-ment on board the Trimotor, and were flying by seven o'clock. Slim Phillips piloted the plane, which landed in Moose Creek to take on Art's chutes, jumpsuit, and fire pack. Flying at an altitude of 10,000 feet, the crew, some of whom slept along the way, arrived within two hours in McCall. After obtaining a harness, the men suited up and took off at 11 A.M.[27]

They encountered the initial fire following a half-hour flight over rugged country. A second fire, which the McCall jumper crew had been battling, could be found on the other side of the canyon. The crew dropped Ted Lewis, Asa Mundell, Art Geisler, and Herb Crocker on that fire, before returning to the first conflagration. Project foreman Carter wanted to drop the jumpers at a spot over the canyon. Art Cochran, an experienced jumper who was not a conscientious objector, vetoed that idea and got Carter to let him parachute first, so that he could scout out the countryside. Land-ing in a cluster of trees, Cochran, as had been agreed earlier, waved a streamer, indicating that the rest of the crew could follow. Stanley and Zim-merman jumped next; Stanley ended up in the same spot Cochran had, but Zimmerman landed about 100 feet up the hill and injured his knee on a rock. Ad Carlsen landed in a tree some 300 hundred yards away.[28]

Shortly after noon, all the jumpers had reached the fire, situated about 1,300 feet up the hill. The fire was spreading but as Stanley later reported, "It soon began to crown out sporadically all that afternoon, night, and most of Wednesday." At different points, the fire "nearly got away from us" and triggered numerous spot fires in dense terrain. "A crown fire," Stanley recalled, "can be a truly frightening experience." Three smokechasers, arriv-ing by foot, showed up in the middle of the afternoon on Wednesday. They applauded the smokejumpers and then helped build a trench to hold back the fire. Seven bedrolls had been dropped from the air but were never found. That evening, four McCall smokejumpers were dropped on the fire. The next morning, the jumpers departed, leaving behind the three smokechasers to finish the mop-up. Stanley and the other men hiked 15 miles to the road's end. There, a pickup truck arrived and took them back to McCall.[29]

By the summer of 1944, the U.S. Forest Service opted to house a batch of smokejumpers at the Priess Hotel in Missoula; it was believed this would curtail response time. On one occasion, the crew that was on call asked to be allowed to frequent the Western Montana Fair. That permission was granted, as the fairgrounds and bleachers were located near Hale Field, which housed the firefighters' planes and loft.[30] That year, Stanley participated in another memorable fire jump, which took place in the Salmon River country. Along with fellow smokejumper Eddie Nafziger, Stanley had just returned from fighting a fire and cleaned up. While lounging on a couch at the Priess Hotel in anticipation of some compensatory time, they received another fire call. Their jumpsuits and parachutes had yet to be returned from the first fire site, so Stanley and his compatriot were forced to grab a couple of outfits and head out in a Trimotor. It was already around 9:00 at night and the crew landed at a fire that seemed to be "burning in nothing." Although there did not appear to be anything flammable present, only goat rock and short grass, a fire was roaring away. The CPS unit battled the fire throughout the night, while awaiting a Pacific Marine pump. By the time it arrived in the morning, the men had no need for it. About midday, they began a 20–25 mile trek along the river to Mackey Bar where a Trimotor was scheduled to await them. They were forced to spend the night near the river, with rattlesnakes slithering about. Later, Stanley, who had been breaking trail, reported, "I remember my left foot coming up with a rattler stretched across the trail right where my left foot was going to come down, and I don't ever remember putting that foot down again, but I must have." In the morning, they encountered a farmer who permitted the men to help themselves to the abundance of fruit and beans found on his orchard. One of the smokejumpers loaded fruit in a box on his back, but by the time they had completed their journey, the fruit had turned to juice as his legs graphically demonstrated.[31]

After the CPS program in Montana concluded with the 1945 fire season, Stanley discovered that he and his fellow smokejumpers received "more understanding and sympathy from veterans than ... from non-veterans. The veterans' attitude seemed to be that they wouldn't do it again. A lot of their time was ... they thought ... wasted." Most striking of all, it was the combat veterans who proved the most sympathetic, in contrast to those who had served in a support role. Those who had experienced the true horrors of war seemed to "never want to do it again," Stanley remembered.[32]

Following his days as a smokejumper, Stanley sought to parlay his experiences into a paying job. For a time, he and another CPS man, Bill Laughlin, considered establishing a parachute rigging service in Ohio, of all places. But nothing came of that notion. He was pleased about his smokejumping experience, believing, as he put it, that "we were the *crème de la crème.*" Stanley also praised the performance of the Forest Service, which he contended "did an outstanding job" during the war. He appreciated the fact that the Forest Service possessed "a great deal more respect for life and limb" than the military appeared to, at least when it came to jumpers.[33]

Still working with the Forest Service as the war came to an end, Stanley, ironically enough, agreed in the summer of 1947 to participate in an experimental water-bombing project that the Air Force conducted. Stanley was asked to serve as the project's ground foreman and photographer. He agreed "without hesitation, but with lots of trepidation." The plan called for the Air Force to deliver the planes and flight crews, while the Forest Service offered the requisite ground personnel. Stanley flew twice, once aboard a B-29 that lost its number two engine thanks to a fire, and again on a B-25 that suffered the loss of oil pressure. As Stanley later quipped, the pilot on the B-29 and another military man, believing the ex-smokejumper was "jinxed," determined that "I was not Air Force material." Shortly after the operation began, the Air Force pulled out, causing the project to terminate. Nevertheless, thanks to this short-lived enterprise, a new firefighting technique, borate bombing, was devised.[34]

For his part, Stanley finally left the Forest Service and then worked for a year as an announcer at radio station KGVO in Missoula. Deciding to remain in that community, where he bonded with a group of Quakers, Stanley became involved with color photography, which was about to undergo a growth spurt. Eventually, he became a businessman himself, which proved a less happy experience. As matters turned out, his self-employment largely precluded him from participating in the succession of progressive movements that emerged in the 1960s. Moreover, while Stanley admired Martin Luther King Jr., he viewed more critically the decision by many young men to resist the draft during the Vietnam War by heading to Canada. Undoubtedly and somewhat ironically, perhaps, this engendered a feeling that those individuals had chosen the easy way out, rather than carving a path that would have required service to their nation. Additional change was in store for the World War II–era conscientious objector. After experiencing financial difficulties, Stanley and his wife, the former Sylvia Goelitz, whom he had met during his CPS days, subsequently moved to Flathead Lake in Polson, some 60 miles north of Missoula.[35]

CHAPTER 3

The Director
ROY E. WENGER

Situated at an altitude of 3,223 feet, the pristine community of Missoula, Montana, covering an area early known to the Salish and Blackfeet Indians, contained a population of about 15,000 people by 1943. The town was located on the bed of a prehistoric lake, right at the mouth of Hellgate Canyon; French-Canadian trappers called it the "Gate of Hell." The Sapphire Mountains stood to the south, while the Bitterroots, including Lolo Peak, could be seen to the southwest. The cold Rattlesnake Creek ran northward from the high country, emptying in the Columbia River's Clark Fork situated close to Missoula's eastern borders; indeed the Salish Indians gave the town its name, with "Missoula" derived from the Salish word representing "by the chilling waters." Mount Jumbo and Mount Sentinel approached Hellgate Canyon's narrow opening, from the north and the south respectively. The northwestern backdrop included Squaw Peak. The shallow but rapid Clark Fork, with its bounty of islands, split the town in half. A trio of bridges tied together Missoula's northern and southern sections.[1]

Begun in 1860 as a settlement called Hellgate, Missoula appeared to offer commercial possibilities, with a log store opened and a search for gold initiated. In 1877, the U.S. Army established Fort Missoula, less than three miles southwest of town. First incorporated as a city in 1885, Missoula grew rapidly, thanks to the presence of the Northern Pacific Railway and the Chicago, Milwaukee, St. Paul and Pacific. In the meantime, electricity, horse-drawn streetcars, and a public library appeared in Missoula. So too, in 1895, did the Montana State University (later renamed the University of Montana), with its initial contingent of 50 students. In 1908, the U.S. Forest Service set up a regional office in Missoula. Two years later, the first electric streetcars showed up in town. Favored with broad, maple and birch-lined avenues,

Missoula came to be known for its fine homes, manicured lawns, diverse gardens, and trees. One popular enclave, located south of the Columbia, contained the academic community with homes of the University of Montana faculty, Greek houses, and other student dwellings joined together. An agricultural trading station for the Flathead, Bitterroot, Blackfoot, and Missoula rivers, Missoula experienced a population boom in the mid–1930s, as Americans migrated westward from the Dust Bowl region.[2]

In 1943, the U.S. Forest Service welcomed a new group of smokejumpers to the area, many of whom initially showed up in Missoula. The first director of the CPS smokejumpers camp in town was a thirty-four-year-old Ohioan by the name of Roy E. Wenger, previously the educational director of CPS camp 5, which was located near Colorado Springs. As usual, eager for the chance to participate in anything new, Wenger had accepted the assignment in Missoula, while his wife Florence became the camp nurse. Working with the U.S. Forest Service, Wenger proceeded to staff and set up the camp, helping to attend to lodging, food, training for the jumpers, and the purchase of necessary supplies. He also helped to coordinate operations involving both the Forest Service and the peace churches. CPS camps scattered across the United States received invitations seeking volunteers for the new project. Eventually 120 men applied, after obtaining approval from their own camp directors, a regional director, and Wenger. Then, Forest Service personnel and Wenger pored over the applications, deciding whom to select. The men had to be in good physical health and express a readiness to engage in the potentially dangerous task of fighting fires. Letters were subsequently mailed out to the successful applicants and training began at Camp Paxson, near Seeley Lake, in April 1943.[3]

* * * * *

The fourth largest state in the United States, Montana contains nearly 150,000 square miles, a more expansive area than Germany possesses. The state acquired its name from the Spanish word for mountain, *montaña*, with the Rockies adding their lustrous beauty to this "great splash of grandeur," as John Steinbeck so artfully put it. The Continental Divide moves both north and south, with summits as high as the nearly 13,000-foot Granite Peak. The Divide allows for more temperate winters, milder summers, and heavier rainfall on the western side of the Rockies. Still, unpredictability is often the norm, with biting storms, warm Chinook winds, and sunny skies cropping up when hardly anticipated. Prairie land, numerous valleys, and

Opposite: Roy Wenger (left) 1940 at Ball State Teacher's College.

undulating hills add to the geographical backdrop. So too do the Missouri and Yellowstone rivers, with terraced landscape abundant. Numerous smaller rivers and lakes, many located in massive national forests, wend throughout the state. Prehistoric remains from plant and animal life have been discovered, making Montana a bountiful find for archeologists. But Montana is richer still, with its abundant flora, fauna, and forest land offering great natural wonders.

For centuries, the Plateau and Plains Indians peopled the Montana landscape. Buffalo provided food, shelter, and tools, and resulted in countless battles between Indian tribes. By many accounts, the Shoshones or another Indian tribe introduced horses to the region, enabling the Plains Indians to become expert horsemen and buffalo hunters. The Plateau Indians, unlike their counterparts, proved skilled fishermen and trappers. War parties, particularly featuring the Crow, were not uncommon sights. The Blackfeet made up another major Plains tribe, while the Sioux, the Cheyenne, the Arapaho, and the Flathead were also present.

Purportedly the first white-skinned visitors to the state were French traders who advanced into southern Montana in the mid–1740s. Sixty years passed before other white explorers visited the region. Commissioned by President Thomas Jefferson to explore the Louisiana Territory recently purchased from Napoleon Bonaparte, Meriwether Lewis and William Clark headed up an expedition party that was instructed to gather scientific information about the region. After arriving in Montana, Lewis and Clark spent several days with the Shoshones, discovering that one chief, Cameahwait, was the brother of Sacajawea; that young Shoshoni, along with her husband, a French-Canadian trader, provided geographical and linguistic instruction for the expedition. The American explorers moved over the Lolo Pass, departing from Montana in September 1805. The following June, returning from the Pacific Coast, Lewis and a small party passed over the site of present-day Missoula before encountering hostile Gros Ventre Indians on the way to Saskatchewan.

Shortly following the conclusion of the Lewis and Clark expedition, fur traders, including John Colter and a group sent by John Jacob Astor, headed back into Montana. The Rocky Mountain Fur Company relied on "enterprising young men," such as Jim Bridger and Mike Fink, to participate in the fur trade. Other well-known visitors to Montana included the painter George Catlin and the naturalist John James Audubon. In 1846, Fort Lewis was established; it was subsequently renamed Fort Benton after Senator Thomas Benton of Missouri. By 1850, the fur trade was drying up, with beavers having become virtually extinct. By contrast, missionaries, who had begun their proselytizing among the Flathead and Nez Perce in the early

1830s, continued to seek out converts. Jesuits came, setting up St. Mary's Mission in the Bitterroot Valley, and the Idaho mission of St. Igatius, later moved to the Mission Valley.

By the early 1860s, a new source of enrichment was turned to: gold mining. Prospectors stormed into Montana, with mining camps and towns like Bannack, Virginia City, and Diamond City appearing virtually overnight. The initial annual yield from Alder Gulch was $10 million. As the opportunity for quick riches mounted, so too did lawlessness, with highwaymen waylaying travelers moving between Alder Gulch and Bannack. In response, a secret band known as the Vigilantes began meting out frontier justice, hanging more than a score of outlaws in a matter of weeks, resulting in the abating of organized mayhem. More big strikes—some that proved short-lived—were made, including those at Last Chance Gulch, Confederate Gulch, and Silver Bow Creek. A boom that began in the mid–1870s turned Butte into "silver city."

The discovery of Montana's riches and the flooding into the region of prospectors, traders, and cattlemen alike led to calls for organized government, particularly as so-called miners' courts proved ineffective. An official from Idaho by the name of Sidney Edgerton urged the creation of a new territory in Montana. That decision was undertaken on May 26, 1864, with Edgerton becoming governor, a trio of justices named, and a territorial legislature convened. After first meeting in Bannack, the legislature relocated to Virginia City, where the territory's original nine counties were devised. But clashes ensued with the judicial branch refusing to accept legislative determinations. The U.S. Congress, in 1867, delivered an enabling act for the Montana legislature.

Although treaties with Native American tribes had been carved out, relations proved difficult, especially after promised goods and funds were not forthcoming. The Sioux, in particular, began targeting travelers from back east. After gold mining in Montana began in earnest, the number of attacks on whites intensified, with the Cheyenne and the Blackfeet conducting raids of their own. In an effort to make passage along the Oregon Trail safer, the U.S. government, almost immediately following the Civil War, set up Fort C. F. Smith, the first army post located in Montana. Placed on the Upper Bighorn, the presence of the fort enraged the Indians, compelling the federal government to remove its troops and proclaim the area an Indian reservation.

Nevertheless, the hostilities between whites and Native Americans only continued to increase, culminating in Custer's infamous "Last Stand" at the Battle of the Little Bighorn in southeastern Montana. In 1876, the War Department initiated a full-scale campaign against Indian tribes, especially the Sioux and Cheyenne. On June 17, the Sioux, led by Chief Crazy Horse, defeated a regiment guided by General George Crook on the Rosebud. At that same moment, Lieutenant Colonel George A. Custer headed for the Little Bighorn, splitting his forces en route. The result proved tragic for Custer and his regiment, which was fully decimated. The final significant battles on American soil pitting Native Americans against the U.S. Army saw Chief Joseph lead his Nez Perce tribe into Montana. Beginning on August 8, the Nez Perce fought against General John Gibbon's unit, before the Indians conducted a retreat across the Montana territory. On October 8, Chief Joseph surrendered.

The reining in of the Indians resulted in the expansion of cattle drives, the appearance of cowtowns, the introduction of sheep, and a population boom. During the next decade, the population of Montana mushroomed from around 39,000 to over 140,000. After a five-year wait, Montana became the 41st state in the Union on November 8, 1889, with Joseph K. Toole serving as the first governor. Montana appeared particularly blessed, possessing more than its great natural beauty. Mines continued to pour out both gold and silver, while copper and coal deposits also abounded. Timber remained plentiful.

Powerful figures such as Marcus Daly, F. Augustus Heinze, and William A. Clark, who became a U.S. senator, vied for economic and political preeminence. Eventually, a giant conglomerate, the Anaconda Company, sprang forth, soon controlling electric power, a railroad, dams, forests, banks, and newspapers. The reach of Anaconda, founded by Clark, became so considerable that it was soon referred to as "The Company." Not all were pleased with the emergence of business enterprises like The Company, and a labor movement, often radically tinged, soon appeared. At various points, workers joined the ranks of the Knights of Labor, with its call for a cooperative commonwealth; the Western Federation of Miners (WFM), which sought to improve working conditions in mining communities like Butte; and the Industrial Workers of the World (IWW), an avowedly radical organization that attempted to spawn the kind of industrial unionism opposed by the American Federation of Labor (AF of L). Labor-capital relations in Montana sometimes proved quite contentious, resulting, for example, in the issuance of martial law on at least a couple of occasions in Butte. There too, vigilante activity thrived at times, leading to the summary execution of a labor organizer by self-proclaimed patriots. Laws against criminal syndicalism helped to fatally cripple the IWW.

Controversies of all sorts thus characterized the first several decades of Montana's statehood, a period of tremendous change for the nation as a whole. Rapid modernization unfolded, leading to an economic boom, albeit one that was often uneven, and producing demands for progressive legislation that would safeguard workers, consumers, and the general citizenry alike from corporate excesses. Like the rest of the country, Montana, of course, later suffered markedly as the Great Depression took hold, with demand for its rich minerals plummeting and drought-tainted conditions depleting farm income. Federal assistance, including the building of Fort Peck Dam, roads, parks, and recreational facilities, helped Montana begin to recover. New Deal programs also focused on soil conservation, irrigation, and rural electrification. These programs, along with a general upturn in the national income, helped improved economic conditions inside the state, benefiting Montana's diverse population of 559,456, as indicated by the 1940 census. A good 40 percent of Montanans or their parents originated from outside the United States, with a substantial number coming from Canada, Germany, Scandinavia, and the British Isles. Only small pockets of Asians and blacks resided in the state, but the Native American population remained substantial, featuring 11 major tribes, many located on seven federal reservations holding over five million acres of land. Schools and churches abounded in the state, with the flagship educational institution, the University of Montana, located in Missoula, and both Catholic and Protestant churches, particularly Methodist and Lutheran, plentiful.

With a citizenry often viewed as conservative, Montana nevertheless produced reform legislation of its own as the Progressive movement sought to ameliorate the worse aspects of industrial capitalism. Measures ranged from a compulsory school attendance law to child labor prohibitions, from statutory provisions for an initiative and a referendum allowing voters to grapple directly with public issues to a direct primary provision, and from mandates safeguarding women laborers to those calling for an eight-hour day and equal wages for men and women performing the same work. Other acts set up a workmen's compensation program and a progressive inheritance tax.

Among those representing Montana in Congress during this same period were several figures who acquired notable reputations in their own fashion. Democrats often controlled the governorship, but a Republican, Jeannette Rankin of Missoula, became one of the best-known congressional representatives from the state of Montana. The first woman elected to Congress, she was the only member of the House of Representatives to vote against a war resolution in April 1917, declaring, "I love my country, but I cannot vote for war." Resoundingly defeated during her reelection bid, she returned to Congress in 1941, once more adopting an anti-war posture. Following the Japanese attack on Pearl Harbor, she again cast the lone vote against a declaration of war. She felt that if she, a woman, was not allowed to fight, she couldn't send anyone else. Other prominent elected officials included Senators Thomas J. Walsh and Burton K. Wheeler, both of whom helped to lead investigations of financial scandals implicating the Harding administration. Following the election of Franklin Delano Roosevelt in 1932, the president-elect named Walsh attorney general of the United States; however, Walsh died before taking the oath of office. For his part, Wheeler, who had run on the 1924 Progressive Party ticket, headed by Robert M. LaFollette, later fought against Roosevelt's court-packing plan, but lost considerable popularity due to his isolationist stance prior to American entrance into World War II. Thus, Wheeler, like Rankin, paid a price for his principled opposition to war, with both on the receiving end of brickbats and their patriotism called into question. Others would suffer a similar fate.

* * * * *

In the fashion of Jeannette Rankin, Roy Wenger's ancestors on both sides of his family adamantly opposed martial conflicts, opposing in the process military conscription. Determined to avoid being ensnared in Napoleon's III's wars, they had departed from Switzerland and the Alsace region of Germany. As good Mennonites, they opposed war, believing that "no one should train for or carry out acts of violence threatening the lives of others." They also were determined individualists, tilling the soil in rural Ohio near Smithville. Wenger remembered singing songs as a young boy celebrating the agrarian life: "The farmer feeds them all, the busy farmer feeds them all!" Growing up in a community of 500 like-minded souls— including many Mennonites—who toiled as farmers, carpenters, or teachers, Wenger and the other children chimed in:

> Hurrah for the jolly old farmer,
> The happiest man in the world,
> Whose life is so free from temptation,
> Whose banner of peace is unfurled.
>
> Hurrah for the jolly old farmer,
> Who whistles and sings at his plow.
> The monarch of prairie and forest,
> 'Tis only to God he may bow.[4]

At the age of five, Wenger experienced how fully his family members subscribed to the Mennonites' nonviolent credo. A friend had given him an "attractive red and yellow pop-gun," which his mother placed before him. After the two conversed at length, the young lad planted his toy in the kitchen stove. Mother and son then rode their horse and surrey to Smithville, where they purchased "the most beautiful, gleaming red coaster wagon." Placated at the time, Wenger always remembered the lesson that his mother had so gently imparted: "We never point guns at people or threaten them."[5]

Roy's parents, Joseph and Emma Gehrig, were proud members of their Mennonite community. Joseph's grandfather had emigrated from Switzerland in 1830 and bequeathed a reverence for the land and farming. His son Elias had seven children, including Joseph. Emma's father, Benjamin, came from Switzerland in 1860, soon joining a group of Mennonite farmers. Benjamin was a farmer, but became a preacher, who, in the time-honored tradition of the Mennonites, had been selected by the community to serve as a religious leader. Later, he was elected a bishop of his church, which required a good deal of travel. A brother too became a church bishop in Iowa. German was spoken at home, where few material resources were found but genuine poverty appeared scarce as well. On their good, productive eighty-acre farm, Joseph and Emma raised wheat, oats, corn, and hay, while cows, horses, chickens, and pigs milled about. The chickens furnished eggs for Saturday night markets and, along with the pigs, provided meat for the family. The cows offered milk. The Mennonite community hearkened to the ideal of non-resistance articulated by Jesus in the New Testament. Its members believed wholeheartedly in the notion that one could overcome evil with good. Emma, more philosophically inclined than her husband, helped to impart the idea that "we were pacifists, who should turn the other cheek," Wenger remembered. Such a belief developed gradually, but dug deep roots in his psyche.[6]

Wenger began attending the first grade at a one-room school, Center College, in Smithville. World War I had just begun and Wenger was impressed with President Woodrow Wilson's 1916 campaign for reelection when talk abounded that "He kept us out of war." By April 1917, however, the United States officially entered the Great War, as that conflagration was called in Europe. While some of Wenger's friends were drafted, he was greatly influenced by three early mentors. Jesse Smucker, who lived nearby and attended the Old Grove Mennonite Church, was one of the bright young men in the area who had been asked to teach in the district school. Smucker served as Wenger's fifth-grade teacher. A World War I–era conscientious objector, Smucker avoided conscription because of ministerial duties he attended to.[7]

At the beginning of each school day, Smucker spent 15–30 minutes reading from the Bible. He sometimes began by distributing one of the books from the sacred text to generate discussion. Smucker, Wenger reflected, "told stories in a unique, wonderful way." He read accounts of Jesus's first miracles, including the turning of water into wine. In Smucker's estimation, there were two ways to examine tales from the New Testament. One involved a literal reading of what was written down. The other called for interpreting matters in an altogether different fashion. The wine, Smucker suggested, might well have been cold water in vats that tasted even better than wine would have. As Smucker acknowledged, "You just don't know" what had actually taken place. When pressed for the "correct answer," Smucker replied, "Don't ask me. I don't know." On another occasion, he related the story of how Jesus supposedly produced enough loaves and fish to feed 5,000 people with a dozen baskets of food left over. Perhaps, Smucker indicated, each individual took a piece and passed the food onto the next person. The miracle for Smucker involved the sharing that a little boy had helped to spark.[8]

Smucker delivered his stories from the heart, but in a non-dogmatic fashion. He told his students, "Use whatever story you want." Students like Roy Wenger felt free to do exactly that. Wenger came to believe that the chroniclers of religious lore, over thousands of years, had possibly embellished stories or had adopted similes or metaphors to impart lessons. That notion proved helpful to him when people asked if the Bible were "really true." In keeping with his mentor Smucker, Wenger reasoned that it "was up to us to decide" what the Bible offered.[9]

Unfortunately, following the Christmas break, Smucker departed from Center College, heading for Aleppo, Turkey, to serve as a relief worker. Smucker kept in touch with the Mennonite community back home and Wenger found his letters "exciting. I longed to be just like him." A second mentor for young Wenger was Jacob Meyer, a third cousin and another World War I–era conscientious objector, who was stationed in a military camp in New Jersey. A member of Wenger's local church, Meyer represented camp COs during talks conducted with Secretary of War Newton D. Baker. Some of the COs at that camp, who had been forced into the army and required to wear military uniforms, had also been tossed in prison for brief periods. Military officials hoped — futilely, as matters turned out — that such treatment would compel them to rethink their opposition to war. When Meyer returned home to Oak Grove, the community fortunately proved tolerant of his wartime experiences; some peace churches, on the other hand, viewed with great suspicion COs who had been obliged to put on military uniforms. Meyer eventually obtained his doctorate in history from Harvard, taught at Western Reserve University, and, like Baker, became heavily involved with the Cleveland Council on World Affairs. Wenger's third mentor was, not surprisingly, yet another conscientious objector, his first cousin, Orie Ben Gehrig. Like Meyer, Gehrig later undertook graduate studies in history, enrolling at the University of Illinois. While working for the League of Nations, Gehrig obtained a Ph.D. in international relations at the University of Geneva.[10]

These three role models taught Wenger a great deal, "but especially that if you do your work as skillfully as you can, if you prepare yourself academically to the best of your capacity and if you are patient with yourself and others, you probably have a chance at doing some of the world's important work in spite of the fact that you are a CO." Not all were willing to afford conscientious objectors such a chance, as attested by the abuse many Mennonites endured during the war. Some, as historian Charles Chatfield records, "were flogged, tarred, and feathered." Some had yellow paint thrown on their houses; others watched as the homes of their neighbors, who happened to be conscientious objectors, were burned to the ground.[11]

While attending high school with Methodists and Lutherans, Wenger "knew they thought differently about war." For their part, Wenger and his religious kin "tried to be peacemakers." At the same time, "we kept to ourselves or did it in a positive way." The first confrontation that Wenger later recalled involved an American history class taught by the superintendent of schools, who was a very outspoken individual. Finally, "I could not hold myself in check," Wenger declared. "I said, 'All war is wrong!'" Afterward, Wenger went to see a Mennonite teacher to verify that what he had said was true. That teacher, like Wegner, believed "you cannot take a life, as Christ" had instructed.[12]

Following his graduation from high school in 1926, Wenger had to determine whether to attend college, a decision his parents allowed him to make. Recruiters from Goshen College in Indiana and Bufton College came to visit; Goshen was affiliated with the Old Mennonites, while Bufton was associated with the General Conference Mennonites, who allowed individual congregations to handle their internal affairs. Wenger opted for Bufton, because his aunt and her family resided in that community, and thanks to a recruiter by the name of Boyd Smoker, a friend of his parents. At Bufton, Wenger majored in history, studying under the likes of C. Henry Smith, a well-known Mennonite who taught all the available history classes and was a friend of Roy's mother. By Wenger's sophomore year, his father, Joseph, was pleased with his son's academic progress but reasoned that Roy needed to teach for a while to help relieve the enormous financial pressures besetting the family. Wenger received a $900 annual salary for teaching in a one-room school, which his grandfather had also attended, with an additional $50 coming his way for attending to janitorial duties. He taught all 45 pupils who were scattered throughout eight grades, but hoped to save enough to resume his own studies at the end of the school year.[13]

After returning to Bufton for his third year, Wenger again was hired at another one-room school, Harmony College, where his father had attended. At the close of that academic year, he had accumulated enough money to complete his undergraduate degree at Bufton. Then, Wenger taught at a new rural school, Holmes Liberty High School. He covered social studies, including ancient history, modern history, American history, sociology, economics, civics, and government, from the seventh grade up. After two years at Holmes Liberty, Wenger followed the lead of the superintendent who had transferred to a larger school, Cuyahoga Falls High School, situated in a Cleveland suburb. Wenger taught history and social studies there and also directed the audiovisual education program. While at Cuyahoga Falls, Wenger took a group of his top students to attend a public forum on why the United States should join the League of Nations. The two speakers were none other than former Secretary of War Newton Baker and Wenger's old mentor, Jacob Meyer, the World War–I era conscientious objector. Did Baker recall that his compatriot had been a conscientious objector during the war?, Wenger asked. Meyer replied, "Yes. We sometimes talk about that, but it makes no difference as we promote the League."[14]

Wenger soon encountered another graduate of Bufton, a former high school principal named Lloyd Ramsire, at Cuyahoga Falls High. Ramsire was working on his doctorate in educational media at Ohio State University, studying under the well-respected Edgar Dale. When Dale visited Ramsire, Wenger met him. After receiving his terminal degree, Ramsire asked if Wenger would like to replace him as Dale's assistant at Ohio State. Wenger took the job, which paid $100 a month, and was informed by Dale, "If you take this job, that means you're going for a doctorate in educational media." Serving as Dale's research assistant for a period of four years, Wenger was "farmed out" to teach courses in audiovisual education at Louisiana State University during the summer of 1939 and at Ball State University the following summer. His studies, however, were interrupted by the United States' entrance into World War II.[15]

Once drafted, Wenger had to decide whether to join the military or "a new outfit called the Civilian Public Service." He had been thinking about the CPS for some time as many of the young men in his church and community had already joined its ranks. Dale, a member in good standing of the American Civil Liberties Union, had himself been attacked by redbaiters, but declined to share his impressions about Wenger's pacifist stance. The head of Wenger's draft board, a law professor at Ohio State, was also affiliated with the ACLU and viewed himself as a pacifist. When Wenger informed his faculty mentor of his decision to enter the CPS, Dale warned, "It'll ruin your career." Wenger responded, "You don't really know what will happen and I don't know either. But I'll do my very best not to disappoint you." Still, Wenger believed that his decision was made easier by the fact that both his faculty adviser and the draft board chair, who refused to either encourage or discourage him, were knowledgeable about pacifism. He was also bolstered by the memories of his three early mentors, all conscientious objectors during World War I, who had gone on to distinguished careers. At the same time, Wenger asked his father to consider retaining the family farm until the war ended, in case his draft record prevented other employment opportunities.[16]

Knowing that he would file as a conscientious objector, Wenger contacted representatives from the Mennonite community, the central committee of the American Friends Service in Philadelphia, and the Brethren Service Committee in Elgin, Illinois; he sought to discover under whose tutelage he could best perform tasks for the CPS. He drove to Philadelphia to see the head of the American Friends Service Committee, Rufus Jones, a number of whose books he had read. When Wenger asked what opportunities existed, Jones replied, "Well, let me tell you. You shouldn't be talking to me. You go to Akron, Pennsylvania, and talk to the Mennonites. You're a Mennonite." Wenger then stated, "Well, I am, but they don't write so much. I've read a lot of what you've written." Jones insisted, "They need help. Go over there." So, Wenger visited Orie Miller, the head of the Mennonite Central Committee, who impressed him greatly. Then, somewhat half-heartedly, Wenger went to see Dan West, a Brethren leader.[17]

After he was drafted in November 1942, Wenger, with his all-but completed dissertation in hand, headed off to become educational director of CPS camp 5, in Templeton, near Colorado Springs. Within two weeks, his new bride, Florence Heineman, a home economics major, joined him at the camp, where she served as the dietitian. Wenger replaced Robert Kreider, who was departing for China to work in a relief training school; soon, however, congressional opposition compelled Kreider to quit that operation. Within six months, the opportunity arose to open the smokejumpers camp in Missoula. Wenger's former director proved somewhat instrumental in Wenger's being assigned to direct the smokejumpers camp. Kreider thought that Wenger might be able to get along with all of the different groups that would participate in the new program. Wenger, for his part, considered it essential to treat Mennonites, Quakers, and Brethren alike. The CPS hierarchy, he underscored, "was very concerned about doing that."[18]

Before the smokejumping program began, Wenger and Albert Gaeddert, who had supervised him in Templeton, headed for Missoula to check out the prospective site and to speak with Forest Service representatives. Wenger met Gaeddert in Missoula, before they traveled to Seeley Lake, believing that the initial training would take place there. Pleased with what he had encountered in Montana, Wenger agreed to direct the smokejumper program. Along with his wife, who would help him to set up the camp, Wenger looked forward to "a new opportunity, a new chance, a new challenge."[19] The smokejumping program appealed to Wenger for a variety of reasons. The peace churches, he recognized, had devised a number of programs to enable members to serve their country in a fashion that would not violate their conscience. He later reflected:

> Some men just didn't want to kill people. They wanted to serve their country, just in more socially conscious ways. In both world wars, that attitude proved to be a problem for the military. More barbaric peoples would just kill these people, but fortunately a group of historic peace churches were [sic] able to put ideas together to design projects for their people.[20]

In a letter to smokejumpers, Wenger referred to discussion at a church service regarding "the problem of making our actions consistent with our professed philosophy." One speaker, he remembered, "stimulated a lot of us to consider more carefully the reasons for our actions—to separate and recognize the acts ... we do because of tradition, because of early habits..., and those which we do because of careful reasoning." Wenger continued, "If we are able to recognize the origins of our actions, we may be better able to make all of them consistent with the gospel of love."[21]

Working hand in hand with government forces, the traditional peace churches—the Society of Friends, the Brethren, and the Mennonites—sponsored the CPS camps. Earlier, Wenger had met with the heads of those organizations, along with the director of NSBRO and Lewis Hersey of the Selective Service. The Mennonite Central Committee helped to supervise the camp at Seeley Lake, which was hardly displeasing to Wenger. He, like many conscientious objectors, recognized that the CPS afforded an opportunity to counter negative stereotypes and, at the same time, to prove something to themselves too. Wenger well appreciated that conscientious objectors often felt stigmatized. "It's a humbling experience," he reported, "to suddenly discover that you're way out of line with everyone else." Having to deal with verbal abuse was not easy. Across the United States, Wenger remembered, conscientious objectors were referred to as "yellowbellies." Consequently, "all COs had to develop thick skin. What else can you do when an entire community turns against you?"[22]

Wenger, along with any number of World War II–era conscientious objectors, had read William James's celebrated essay, "A Moral Equivalent of War." As Wenger recalled, James had contended, "We ought to organize ... to develop as a society ... some kind of an equivalent for war." James argued, "This equivalent should be something that would challenge the bravery of the person, something in which ... you ought to ... be able to risk your life in a good cause, and something that would be physically challenging and ... intellectually challenging." To Wenger and many of his compatriots, the smokejumpers' experience appeared to offer the possibility for something like "A Moral Equivalent of War." They reasoned: "Here is a project that is certainly constructive ... we could save the country's forests ... we could save some of them from destruction, and it would ... require physical strength and ... intelligent approaches to this whole job." The appearance of pacifist leader A. J. Muste in Missoula heartened Wenger, while the Bible and the life of Jesus provided "inspiration and guidance," Roy noted. Discussion was wide-ranging, with "a variety of opinions" expressed.[23]

Still, directing the CPS camp in Missoula, Wenger believed, was no easy task. As was generally the case regarding conscientious objectors during the war, any number of individuals, including Forest Service personnel, viewed them "with some suspicion." There were concerns, in fact, that these opponents of war might be "pro–German, pro–Italian, pro–Japanese." Such concerns were misplaced, Wenger reported. "These men were opposed to war as a means of settling disputes, no matter who it might be." There were other doubts expressed about the CPS men, including whether they simply lacked guts and thus had opted out of the military because of fear of combat. That too, Wenger insisted, was hardly the case. Still, serving as volunteer smokejumpers might help to dispel such sentiments.[24]

With the passage of time, a thaw in the relations between the smokejumpers and Forest Service representatives took place. Wenger, who helped to mediate potential problems involving the Mennonite Central Committee and the Forest Service, came to greatly respect the "remarkably fine people" associated with the government agency. They included Earl Cooley, who worked with the CPS men from the outset, and Cooley's superior, Ralph Hand. Wenger came to see Cooley as "a fine person to work with" and as one who was "immensely" respected by the CPS volunteers. Hand too "was just a marvelous person." For their part, many of the Forest Service representatives also grew to admire the smokejumpers, who were receiving but a pittance — a monthly allowance of only a few dollars—for their wartime service. Fortunately, the Forest Service officials recognized that certain needs had to be addressed. They believed that "the way to keep a man in the forest is to feed him well. To feed him, he's got to have good steaks for this hard labor in the forest. He's got to have all he can eat, and good desserts." Consequently, they offered cooks and special food supplies for CPS smokejumpers. Eventually, the Forest Service also determined to address the matter of the patchwork nature of the clothing that the CPS men sported. Subsequently, volunteers were provided with "two pairs of pants and two shirts and a pair of shoes" each year.[25]

As the project began, the first 15 or 20 men from the CPS went to the Seely Lake Ranger Station. They, along with the other prospective smoke-jumpers, eventually went to the Forest Service lodge at Camp Paxson. Wenger later pointed out, "It was the most beautiful forest area I had ever seen and that the men had ever seen." Two types of training ensued: one involved how to jump out of planes, while the other pertained to fighting forest fires. In Wenger's estimation, about 80 percent of the training was designed to ensure that the men were in tip-top physical condition. The program proved successful, with few injuries resulting and financial costs held in check. Wenger discovered that

> not all COs are easy to get along with. They've got these hang-ups about what they can and cannot do. And they've got all these religious backgrounds. Some take their backgrounds very seriously and very literally. But for the most part, they don't. This group of CPS men, this group of smokejumpers ... turned out to be a serious group in half a dozen ways. First of all, they were smart. They were intelligent and did not quibble over small points, especially the big points.

In addition, they were, for the most part, "husky, muscular men who could do hard work." In contrast to many other conscientious objectors in the large base camps, they had desired "a chance to do something more ... [in the way of] direct personal service." They wanted to do more than simply plant trees or clear brush from trees. "They wanted to do something more challenging."[26]

Wenger was impressed by the fact that the men, who had been care-fully selected, had all volunteered for their latest assignment. Consequently, he believed, they were "a step removed from the feeling of being involun-tarily conscripted" and were pleased to be afforded an opportunity "to risk their lives in a cause for the benefit of humanity as a whole." Some small material perks came the way of CPS volunteers, including decent food, a slightly higher monthly allowance, and the ability to accumulate overtime for firefighting, thereby resulting in more leave time. The professional nature of the Forest Service was beneficial too, as was the staff's tolerant nature and evident desire to ensure the project's success.[27]

The Amish and the Hutterites, considered among the most conserva-tive figures in the camp, proved to be among the most liberal in their think-ing, as Wenger discovered. "I mean giving everybody a chance to express themselves, giving everybody a chance to do what they think is best for the group." Dale Yoder, one of the Amish, turned out to be "one of the most accepting and the most cooperative." Levi Tschetter, a Hutterite school-teacher, "was one of the most creative people we had in our whole group."[28]

Florence Wenger was herself an invaluable member of the CPS team in Missoula. Not having been raised in one of the peace churches, she initially "had no idea what these guys were all about." Nevertheless, they came to appreciate her greatly. At one point, Florence decided that she was going to undertake all the smokejumper training herself. She proceeded to do exactly that. Her worst moment occurred when, in seeking to duplicate the experience of falling from a plane, she jumped from a tower, receiving quite a jolt as a consequence. Gender considerations came into play, however, and Florence was denied the opportunity to go up in a plane.[29]

Still, she was highly regarded by the CPS men who passed through Missoula. Many recalled the time when Roy attended a CPS conference in Colorado Springs. Florence stayed behind and proceeded to organize a square dance for the smokejumpers, whom she considered to be "great guys," and young women from town. At least two smokejumpers, Phil Stanley and David Flaccus, later married women they met on that occasion. When Roy returned home, he was "just appalled" at what had transpired. After all, as his daughter Susan Duffy later pointed out, "Mennonites don't dance." Responding to her baffled husband, Florence declared, "Look, Roy. They all had a great time. I didn't see anyone standing around." Duffy considered the dance to have been "one of the best experiences in Mom's life."[30]

In late 1944, Wenger produced a report on the smokejumpers. In rhapsodic language, he declared that "the wilderness has not yet completely vanished from the face of America." Pointing to Montana, Idaho, and Washington state, he asserted that there could be found "the country's last undeveloped primitive areas — vast, rugged, forested regions not yet invaded by roads, stump ranchers, and the accoutrements of civilization." All of this, Wenger continued, "is our country. To us, the Smoke Jumpers, is entrusted much of its protection from the ravages of fire." In addition to the aforementioned states, Wenger noted, the smokejumpers had been called on in Oregon and Idaho, which contained three Forest Service regions. During their first two years of operation, the smokejumpers had vanquished more than 100 fires, saving hundreds of thousands of dollars "in suppression costs." Timber resources had been shielded, but so had the habitat for animals and forest land that helped to prevent soil erosion and ensure flood control. Equally important, Wenger suggested, was the fact that "some of the finest opportunities for soul-satisfying recreation" had been safeguarded. After all, "to Americans the forest means adventure — breadth, freedom, great spaces, fragrant air, clear water, and perhaps a sad but sweet feeling of lonesomeness."[31]

After two firefighting seasons, Wenger departed from Missoula to help supervise the Mennonite Central Committee hospital located at the organization's headquarters in Akron, Pennsylvania. While there, he buckled down and completed his Ph.D. The graduate school at Ohio State was virtually empty, so an entire room of professors and graduate students showed up for his doctoral defense. To his surprise, no questions were forthcoming about the CPS or pacifism. In December 1944, Wenger received his doctoral degree.[32]

The following November, he was discharged from government service. Although inflation rippled across the American economy in late 1945 and 1946, postwar prosperity generally prevailed. That enabled Wenger to obtain a position in educational media and his wife to acquire one in the university kindergarten at Kent State University. Wenger's academic career proved lengthy and highly productive. A longtime faculty member at Kent State University, he served for a time as dean of the College of Education. Along the way, he was a Fulbright fellow at the International Christian University in Tokyo—where Florence was involved in kindergarten and elementary education—and director of the Office of Institutional Research at Kent State. The Wengers traveled widely, coursing through 20 countries at one point as they returned from Japan. Their summers often found them accompanying university students who were off to study at Oxford University, but Florence spent time on her own traveling through Africa. Another occasion saw her participate in an American Friends Service project that sought to ready African American youngsters for school integration in Powhatan, Virginia. Both Roy and Florence were also instrumental in spearheading reunions of veterans of CPS 103.[33]

To assist their daughter Susan Duffy and Keough, her friendly, though mentally challenged first child, the Wengers moved to Missoula, which they considered "a great place to live." Wenger maintained his hopeful nature, notwithstanding Florence's death in 1989. His subsequent happy marriage to Lillian Alischewsky, and his general perception "that much hopeful progress" had occurred since the end of World War II, caused him to view developments optimistically. Moreover, as Wenger asserted, "I believe we can organize a war-less world for ourselves and our grandchildren. Never give up! Peace be with you."[34] On November 30, 2004, the ninety-six year-old Wenger died in Missoula, where he had lived for over six decades.

CHAPTER 4

The Committed

OLIVER PETTY

He had watched the antiwar classic, *All Quiet on the Western Front*, the 1931 film that brought Erich Maria Remarque's heart-wrenching story of World War I trench warfare to the silver screen. "I knew that I would never be able to carry a gun against anyone," Oliver Petty recalled. As for war, he considered it simply "folly." He listened as representatives from the Fellowship of Reconciliation, who were visiting the Corvallis First Christian Church, spoke of what war entailed. Petty, along with four other young men, agreed to sign a pledge promising "never to take part in war, the business of killing." However, when the United States entered the conflagration, the others reneged on their promises, with one accepting a 4-F deferment and three joining the American armed forces. That trio had hoped to enter as non-combatants but soon were handed rifles instead. "I was the only one who remained true to the vow," Petty remembered. His determination to file as a conscientious objector and his involvement with the pacifist Fellowship of Reconciliation would be rewarded with receipt of a 4-E classification from his local draft board.[1]

* * * * *

Petty was born on June 9, 1914, into a farm family that resided in Bear Creek, outside the town of Creswell, Oregon. His Oregon roots were lengthy, as his father's family had taken to the 1853 Lost Wagon Trail, bound for the Oregon territory. His mother's family departed Nebraska for Oregon in the early part of the century, settling in Eugene. His father, Riley Petty, was a farmer, who also served as a part-time appraiser for Lane County, while his mother, Mamie Sheridan, taught at the one-room Bear Creek School, located half a mile from the family farm, and other schools in the area. The family purchased a 1923 Model T Ford for $700, to transport Mamie to work.[2]

Because his mother was the local schoolteacher, Petty showed up at Bear Creek School before he officially enrolled in the first grade at the age of five. When he did so, his mother was his first-grade teacher but his small size hardly did much for his self-esteem. Petty later attended Pleasant Hill Union High, located only two miles from where Mamie was then teaching. She dropped off Oliver and his sister Ethel at the high school, before heading for her own classroom. When the school day ended, they walked to Mamie's elementary school to get a ride home. Pleasant Hill Union High was hardly a happy experience for him, as he continued to suffer from a shaky self-image and experienced hazing by upperclassmen. Eventually, Petty transferred to Creswell High, where his social standing improved, along with his grades. Frequently, he undertook the four-mile journey from home to school on foot.[3]

Oliver Petty (courtesy National Smokejumper Assn.).

Christian values were imparted to the Petty children, largely through the determination of their mother. As Petty recalled, "She read the Bible to us and played the organ while we sang hymns." On the other hand, "If Pop came in, we stopped what he considered to be foolishness." Mamie took the children to Cloverdale Community Church whenever she could. There, they encountered missionary teams sent by Eugene Bible College. Later, the Pettys frequented a Methodist church in Creswell. The children "were always clean but often wore patched clothes and went barefoot." Consequently, "we sometimes took a ribbing" from the better-dressed young people who attended the church, Petty recalled. One afternoon following Sunday school, he stopped in at the Christian church, where an evangelical meeting was about to be held, and was greeted "with open arms." That experience was an important one for Petty: "I was moved to become a Christian that day and gave my life to the Lord. Mom brought me back that afternoon and I was baptized at a special service. Mom was very happy for me. Pop accepted it." Petty became quite active in the Christian Church, which was tied to the Disciples of Christ. He served as president of Christian Endeavor and superintendent of the Sunday school, and taught a class for young people. He also became a deacon of the church board of directors.[4]

In 1931, the then 16-year-old Petty graduated from Creswell High. Having dedicated his "life to Christian service," Petty enrolled at Eugene Bible College, thanks to financial assistance from his church, savings he had accumulated, and funds "Mom slipped to me." Still, afflicted with something of an inferiority complex, Petty doubted that he would be able to preach, yet while at Eugene Bible College he became a student pastor. He envisioned teaching or missionary work as his life's work. Unfortunately, financial difficulties forced his departure from the college after his freshman year. Petty's mother had just died and his father was unable to help finance his education.[5]

For the next four years, as the Great Depression continued to befall the United States, Petty worked in a series of small lumber mills, trying to save enough money to return to school. His brothers helped him learn how to work sawmills and logs. He also assisted his brother-in-law with a shingling business, loaded railroad cars, and held all sorts of odd jobs. One summer, Petty went to Oakridge, Oregon, where he got a job at a pencil cedar mill run by the Westfur Lumber Company. The pay, when he received it, was a dollar and a half a day.[6]

Due to his love of nature and forestry and his determination not to be tied to an office, Petty moved to Corvalis to attend the School of Forestry at Oregon State College, beginning in 1936. He had saved some money, even loaning a bit to help his preacher purchase an automobile. Petty also doled out a loan to his new landlords, who were scrambling to cover the mortgage. He took a room at a boarding house, just across from the college, but within two months, realized that his funds were rapidly becoming depleted. At the Corvalis First Christian Church, Petty met two fellows who rented a bachelors' quarter in the basement of a house and invited him to stay there. He also got work through the National Youth Administration, a New Deal program that provided work-study jobs for needy college students like himself. For two hours each morning, starting at six o'clock, he labored as a janitor on campus. During two of his summers in Corvalis, Petty also worked at a forest lookout in the Bohemia District east of Cottage Grove. At the same time, Petty became actively involved with the Corvalis First Christian Church, once again serving as president of Christian Endeavor and as a church deacon. His commitment to Jesus Christ soon dramatically recast his life in other ways, shortly after he graduated from college. Before World War II unfolded, the Disciples of Christ adopted one of the strongest stances against war of any religious group in the United States.[7]

Petty completed his education at Oregon State College in 1940, having majored in technical forestry and minored in education. Hoping to return to complete a graduate program in education, he was dissuaded from doing so by his local draft board once he acquired his draft number: 68. Having filed as a conscientious objector, Petty briefly worked with the Snow Peak Logging Company in Linn County, serving as a chainman on a road location gang. In June 1941, the 27-year-old Petty was ordered to report to CPS Camp No. 2, located in San Dimas, California, and run by the Friends. The initial CPS camp along the West Coast, it later was referred to as Camp 76 and was based in Glendora. Before he left for California, Petty witnessed his father break down in tears for one of the few times he could remember. Riley Petty told him, "Oliver, at least you will have your hide left when this war is over." Riley's son Joe received a 4-F classification because of a hernia, while Earl served for only a few months before obtaining a medical discharge.[8]

As Petty readied to go to the CPS camp, he anticipated that his service too would prove quite abbreviated. He was less than a year from turning 28, when he would enter a different draft category altogether. The attack on Pearl Harbor and the subsequent declaration of war by the United States compelled the Selective Service to make men eligible for military service up to the age of 46. Consequently, Petty remained in the CPS for the duration of the war.[9]

Preparing to depart from the train station in Eugene, Petty ran into another CPS man from Cottage Grove, Ellis Decker. The two shared a single berth for the full 24-hour ride to Los Angeles. Subsequently, they went to Tanbark Station, located in the rugged hill country of the San Dimas Experimental Forest, situated nine miles outside Glendora. Petty was assigned to study the effects of water run-off through different vegetation on below-surface tunnels. The studies were highly technical and Petty's undergraduate studies at Oregon State College undoubtedly served him well. Eventually, he was appointed to run and supervise lab operations pertaining to the soil.[10] While at the Tanbark Station, Petty slipped on a steep bank one morning, fracturing his kneecap. Petty refused to take any time off, reasoning that he could continue running the show in the lab, perched on a high stool, with one leg propped up and the other wrapped in a cast. "They said I would be crippled the rest of my life because I wouldn't give up and 'enjoy' my broken kneecap," Petty recalled. As matters turned out, it healed and never bothered him again.[11]

Like many others in the CPS, Petty came across announcements of openings for the smokejumper program in Montana. He immediately applied, was screened and was soon accepted. Before he departed, Petty's supervisor at San Dimas, Mr. Coleman, insisted he return to California after the fire season. For the next three years, Petty did exactly that, going to Montana during the hot summer months to help fight fires and returning to San Dimas in the wintertime to work in the soils lab. On one occasion when Petty was serving with a ground crew, the fire they were battling blew up. He became quite frustrated at various points and was reduced to gasping for air. Such experiences led Petty to declare, "I can see how a person could burn to death." Later, he well appreciated what Wag Dodge and his crew encountered during the Mann Gulch affair in August 1949, when a terrible firestorm took the lives of 12 smokejumpers.[12]

While not selected as one of the initial six or eight men who helped to set up the training camp at Nine Mile, Petty was part of the first large group of smokejumpers that the Forest Service turned to in 1943. Some Forest Service personnel, like those residing in surrounding communities, viewed the CPS men with distrust or outright disdain. As Petty put it, "They didn't know us. They'd look at us as a bunch of yellowbellies." But Petty himself was soon to become the second oldest CPS smokejumper; only Joe Osborn was older. He eventually made 29 jumps, including some in Washington, Oregon, and Montana.[13]

The actual training required Petty to jump off the tower, rather an unpleasant experience. Nevertheless, Petty, who was well accustomed to physical activity, considered the rest of the training "not too difficult." His first jump occurred with an Eagle chute, which offered "a fairly severe opening." His adrenaline was at a typically high pitch for that initial leap from the sky. "I never got the sensation of falling," Petty remembered. Rather, it seemed like "approaching the earth." In characteristic fashion, Petty undertook seven practice jumps at Seely Lake, encountering difficulties only during the third session. On that occasion, "I began to wonder why I was doing it," Petty later reflected. With that jump behind him, however, he experienced no further problems. After completing his practice jumps, Petty transferred to the work camp at Basin Creek where Wag Dodge served as his supervisor. Once the fire season was underway, the CPS smokejumpers moved to the Big Prairie Ranger station. Big Prairie was located close to an

Eagle parachute: the opening shock was tremendous. Note the limp jumper (courtesy National Smokejumper Assn.).

airstrip and was situated along the Flathead River, where the CPS men could fish. While waiting to be called out to a fire, they performed a variety of tasks, including beginning construction of a bridge across the river. That first season, he undertook three fire jumps, with the initial one compelling him to carry 80 pounds of jumping gear. The fire itself, triggered by lightning, was a small one but the gear Petty lugged proved so heavy that he was forced to make two trips to transport it the requisite mile and a half down a trail.[14]

On November 20, 1943, Petty started a two-week furlough that allowed him to spend Thanksgiving with his family in Bear Creek, Oregon. While there, he attended his brother Joe's wedding. For the winter season, he went back to San Dimas to conduct soil samples and to measure rainfall. The next spring, he returned to Montana, where he resided in a fraternity building at Nine Mile called Waffle Bottom Lodge. He undertook his mandatory practice jumps and helped to maintain the phone line at Fish Creek Ranger Station, in Superior, Montana. Once the fire season began, he remained at Nine Mile and assisted with both the Forest Service's remount station and the tree nursery at the University of Montana, which, not surprisingly, had a fine program in forestry.[15]

For many smokejumpers, the 1944 fire season proved to be a relatively light one, but not so for Petty. Operating on a Forest Service boat on Lake Chelan, near Winthrop, Washington, he participated in a pair of fire jumps. On one, his crew departed from a fire, rested for two to three hours, and then moved along to face another blaze. Landing amid low brush and alpine trees, the men eventually walked out with snow all around. On yet another fire, he became known as the "jumping cook." The men "ragged on my cooking, especially on that first fire," Petty admitted. Petty also helped out Gregg Phifer with a magazine that the camp at Nine Mile was publishing: the *Smoke Jumper*. While Phifer served as editor of the publication, Petty became the photo editor.[16]

On November 20, Petty began another two-week furlough. Afterward, he was stationed in San Dimas, with former Camp 2 now referred to as Camp 76, Glendora. He returned to the lab but spent more time heading a phone line survey crew that operated between Fern and Tanbark. One evening, while standing in the look-out, Petty and other CPS men watched an eclipse. In early May, he moved back to Nine Mile to begin his third year as a smokejumper. Prior to the fire season, he trained and worked on trails and phone lines along the North Flathead River, close to the Glacier National Park.[17]

One of that season's highlights involved a bear that had managed to barge into the jumpers' garbage pit. Petty and five or six other CPS men were about to depart from cabins operated by the Forest Service. Opening the door, Petty spotted a bear on the porch but fortunately, the bear veered for a garage pit. Subsequently, Petty and Raymond Phibbs watched from the back door of their cabin as Phil Thomforde sought to bring down a splitting ax on the bear's head. Petty and Phibbes shouted at Thomforde to leave the bear alone, but their voices induced the animal to depart from the pit. Thomforde's attempted swipe at the bear produced only "a glancing blow." The bear then walked away before glaring back questioningly at Thomforde as if wondering, "What the hell do you think you're doing?" A Forest Service employee later spotted a bear with a wounded head. Petty discovered a lesson in this story: "Phil was lucky the bear was a pacifist."[18]

As the war ended in the summer of 1945, Petty and his CPS compatriots awaited news about their release from government service; at the same time, he wished to continue smokejumping, something that proved impossible once military veterans returned from overseas service. The CPS smokejumper program came to an end. For a brief spell, Petty, still seeking his niche, served as a cook for a timber cruising crew that operated on Boulder Creek near Butte, Montana. Then, on November 15, 1945, he received his discharge physical from the CPS. Calling on accumulated furlough time, Petty hitchhiked to Seattle, where he purchased photography paper for his fellow smokejumpers. He then headed for camp headquarters, now based in Savenac. There, he photographed a series of newspaper articles regarding smokejumping.[19]

Having purchased a 1942 Harley Davidson motorcycle from Thomforde for $380, Petty grabbed a bus bound for Bonners Ferry, Idaho, to pick up the bike. His possessions fitted into a box that Thomforde had built for the motorcycle. Departing from Bonners Ferry just before noon, Petty began his ride to Spokane, ignoring the snow alongside the road. Having reached Spokane during daylight, he began coursing to Pasco, where he planned to rest that evening. As he approached Colville, Washington, however, an automobile's headlights blinded him, resulting in the bike and Petty's going off the road and landing in a plowed field. The local police helped him find a place to stay that night, and the next morning he went to get his motorcycle repaired. Subsequently, he returned to Oregon and, on December 10, his CPS service came to an official close.[20]

Returning to California, Petty helped out a couple of beekeepers for the first several years following his days as a smokejumper. In 1950, Petty, who had saved up a little money and desired his own independence, moved to Albany, Oregon, to begin his own beekeeping business. During that same period, he married Loretta "Connie" Vaughan and soon began a family. Eventually, the Pettys had five children: three boys and a pair of girls. He continued running his beekeeping enterprise for some time, even serving as president of the state chapter of beekeepers for 22 years.[21]

Many years after his days with the CPS had ended, Petty admitted that he was uncertain if he would now be as adamant about his pacifist stance. Still, he asserted that he had never regretted carving out that position. In addition, Petty indicated, "I cherish the memories of smoke jumping." He looked forward to reunions with fellow CPS veterans.[22]

CHAPTER 5

The Methodist
T. RICHARD "DICK" FLAHARTY

During the midst of the Great Depression, his involvement with a poor, inner city Methodist church situated near Chicago's north side drew Dick Flaharty to pacifism. The Reverend Bailey Waltmire of the Humboldt Park Methodist Church was, in Flaharty's eyes, "a real fighter in terms of trying to make the church meaningful to people during the Depression years." Among Waltmire's most significant acts was to establish a youth group, composed of some 85–100 young people from various denominations throughout the neighborhood. Flaharty viewed Waltmire, who "would do anything to further the betterment of man," as "a militant pacifist — a real fighter for social justice — and a great inspiration to those of us who were growing up under his influence." The minister battled with government officials, whom he saw as doing too little to alleviate economic distress. For his part, Waltmire founded a cooperative grocery in the basement of the parsonage to help the people of the neighborhood survive. Along with other ministers, he also organized food marches. Recognizing that communists were trying to take over such operations, Waltmire nevertheless refused to pull back, reasoning that he could maintain control.[1]

Waltmire introduced his young audience to pacifists like Mahatma Gandhi and Toyohiko Kagawa of Japan, the Christian activist who founded the Anti-War League and apologized for his nation's invasion of China. Chicago, moreover, was the home base of the Methodist Church's Commission on World Peace. Flaharty and some other young people asked themselves, "If everybody were conscientious objectors, what would we do against people like Adolf Hitler and the like?" They learned that the commission was seeking peaceful solutions to international turmoil, including supporting economic sanctions against Germany. "This made sense to us," Flaharty recalled.[2]

Dick Flaharty (left) and George Leavitt (courtesy Dick Flaharty).

The Methodist Church, of course, was not one of the historic peace churches. Nevertheless, the horrors of World War I and its immediate aftermath induced a number of Methodist ministers, like those in other Protestant denominations, to adopt an anti-war position during the inter-war period. In 1934, the *World Tomorrow*, published by the pacifist Fellowship of Reconciliation, proclaimed that "unqualified repudiation of war is now becoming commonplace in religious conferences." The following year witnessed the General Conference of the Methodist Episcopal Church insist it would refuse to back, support, or join in war. In 1939, the church's northern and southern branches both affirmed that position. The Reverend Walter Van Kirk suggested that Christians in general, like many religious leaders, were subscribing "to the pacifism of the early church." Still, pacifists remained a minority within the Methodist Church and other Protestant churches.[3]

The guiding dogma of the Methodist Church did allow for conscientious objection. The church believed that if an individual went into the military, he should be supported, but so should those who subscribed to the biblical edict, "Thou shalt not kill." The church eventually reassigned Waltmire to a conservative community in Libertyville, Illinois. His replacement, "an old, ready-for-retirement minister," was supposed "to undo some of the teaching Waltmire had laid out to the young people in the church." On one occasion, the new minister stood up during a church meeting and declared, "I can understand that it must be very difficult to think about taking a gun and shooting somebody, but couldn't you possibly think about taking a job where you're loading bombs in a plane and not out-in-the firing line." An enraged Flaharty retorted, "You couldn't take a gun and shoot somebody but you could put a bomb in a plane that's gonna kill them by the thousands." The minister simply declined to discuss the issue any further.[4]

*   *   *   *   *

Flaharty's mother, when she was four years old, emigrated with her family from Altona, Germany. Her father was supposed to follow suit but died before undertaking the transatlantic passage. While in her teens, her mother also died, leaving her in the care of an ill-tempered maiden aunt. His father — who discovered during his late teens that he was illegitimate — had been raised by his grandparents, both Irish Protestants. Flaharty's father bounced from job to job, trying his hand at firefighting, cab driving, policework, and auto mechanics. The marriage split apart when Flaharty, who was born in 1920, was around eight years old. From that point onward, his father, who ran a garage nearby, flitted in and out of the neighborhood.[5]

For the Flahartys, the Humboldt Park Methodist Church served as the center of much of their existence. Flaharty's mother worked as the custodian there, but the income she received hardly sufficed for her brood of three boys. Fortunately, the minister of her church, Bailey Waltmire, helped her obtain a job at Lawrence Hall, a Home for Good Boys, where the family came to reside. From the ages of 10 to 16, Flaharty remained at Lawrence Hall, alongside 150 other boys. They stayed in dormitories and attended public schools in the area. On more than one occasion, fights broke out when other classmates sneeringly referred to a Lawrence Hall resident as "one of those Hall boys." On a more positive note, Lawrence Hall featured a summer camp, Camp Hardy, which was situated on Little Blue Lake in upstate Michigan. There, Flaharty thrived as he swam, caught turtles, learned about nature, and collected Indian arrowheads.[6]

Lawrence Hall possessed a band of its own that enabled many of its members to obtain "first chair positions" in the Von Steuben Junior High School band, which won a citywide contest. During high school, Flaharty performed as the lead percussionist in the concert band, the theater orchestra, and, ironically enough, the ROTC marching band. He also played tympani or kettledrums for the concert orchestra, along with his brothers Ed and Earl. Flaharty recalled: "We had our own drum major dynasty at our high school." During his junior year, Flaharty joined a dance band that performed swing music. The next year, his mother obtained a new job, which resulted in the family's move back to the Humboldt Park area. Flaharty continued playing music, obtained a series of odd jobs, and attended downtown theaters to take in the big bands that came through Chicago.[7]

All the while, the Humboldt Park Methodist Church remained a focal point of Flaharty's existence. He finished high school as the drumbeats of war mounted in Asia and Europe. In his church, there were 26 young men who were drafted, with six becoming conscientious objectors, "a very high percentage" for a Methodist church at the time. Flaharty was the second individual to appear before the local draft board; the first, who was called before the United States entered the war, had proclaimed himself a CO. Reverend Waltmire went along with his congregant to the draft office, where "a lot of static" resulted. Nevertheless, he received the cherished 4-E classification. When Flaharty's term arrived, the board "didn't challenge me at all. They said, 'Oh, he's from that church,'" with its well-known minister, Bailey Waltmire, who had helped other young men acquire 4-Es. Few questions even came his way. On the other hand, the doctor who later examined him seemed to resent that he was a conscientious objector.[8]

Fortunately for Flaharty, his mother was highly supportive of his attitude regarding war and peace. Both his brothers also supported Flaharty's stance; his younger brother, who was eventually drafted into the military, understood Flaharty's position but did not believe he could accept some of the criticism and abuse that invariably came the way of conscientious objectors. A few people did challenge Flaharty, who was now picking up extra money as a drummer. The parents of the leader of his band wondered, as Flaharty recalled, "How I could do that when their son was going into the military?" Flaharty worked in an X-ray factory that employed his mother and when the word got around that he was filing for conscientious objector status, he received an envelope with a yellow feather cut out of paper. His antagonist "was such a brave person that he failed to sign the notice to me indicating that he was critical," Flaharty later charged. In the same fashion, "nobody approached me and challenged me," he declared. However, "my mother took a lot of static after I was drafted and gone. She'd get people who would question her as to why I took that position. One lady came to her and said that she had heard a rumor that I had thought the Nazis were going to win the war and take over the country and therefore because I was a conscientious objector I would be in their good favor."[9]

Such criticism never induced Flaharty to reconsider his stance. "I was, of course, upset and very uncomfortable dealing with the feelings about it.... I didn't feel capable of discussing the position openly with people and challenging them or being able to get into a conversation and challenge people back regarding their questioning my position. I didn't feel intellectually up to coping with that sort of discourse at that time." Flaharty did believe that the United States, owing to economic considerations, was failing to contest fascist aggression on the European continent. He and those of like mind continued to reason that economic sanctions might have worked against Germany. They also wondered if Roosevelt was heading toward war in an effort to pull his country out of the Depression. However, most significant, as Flaharty recalled, was the question "of whether I as a human being could go out and shoot somebody and take a life. I didn't feel that I was up to doing that sort of thing."[10]

In February 1942, Flaharty boarded a "Pennsy" train for Coshocton, Ohio, the home station of CPS camp 23, which was undertaking a soil conservation project involving an examination of the effectiveness of contour plowing in the hilly terrain of rural Ohio. Soon, he encountered a handful of COs, all, like himself, anxious of what lay ahead. One of the men was his friend Murray Braden, another Methodist and a former student antiwar activist. "There was an instant camaraderie that built up," Flaharty declared. "We all were a little apprehensive about what we getting into. But the fact that there was a group of us made it a lot easier for us." Still, "we didn't know what the work experience was actually going to be other than ... that it was a soil conservation project that we were assigned to."[11]

While aware that the Society of Friends ran the camp, the CPS men did not know what the role of the military would be. Occasionally, army officers would come around to inspect the camp, which bothered some of the men. On the other hand, "some of us just rolled with the punch," Flaharty stated. "There were some who fought it." This was more apt to occur in the Quaker camps, rather than the ones run by Mennonites. Some 40 denominations were represented in 151 CPS camps. There also could be found "some absolutists, including political objectors." At Coshocton, Flaharty continued, "We had quite a variety of philosophies, quite a variety of backgrounds, much more of a mixture than would be found in the camps run by the Brethren or the Mennonites. At Coshocton, there was one fellow who ... refused to work for the government project. He said, 'That's giving into the military structure, being dictated to in the military situation.'" That individual carved out his own living quarters and only grudgingly accepted work assignments.[12]

Flaharty understood the position of the absolutists, appreciating that they disliked "being under military direction." He and those of like mind, on the other hand, reasoned, "We felt that we had a mediated force between us with the Society of Friends being the mediator there directing the operations of the camp." Flaharty acknowledged, "There were a lot of us ... of my thinking who thought we might have served even in the military if we could have served, as Lew Ayres ended up, in the medical corps." They had heard tales of other conscientious objectors, who, after being classified 1-A, ended up in regiments where the military commander "felt it was his duty to break that spirit." The commander might order them to the parade grounds, tell them to pick up rifles, and then send them to the brig for several months when the men refused. At the end of that period, the same scenario might be repeated.[13]

Initially, Flaharty, like the other CPS men who had not attended college, received assignments at Coshocton to dig ditches to shovel silt out of flumes. Eventually, he joined a survey crew that went through the countryside to check water areas. During the winter and when it rained, he could be found in a drafting room examining survey results. He considered the work more useful than many of the tasks that CPS branches handled. By mid–1942, the Coshocton camp contained 300 CPS men. Situated miles from the nearest town, they proceeded to establish a library, a cooperative candy store, a recreation area where plays were put on, a woodwork shop, a tennis court, and the infamous "Fracture Field," a baseball field riddled with gopher holes. To Flaharty's delight, an orchestra was formed, along with a choral group. A series of study and discussion groups also cropped up, while the camp's sponsors offered guest speakers on occasion.[14]

The seemingly idyllic nature of the camp was soon disrupted when the local congressman began receiving flak about the presence of "yellowbellies." Previously, that same elected official had patted himself on the back for providing cheap labor to the community. Now, he insisted that the camp be "cleaned up." Within a short while, the size of its operations was scaled back and only 50 CPS men remained. The federal government, Flaharty believed, "was making an effort to hide us away, to make use of us, but to hide us away."[15] At one point, Flaharty returned from a visit to Chicago, where he had broken up with a girlfriend. Her parents, as matters turned out, "didn't appreciate her association with a CO." By chance, however, a group of young women from Denison University stopped off for a visit. As a consequence, Flaharty met Betty Putnam, his soon-to-be spouse.[16]

With the exception of the summer of 1944, Flaharty spent the full 35 months of his CPS tenure at Coshocton. The operations of the smoke-jumpers largely ceased during the winter months, with many men returning to their previous units. Only a small group was stationed year-round at Missoula. Nevertheless, for Flaharty, his short stint with the smoke-jumpers was a highlight of his CPS experience. Flaharty had become concerned about his own work habits, believing that they had to change, increasingly feeling, as he had at the outset, that he was engaged in debilitating "made-work." Consequently, Flaharty volunteered for the smoke-jumpers program in early 1944, but "was crushed" when Murray Braden was selected, but he was not, perhaps because he weighed 160 pounds, the cut-off point for smokejumpers. Readying to participate in the Malaria Project involving human guinea pigs, Flaharty heard that the Forest Service intended to train one more crew.[17] At that point, Flaharty recalled, "I was getting rather depressed," having lost "much of the initial enthusiasm" he had possessed at "making ... witness." Flaharty continued, "I felt a need at making a change in my life" and was becoming "rather desperate." Thus, the idea of applying for the smokejumpers program proved attractive. Indeed, for Flaharty, "there was a certain amount of thrill involved" in the idea of becoming a smokejumper. He welcomed the fact that smokejumping involved "a certain amount of danger.... We were combating this whole feeling that we're cowards and we're afraid of risking ourselves, our lives." Naturally then, Flaharty was pleased that he was finally accepted.[18]

With travel papers in hand, Flaharty boarded a train to Chicago, where he saw his mother before heading out west. He ended up in Missoula, "a little quiet and backward" town at the time. He was taken aback to encounter an Indian, with "a squaw" walking three paces behind him. Picked up at the train station in Missoula, Flaharty was driven out to the Nine Mile Remount Station, a good distance from Missoula. He was assigned a bed in one of the dormitories. At that point, there were about 120 jumpers involved in the program. Flaharty met with Roy and Florence Wenger, who briefed him on camp procedures. The Wengers checked out his wardrobe, which the jumpers had to provide for themselves, and they found it lacking. So they scrounged up some World War I castoffs that they handed to Flaharty. Later, he, along with some other CPS men, drove into Missoula and the Forest Service bought them some boots.[19]

Flaharty proceeded to train at Nine Mile, along with the D unit. There followed a couple of weeks of rather intense, physically taxing training sessions, including running exercises, designed to acclimate the men to the altitude, and leaping off platforms. The men were informed that coming off a chute was equivalent to jumping from an eight- or ten-foot platform. They were taught how to put on a jumpsuit and a harness. First lifted by pulleys, they then had to learn how to maneuver a letdown rope through the harnesses to descend to the ground. Classroom sessions were offered on reading a compass or following a topographical map as smokejumpers sometimes jumped into country without any trails. Running proved the most difficult part of the training, perhaps because Flaharty was at the top of the weight scale allowable for smokejumpers. While at Nine Mile, Flaharty strove diligently to keep his weight in check. Perhaps fearing that he might lose his nerve, Flaharty also invariably volunteered to be the first CPS man to jump from the tower. But in spite of his weight, he encountered no difficulty completing the operation on the ground, by "hitting and rolling." He wanted "the full experience" and desired "to feel good about [himself] physically." No CPS men were ushered out because of the physical training and no serious injuries occurred during practice sessions, although one individual suffered a shattered thigh when he fell out of a snag (a standing, dead tree) and landed on the ground. Strikingly, no one ever refused to jump.[20]

Flaharty's first several practice jumps resulted in no difficulties, but his fifth jump proved more troublesome. One of the lines in his chute got twisted, so that only half the canopy opened. Consequently, Flaharty began to fall much faster than was desirable. "I could hear the wind rushing through my helmet and realized that I was falling much faster than I was supposed to be falling. So I started to panic." A voice through a battery-power amplifier blared out, "Take it easy, Flaharty. You'll make it all right. Just get the silk away from your face so you'll see what you're doing." His anxiety had led Flaharty to try, unsuccessfully, to pull open his emergency chute. The jump instructor wanted him to be able to see when he hit the ground. Flaharty rolled when he hit the ground, but sprained both ankles. But he was soon back in the air, completing two jumps one day to catch up with the other volunteers. His last training jump occurred in the midst of a demonstration that the Forest Service put on for visitors. "Caught in a thermal," Flaharty nevertheless had "a nice ride."[21]

The time spent in Montana, which included fixing fences and baling hay, Flaharty noted, amounted, to "a great experience." Nineteen forty-four was not such a difficult year and he made 10 jumps: seven practice and three fire jumps. His initial fire jump and the last one proved the most noteworthy. On standby, Flaharty, Murray Braden, and eight other volunteers awaited in a loft in Missoula. In the late afternoon, they reasoned that a call would not likely occur. So they went to purchase soda water at a nearby shop. Looking across the way, they noticed considerable movement around the loft and hurried back over, where they discovered that a fire jump was now impending. Soon, eight smokejumpers, including Flaharty and Braden, boarded a Trimotor headed for the western sector of Idaho. The largest fire, however, was situated on private land opened by the Potlatch Timber Association, and the Forest Service had determined to attend first to other fires on public territory. A pair of men landed at one of the fires, but Braden and two others experienced motion sickness. Flaharty engaged in "some deep breathing" to avoid becoming ill. The six remaining smokejumpers now went to the Potlatch Timber fire, which had grown in size. With the sun threatening to go down, the men jumped out in pairs although no clearing had been found; instead, they sought out the timber on the ridge above the fire. "The principle of jumping into trees," Flaharty later explained, "is you try to hang your chute over the top of the tree and it's like ending up on a spring. And then you just work your harness and you work your letdown rope to get down." But this timber was at least 150 feet tall and the branches were all bunched at the top.[22]

Braden and another volunteer were the first to depart the plane, while Flaharty jumped next. Hoping to land on "a nice big spruce," Flaharty shot past that point and his chute began to bunch up behind him as he flew into the top of a batch of trees. An adrenaline rush lasted for several moments.

> My chute didn't catch and it rolled down behind me and I fell down through the branches. And then I was going down what seemed like falling down an elevator shaft because here's this trunk of a tree flashing up alongside side of me. I could see a log on the ground that I was going to crash in on and I was just ready for that landing on that log when my chute unfurled and snapped around the trunk of a tree. And I was left hanging. There was a stub of a branch where it had caught the chute and was holding it. And I was able to shift my weight and put my foot on the log and slam my harness and step out. I think that's when my hair started turning white.[23]

Once on the ground, Flaharty looked up and spotted Phil Stanley, dangling at the bottom of an 80-foot-long rope, which was wrapped at the top of a 150-foot-tall tree. Flaharty climbed up to help bring Stanley down. Three men soon began to work on the fire, while Flaharty searched for Braden, who had yet to be found. Flaharty soon discovered a dazed Braden, who had set out streamers after falling through several branches. When the fire was under control, Stanley, serving as squad leader, sent Flaharty and Ed Vail to scout out a Forest Service trail appearing on their map, to enable the men to depart the next morning. After spotting recently clawed bear marks, Flaharty and Vail returned to the group. Following dinner, provided by firefighters from the Potlatch Timber land, Flaharty had trouble sleeping, "lying awake most of the night wondering if [bears]were nocturnal wanderers."[24]

Flaharty's final jump took place in the Bitterroots, after a small fire, set by lightning, broke out 300 yards from the lookout tower at Wahoo Peak. Along with Ad Carlsen, Flaharty quickly attended to the fire. Afterward, they were ordered to stay at the site, which they were to help shut down for the winter. Awaiting a packer who was supposed to assist them, the two smokejumpers headed for the spring to obtain fresh water. Carlsen spotted a "fool hen," which he nailed with a rock, thus providing the main course for dinner. The following day, Flaharty and Carlsen hiked toward Hamilton, Montana. Flaharty kept teasing elk that appeared to be all about, until Carlsen warned him, "Have you ever met a bull elk in mating season?" Before the end of their jaunt, they ran into the father of another smokejumper, who was riding with a pack of mules along the trail.[25]

At the end of the 1944 fire season, Flaharty interviewed a number of his fellow smokejumpers, seeking to discover why they had joined "the parachute fire-fighting unit." Many, not surprisingly, were interested in flying. One CPS man, with 12 jumps to his credit, acknowledged this, while declaring, "This seems to be the closest I could get to it in CPS." A thirty-year-old former bank teller confessed, "The lure of chute jumping got me." Others were attracted to "the great out-of-doors." Another CPS veteran, who had completed 18 jumps over two seasons, was a fisherman, hunter, and hiker. Several appeared drawn to "a job 'with a risk.'" One smokejumper, with 17 jumps behind him, reasoned that this unit afforded him "an opportunity to take part in something dangerous for me and to make a better witness than in other non-hazardous projects." Of no small import was the sense that smokejumping amounted to "work of national importance." As one man, having carried out 10 jumps, stated, "I figured that in the Smoke Jumpers I would be doing a more important service."[26]

Determined to marry in the summer of 1945, Flaharty chose not to return to the smokejumpers camp that year. Instead, he went back to Coshocton to participate in a soil conservation program. He discovered that the camp cook crew worked a different shift. Rather than working six days a week, with one day off, that crew operated for longer stretches but also received more time off. That enabled him to visit Betty, who was completing her master's degree in social work at Western Reserve University. To do so, he hitchhiked to Cleveland for the weekend. On one occasion, an army captain gave him a ride. When he informed the soldier that he was a conscientious objector, Flaharty related, "He accepted that." However, when they started to discuss the war, the captain declared, "You know, it was a battle. Who the hell cares about the Jews?" Flaharty immediately reflected on the fact that a number of the men at Coshocton were Jews (only 50 Jews were in CPS altogether), including, interestingly enough, one from Germany who believed that "the military way was not the way to defeat Hitler." The captain stated, "Well, it takes all kinds." The following January, the Selective Service ushered out Flaharty.[27]

To its credit, the Society of Friends had CPS men tested and queried about their plans following the war. It was recommended to Flaharty, who had "never felt able to attend college," that he might be able to do so and end up "working with people." Like Betty, Flaharty was interested in the possibility of social work. Fortunately, the Friends provided a small scholarship to get him started. Flaharty began attending Roosevelt College, a university affiliated with the YMCA, which was fighting the quota system that targeted Jews and other minorities. Roosevelt College was located in the Chicago Loop, on LaSalle Street. Flaharty began attending the school a month after he left the CPS. He eventually received his undergraduate degree from Roosevelt College, which he completed in two and a half years, and then took a master's degree at the University of Pittsburgh.[28]

For Flaharty, what was so unique about his particular CPS experience involved more than the smokejumping. The CPS camp included some remarkable people, including full professors and Doc Muldenky, the assistant head curator of the New York Botanical Gardens. The camp also featured a mathematical engineer who reconfigured some of the formulas the soil conservation unit relied on. Flaharty recalled:

> The smokejumpers accepted people from all of these units. Here was this tremendous range of educational experience of philosophy of background. And yet out of the working together on the smokejumping experience there was a tremendous bond that took place. And it was really a very unique experience. We'd get into some theological discussions. We get into all kinds of discussions in the camp. There was an acceptance of the differences. That was very unique. And I think this is why probably the smokejumping unit has been the most ongoing group in the whole CPS experience.[29]

Flaharty remained quite proud of having provided "service to his country," which was undertaken despite "the antagonism" against CPS operatives in Montana that was sometimes exhibited. Decades later, he looked back fondly on "the tremendous *esprit de corps* that I felt in this unit," the kind of commitment that "cut across lines" and involved "an element of physical risk."[30]

Chapter 6

The Academic
Gregg Phifer

He had told himself, "I am not going to be part of this war machine." At the same time, Gregg Phifer jumped at the chance to become a smokejumper. As he reasoned, "If I could work for my country, I would do it," and he hardly thought he could do more than serve as a smokejumper during the period when the Forest Service was desperately short of manpower.[1] Phifer undertook a total of 10 fire jumps in 1944 and 1945. His third and final jump in 1944 proved somewhat memorable. That involved the Wahoo or Cox Creek Fire, which broke out at an altitude of 7,500 feet in the Bitterroot National Forest in Idaho. The smokejumpers realized, as they flew with their spotter Earl Cooley in the red Travelair, that the jump itself would prove "our biggest thrill and greatest challenge." The landscape was panoramic as they approached the fire just before noon on Saturday, September 9. They saw "rocky crags and razor-sharp ridges, jutted at wild angles from the forest cover of the Selway Bitterroot Primitive Area."[2]

Loren Zimmerman, one of three smokejumpers sent from the Nine Mile station outside Missoula, spotted the fire. "It's not smoking very much," he said. "But it's crowned out. And there I see a chute. Must be a couple of jumpers already on the fire." They discovered a lovely mountain meadow some 1,000 feet below, perched on a ridge-top, but no more than 75 yards long and 25 yards wide. The surrounding terrain was considerably less appealing. There were cliffs, snags, great rocks, a pair of lakes, including one situated close to the fire, and, of course, the fire itself. Simply put, "prospects did not look good." The drift chute was caught by the wind and ended up in the fire. Having headed up to 1,600 feet, the pilot prepared for the first jump. Zimmerman undertook it, and then Cooley instructed Phifer to hook up and get ready to leap himself. Phifer, like Cooley, saw that Zimmerman had landed in the middle of the meadow. Cooley shouted encouragement to Phifer, "Loren did a swell job. I want to see you do as well. Turn into the wind and away from the spot until you get the feel of the drift."[3]

Cooley signaled to the pilot, "Cut the motor." After the prop blast dissipated, Cooley slapped Phifer on the back, signaling for him to jump. As Phifer recalled, "My opening shock was light and after a glance upward to check my canopy, I turned into the wind." His parachute readily emerged, but within 10 seconds, he sensed that the wind drift was less severe than had been anticipated. He detected slide rocks beneath him and a cluster of "snag-dotted trees" located between rocks and his hoped for landing spot. In the next few seconds, as Phifer remembered, "I planed hard for my jumping target, let up for a moment, then worked harder than ever." Having reached the three-quarter mark, Phifer knew that he had floated past the rockslide. However, ominous-appearing boulders still awaited if he failed to alter course. Just ahead, snags in trees seemed far more inviting. Consequently, "I planed for the trees, then at a hundred feet grabbed my guide lines, trying to select my spot," Phifer later wrote. "The ground rose with a terrific wallop and I fell flat on my face, no chance for a good roll on Wahoo." Fortunately, his parachute wrapped itself around a thin pine tree.[4]

The third member of the team proved less fortunate. As Ed Harkness landed hard — "What we sailed over he hit squarely" — the Travelair headed close to the ground and Cooley called out, "Harkness ... hurt." When Phifer and Zimmerman arrived on the spot, they saw Harkness lying on his back with one foot raised in the air. "Broken?," Phifer questioned him. "Yes," answered Harkness. "I landed on the point of that little rock right in the middle of all those big ones. Something snapped — here, in my foot." His jump mates attempted to make the injured man as comfortable as possible. Then, they retrieved their equipment, discovering that the radio was malfunctioning. "The cargo bounced when it hit," Zimmerman noted. "I dug a couple of post holes myself. It's partly the altitude." Zimmerman and Phifer walked across the meadow and hiked down a 1,000-foot drop that took them to the scene of the fire. The spotter in their plane, which had briefly departed, now returned and discovered, through the relay of signals, that Harkness was pretty badly injured. Zimmerman headed up to the ridge once more, before hiking to the lookout spot where a packer would arrive. Phifer remained there to battle "his private ... two-snag fire."[5]

In the meantime, two other smokejumpers already on the fire — Dale Entwistle and Louis Goosen — had joined Phifer at the fire site. "Whistle" informed Phifer that the forest supervisor in the area had referred to this as a "one-man fire," but indicated, "We'll drop two of you on it. You'll probably be back at the Wahoo lookout by tonight." The previous afternoon, only

Gregg Phifer (courtesy National Smokejumper Assn.).

minutes after Entwhistle and Goosen had landed, the fire "had flashed up the canyon on the north, growing in one fell swoop" to all but envelop a dozen acres. Fortunately, rocks and steep cliffs prevented the fire from darting over the ridge. That was the case, the men recognized, "at least as long as we exercised reasonable caution against spot fires."[6]

In contrast to most blazes, this one appeared most threatening at its bottom corner. Ignited tree limbs or cones could slide down the slope, thereby setting thick underbrush afire. The three men worked to trench the fire line. "Our fire flashed once," Phifer reported, but it burned "only the top layer of needles and dry grass." At that point, the fire "crept through the duff, catching in the green but highly flammable buffalo grass and leaping to crown out one tree after another." Because only Phifer, Entwistle, and Goosen were present to battle it, "we couldn't worry too much about the center." At the same time, they recognized that "the creeping and crowning along the edges had to be stopped." No additional manpower was available as fires were raging, including one on Bell Lake that required 29 smokejumpers. Planes frequently flew overhead, tracking the crew's progress in fighting the Wahoo fire. Although comforting, "no reinforcements, messages, or cargo" came their way.[7]

On Sunday morning, a packer's horse carried away the injured Harkness. In the late afternoon, the Trimotor kept circling over the meadow, before the spotter let loose "a full fire camp—food, radio, tent, lanterns, bed rolls." At that point, the first five men of a six-man walk-in crew also showed up. Another member of that crew, a young veteran who had been wounded in the attack on Pearl Harbor, lagged behind until the evening. The nine men finished attending to the fire at Cox Creek on Monday and Tuesday, allowing for a departure early Wednesday. Goosen and one of the new men remained to ensure that the fire didn't reignite. By that point, the snags that had appeared smoky or were smoldering had been knocked down, and dirt or water called on to mix "large areas of smoking duff and buffalo grass." Now, the men hiked to Wahoo Creek, before beginning the ascent of Wahoo Pass, which was situated at 7,500 feet and the border separating Idaho and Montana. At Twin Lakes, they went along a Forest Service road, and proceeded to a cabin at Lost Horse. There, they had dinner before going into Hamilton to check on Harkness, who had been hospitalized with three broken bones in his foot. Finally, the Inter-Mountain bus carried them to Missoula, and they soon proceeded on to Nine Mile. "Our Wahoo fire had become a tiny part of Smokejumper history," Phifer noted.[8]

* * * * *

Lyndon Gregg Phifer was born in Cincinnati, Ohio, on May 17, 1918, to a father whose ancestral roots were German and a mother whose family heritage was English. Lyndon Burke Phifer completed his undergraduate education at the University of Missouri in Columbia and took an M.A. in political science from Columbia University, before serving as an editor for the Methodist Book Concern, a publishing house. He also became an ordained Methodist minister. Wilma Louise Phifer was a homemaker until Gregg entered college, at which point she taught in a series of public schools in Cincinnati. Relatives dwelled close by, in Kentucky and Price Hill. During the period of American involvement in World War I, Lyndon Phifer filed as a conscientious objector, something that was greatly frowned on by the Wilson administration. As matters turned out, the Selective Service eventually reclassified Lyndon because his wife was pregnant with Gregg, ironically enough; he would only learn about his father's conscientious objection many years later.[9]

When the Phifers moved briefly to Newport, Kentucky, Gregg started kindergarten there. After his father constructed a house in Westwood, Ohio, Gregg attended the elementary school located three blocks away. He later took a bus to Western Hills High School, where he entered the seventh grade. The Phifer home was situated across from both a cornfield and a good-sized farm, while a playing field, where he played baseball and tag football, was a mere block away.[10] Thanks to his hardworking parents, Phifer's summers proved somewhat idyllic. They were spent in Bear Lake, a small community in northern Michigan, less than 20 miles north of Manistee where Wilma Louise had been raised. Phifer spent part of the time picking cherries at an orchard owned by a cousin or wild strawberries near a house his grandfather had purchased. For his cherry-picking work, Phifer received his "pay in cherries for eating, pies, juice, and even cherry ice." He also swam in nearby Bear Lake, where he received Red Cross lifesaving training from a laborer employed by the Works Progress Administration. In addition, the family conducted a number of trips, including one that took the Phifers, along with Gregg's grandfather, to eastern Canada.[11]

As Phifer later recalled, his relatives shielded him from the ravages of the Great Depression. True, his father suffered a number of pay cuts and his aunt was at times reduced to receiving script rather than cash for her teaching job. Still, "we never worried about a place to sleep or the next meal," Phifer later wrote. Rather, his mother determinedly purchased "something (a spool of thread, a pack of needles) from those who came to our back door selling notions to earn a precarious living." And she never denied anyone who came by in need of a meal. In Cincinnati, the Phifers joined the Westwood Methodist Church, which then "emphasized peace issues, even pacifism." The pastor was Clifford C. Peale, a liberal theologian and the father of Norman Vincent Peale, while James N. Gamble of Proctor and Gamble was one of the church's best-known congregants.[12]

While in high school and college, Phifer excelled both athletically and academically. He was a letterman in track, running the sprints, participating on the 440, 880, and medley relay teams, and serving as a broad jumper. He also helped to edit the school magazine, the *Maroon*, and was the top male student, which garnered him the Harvard award and a book. In addition, Phifer continued playing softball and helped to organize a school volleyball team.[13]

Encouraged by his uncle Leon Gillespie Phifer, who ran an insurance business in Stockton, California, Gregg attended the College of the Pacific, based in Stockton. There, Phifer thrived on the college's liberal arts emphasis, while majoring in both history and public speaking. While attending school at the College of the Pacific, Phifer lived with Uncle Leon, Aunt Ardene, and his paternal grandmother. Leon purchased for Gregg, to his delight, "the Gray Ghost, a rumble-seat equipped Ford with wire wheels and a rag top." That car, Phifer recalled, "helped me win dates with several college coeds." He achieved a letter in track, having placed in the Far Western Conference meet, and worked on the *Pacific Weekly*, the campus newspaper, where he ran a column, "On the Sidelines," and which he edited during his senior year. The Associated College Press accorded the school paper All-American status in 1939-1940. In addition, Phifer was actively engaged in the Life Question League at Central Methodist and the campus Y program.[14]

Throughout his undergraduate days, Phifer served on the debate team, which traveled along the West Coast and to the American heartland. One debate held at Stanford University in Palo Alto resulted in a congratulatory note from the director of the campus Y. The address on the postcard read, "College of the Pacifist." Phifer, who had heard radio reports about the German invasion of Poland, articulated a pacifist response to world affairs, which he and other members of the college debate team read over a radio station in Stockton. While in college, he also registered as a socialist, during the period when Norman Thomas headed the party.[15]

At the College of the Pacific, Phifer graduated with highest honors, proceeding to establish a record for the highest grade point average in school history. He subsequently received a scholarship to attend the University of Iowa, where, in the summer of 1941, he completed a master's thesis on University of Chicago Round Table discussions, then aired over the NBC Blue Network. Phifer even received an audition with the Crosley Corporation, which offered a job to write newscript for its radio station. Turning that down, he accepted instead a teaching assistantship to cover seven sections of the Principles of Speech course. His pay was $45 a month.[16]

Compelled to register with the Selective Service, Phifer sought conscientious objector status. "I insisted on marking on my card that I was a conscientious objector to military service," Phifer related. Eventually, the registrar, after attempting to dissuade him, agreed that notation would be made. However, his local board, situated in Cincinnati, denied Phifer's request as he was not associated with one of the peace churches. A subsequent appeal hearing took place in Nashville, Tennessee, where his father now worked for the renamed Methodist Publishing House. During the summer of 1942, Phifer, while awaiting final determination of his draft status, enrolled at a series of local colleges and universities, including Vanderbilt. Soon, he was reclassified 4-E but his induction notice was delayed. Consequently, Phifer attended Draughon's Business College, where he took shorthand and typing. Just prior to the end of the year, he received his orders to report for Civilian Public Service.[17]

In December, Phifer showed up at CPS 19, Buck Creek Camp, run by the American Friends Service Committee and situated outside Marion, North Carolina. The camp director was Roy Binford, who had served as president of Guilford College. The U.S. Park Service oversaw camp operations. Phifer arrived as a batch of Quakers was departing for Christmas furlough. Along the Blue Ridge Parkway, he helped knock down decayed chestnut trees and transported wooden rails to be used in a local park. On one occasion when he was serving on a rock crushing crew, steel lodged in his knee. Taken to Marion, Phifer had the steel removed by a physician. He battled forest fires in the region, including a large one that broke out in the Pisgah National Forest; Brethren from a nearby camp helped out. Firefighting proved a welcome relief from the boredom that sometimes enveloped the camp.[18]

Phifer considered many of his fellow conscientious objectors at Buck Creek to be fascinating. The large group of descendants of "North Carolina birthright Quakers" who were stationed there intrigued him. He came to appreciate a number of Jehovah's Witnesses with "their eccentric beliefs." And in a prescient manner, Phifer penned a note for the camp newspaper, *Calumet*, regarding three veterans of Buck Creek who had been assigned to undertake an "unusual" operation at Seeley Lake, Montana.

While at Buck Creek, Phifer joined with other CPS men to run a series of classes, including some designed to teach foreign languages, which might lead to their participation in the postwar reconstruction of Europe. Although that hoped-for order never panned out, another opportunity soon occurred. After Phifer had worked there for about three or four months, Buck Creek Camp was closed, with a number of the men shipped out to a camp in Gatlinburg. Approximately 50 were transferred to CPS 37, Camp Antelope, located in the midst of sagebrush country in Coleville, California. Phifer, having volunteered for the assignment, was part of that group. The Selective Service furnished a sleeping car to transport the men to Reno.

In Asheville, the men encountered a group of women who bore gifts and referred to themselves as "the USO for the CO!" When the train stopped in Kansas City, Phifer was able to see his Aunt Nora Warren. Along the way, the CPS men were attached to a pair of troop trains. On being informed that the COs were headed for a military camp, the soldiers warned, "You'll be sorry." At the same time, no friction developed between the two groups, separated by divergent beliefs but united in their determination to serve their nation during wartime. The soldiers exhibited no hostility, appearing in fact to be quite friendly. Moreover, some expressed genuine interest in what the COs would experience.[19]

While stationed in Coleville, where he thought he would remain for the rest of the war, Phifer participated in a few firefighting operations. He volunteered to join the Dog Valley Pumpers, a well-regarded flying contingent that fought fires along the West Coast. For a few months, he worked near the old Lincoln Highway, close to Reno. When the Forest Service determined that it had enough firefighters, it shut down the Pumpers. Phifer moved on to the Inyo Spike Camp, where he toiled in the mountain at an altitude of 8,000 feet. Phifer helped to string telephone wire that linked ranger stations across the mountains. He did so, despite having the opportunity to work "the salad detail—collecting garbage from Forest Service camp grounds—instead." Nevertheless, he viewed the outdoor works as "more enjoyable."[20]

His "Big Adventure" while at Inyo involved a rescue of another CPS man, Herschel Asbury, in the High Sierras near Bishop. Asbury had been part of a team that had climbed the 14,250 North Palisade Mountain, but he suffered a broken leg from a falling rock. Paul Olmstead, Phifer's camp leader, awakened Phifer and his compatriots at 6:00 A.M. Ranger Fred Meckel, Olmstead reported, needed six men for a rescue operation. Phifer and the other volunteers quickly dressed and after Meckel arrived, they headed for Bishop within thirty minutes. When they arrived at the warehouse at the Inyo National Forest to obtain additional supplies, the forest supervisor asked, "Are you ready for an adventure, boys?" After reaching the Glacier Park Station, they acquired still more supplies— some loaded on two mules— and the men mounted horses. Once they reached a grassy hollow located high above Big Pine, the crew proceeded on foot the rest of the way.[21]

At the top of the icy moraine, the men could envision the task awaiting them. Beneath them was stationed "a jungle of huge boulders, then Palisade Glacier. Mountains formed a semi-circle around the glacier and, with the terminal and middle moraines, gave the effect of a huge bowl." Bruce Colbert, who along with a head packer had joined them at the Glacier Park

Station, hardly expressed confidence in asserting, "There's not one of you fellows who can make the climb on the other side of the glacier. You're not equipped for it. I believe the injured man is at the lower right-hand corner of that snow rectangle just above the long snow chimney." They waited for a guide, Norman Clyde, to descend from the mountain. On spotting him, they carefully edged out to the glacier. As Phifer recalled, "Stumbling, slipping, occasionally falling, soaking our feet in pools of melted ice or in the tiny streams that crisscrossed the lower section of the glacier, stopping at a big rock here and there for a blow, we hastened across the glacier." Their task was made still more perilous by the fact that the climb was undertaken at an altitude of over 12,000 feet. Moreover, after Clyde delivered his report, they overheard Colbert mutter, "Almost hopeless." It was agreed that Fred Meckel, Clyde, and Olmstead would continue up the mountain to bring Asbury down. The rest of the crew returned to the Upper Glacier Lodge to get a meal, additional rope, and poles. But first, Wallace Dunn and Phifer helped the climbing team take a stretcher and other equipment "to the crevasse, half-crawling the last twenty-five yards diagonally in steps cut by Norm's snow axe."[22]

Early the next morning, Phifer and four others went back up the trail to await the rescue team and the injured Asbury. Hour after hour passed, resulting in their feet becoming numbed with cold taking over and sunlight fading. Finally, a voice from the mountain could be heard. Tossing off their blankets, they hurried to the edge of the crevasse, which winded Phifer and left him shivering hard, something he had avoided up to then. Finally, the team came down and Phifer helped to transfer Asbury to a wire stretcher on which he would be transported across the glacier. It was now close to midnight and movement at times was painstakingly halting. Footing was slippery at best, while the men were unable to lift the stretcher past the point they could reach because of "deep snow cups." Consequently, progress was made "one foot, one yard, two yards at a time." The rocky cliffs appeared to stand "appalling close behind" them as they plodded along. Moreover, whenever they stopped for short breaks, the icy wind chilled them.[23]

All in all, nevertheless, "We made amazing good time getting up there," Phifer remembered, although the ranger warned, "Get out of the way. There will be stones falling." Moving over a vast array of potholes in the ice, the crew continued its odyssey, stopping after reaching a ledge large enough to hold Asbury. The rescuers, some of whom had been toiling for up to 13 hours without eating, prepared to rest. They also decided to wait until the morning when the sun would generate some heat. Around 9:00, they started down the last portion of their journey, or so they hoped. They initially thought their destination would be reached by noon, then late afternoon, and finally when it got dark. But as light faded, there remained still two more ledges to finesse. They also had to contend with falling stones. The mountain had proven "a long, long, icy, miserable thing to walk down." They couldn't navigate easily, being compelled to take one lone step at a time. "We were just anxious to get off that ice as soon as possible," Phifer reflected.[24]

The men, thoroughly exhausted from their travails, finally reached the point where a physician was waiting for them. They also were greeted with hot coffee and soup from the lodge. The doctor determined that Asbury could not be transported on horseback across a very rough stretch of terrain, so the men had to carry him to a juncture where a Forest Service truck awaited. Asbury was then taken to the closest hospital. When the badly chapped Phifer returned to camp, Meckel said goodbye and joked, "I suppose I'll see you bright and early tomorrow morning." The story of the Inyo Spike Camp's Mountain Rescue appeared in a newspaper in Reno. Five inches were devoted to the story but not a word about the CPS was included.[25]

During the spring of 1944, Phifer heeded the call for an additional batch of smokejumpers. A number of men who had served at Buck Creek had already joined CPS 103. Phifer informed Wes Huss, who headed CPS 37 in Coleville, that he wanted to apply to become a smokejumper. Now, with the backing of Ranger Meckel, Phifer was admitted to the program. In fact, as Phifer later indicated, "His words may well have been the deciding factor in my acceptance." Small in stature but in the finest physical shape of his life, Phifer just skated past the 130-pound minimum. He got aboard packed trains, starting in Reno and ending up in Missoula, where he was greeted by a Forest Service representative. Phifer headed for base camp at Nine Mile, just outside Missoula.[26]

The training that Phifer participated in at Nine Mile was "rigorous." Prior to breakfast, a typical regimen involved running and exercising on an empty stomach at seven in the morning. Working on a crosscut saw, referred to by Phifer as "the misery whip," was a standard part of the morning routine. The men were required to jump from the tower, using a harness and rope, which was intended to replicate the phenomenon of a parachute opening. As Phifer remembered, that practice run proved more jarring "than I ever experienced on a real jump." Because the Forest Service anticipated that the smokejumpers would inevitably land in trees at some point, they had to learn how to descend from trees. This proved taxing for Phifer, who admittedly never fully mastered the procedure. The men also practiced readying to jump from the planes, after receiving a slap on their shoulders from spotters in the increasingly time-honored fashion of smokejumpers. The men bolted down an inclined ramp and then jumped, moving into a "hit and roll" pattern, which Phifer eventually managed. At one point, when traversing the obstacle course, he badly injured his right shoulder.[27]

During Phifer's training session, smokejumpers were required to undertake seven practice jumps. The injury to his shoulder, injuries suffered by other CPS men, and inclement weather delayed his first jump. Finally, on Wednesday, June 28, Phifer boarded a Ford Trimotor, operated by the Johnson Flying Service in Missoula, for that long-awaited leap. Another CPS man, Harry Burks, who had made his initial jump a year earlier, attempted to encourage Phifer, while asking, "Do you know where your emergency handle is? You won't have to use it, of course, but you should remember." Readying for his jump, Phifer chewed furiously on his Wrigley's gum, stood "with a death grip on the wire cable running just above the gaping door" of the plane, and delivered what he "wished were a more reas-suring glance at my securely-locked static line." Was he afraid?, Phifer later reflected. "Every jumper is convinced—consciously—before making his first training jump over the airfield that chances of any injury are small and of serious injury quite tiny. Perhaps the most difficult problem is the fear of being afraid, of freezing and being unable to take that big step. Part of our training was designed to make that step out of the plane automatic."[28]

All too soon, it seemed, his turn arrived to bolt out of the Trimotor, following a jump by Burks, who, like Phifer, had battled with the draft board in Nashville. Admittedly lacking "a sense of either time or falling," Phifer felt his shoulders being tugged at. "I've done it," he told himself as he stared at the ground below, experiencing both jubilation and a sense of weakness. Forgetting to check out his parachute, Phifer pulled hard on his left guide line twice before the chute came around. Avoiding a fence, he landed with his face being jarred and no roll forthcoming. As Phifer recalled,

> I ... suddenly realized that I was falling through space toward a fence beside the airstrip. I avoided the fence but my "hit and roll" left something to be desired. Since after landing my parachute remained inflated, I pulled the lower load line toward me until the chute flattened on the ground.

He stood, managed to take off his gloves, and unbuckled his helmet. "My jump one was history," Phifer remembered. "I knew then what veterans meant when they said that the time one feels most like jumping is just after landing successfully." Returning to camp, Burks slapped him on the back and asked, "Do you realize it? You're a Smokejumper!" Phifer replied, "Not so fast. *You* made this first one for me. I just followed you blindly out the plane. The next one will be on *me*."[29]

Subsequent jumps, some 19 in all, proved more successful. He came to view jumping out of planes as less frightening than peering over the top of a tall building. He was, Phifer later appreciated, "lucky" for his parachute worked "perfectly" each time out and he reached the ground on each occasion, even the one time when he was supposed to end up in a tree.[30]

His third practice jump led to his parachute being draped "across our target circle at the center of the airfield." He was fortunate that his parachute operated smoothly on each of his first five practice jumps and never caught up in a tree. On his sixth jump, the trainers issued an order: "Hang up in a tall tree." Phifer attempted to do so, but banged into a small pine and then slid virtually all the way to the ground. Following the final practice jump, Phifer and his fellow training mates built their own fire camp. Now, they awaited "the call of Fire on the Mountain, the Smokejumper battle cry taking us into action," he remembered. In the meantime, the smokejumpers toiled at the Forest Service Remount Station, stacking hay for horses and mules. The work was hardly what they had foreseen, but it undoubtedly helped to keep them in shape for fire jumps yet to come.[31]

Nineteen forty-four proved to be a relatively light fire season, resulting in only three fire jumps for the new smokejumper. He missed the largest one of the season, which required 40 smokejumpers to subdue a blaze near Bell Lake. From the base camp, Phifer and his colleagues merely wrestled with "a 'walking fire' or two." For smokejumpers, he admitted, "that was no fun at all." Because of compensatory time they had accumulated, Phifer and several other CPS men were able to work for a week or longer picking potatoes near Pocatello, Idaho, a job that paid $1 a hour and included good meals. Afterward, as the winter season approached, Phifer and the rest of the smokejumpers moved on to side camps. He was stationed at the Quartz Ranger Station, where he worked with the Forest Service on a bridge project. He also helped out in the kitchen, before being summoned back to Missoula for refresher training.[32]

Before the 1945 fire season opened, camp director Art Wiebe visited all the side camps to inform the CPS men about a new stratagem that the Japanese had concocted. They were attempting to send balloons, complete with explosives and incendiary materials, to spark fires in forested areas in the American Northwest. Phifer heard Wiebe indicate that no major fires had yet been ignited by Japanese balloons. Apparently at the Forest Service's request, Wiebe asked if any CPS men were averse to fighting such fires if they developed. None objected. As Phifer remembered, "After all, to us all forest fires offered the same threat and ... became candidates for quick suppression, whether caused by lightning, human error, or an incendiary device." However, as far as he knew, neither he nor other CPS men had to contend with such fires.[33]

In the springtime, Phifer returned to Nine Mile for additional training and a trio of "refresher" jumps. One of those proved more striking than the others for the pilot agreed to take the men above the standard 2,000-foot altitude from which they normally jumped. On that occasion, they went up to 3,000 or possibly even 4,000 feet before descending with their parachutes, which afforded them more time to float through the air. Actual fire jumps usually saw the men depart from planes at an altitude of some 1,500 feet to ensure a more precise landing. Now, most of the men were no longer using the silk Eagle parachutes, which had been replaced by slotted Irvin chutes.[34] Since the last fire season, Frank Derry had switched parachutes, opting for the Irvin ones that seemed "to respond more quickly when we reversed the direction air spilled from our parachute slots." The previous year, a few smokejumpers continued to rely on the Eagle, a lovely silk parachute referred to as the "porch and ears." Unfortunately, grasshoppers were fond of them too, and by 1945 all the men were jumping with Irvins.[35]

Following completion of his refresher jumps, Phifer worked at the Savanac Nursery, which was situated on the main road leading to Spokane. After helping to set seedling trees, Phifer and his colleagues returned first to Nine Mile and later to Missoula. The new fire season proved to be a very busy one, with the Forest Service having "more fires than it knew what to do with them." There was "no chance to get bored in '45," Phifer recalled. The men would go fight a fire, depart when a clean-up crew arrived, return to camp, and end right back on top of the chart indicating which crew would fight the next fire. A stakeside or pickup truck transported the men from the fraternity house, located on the campus of the University of Montana, where they resided, to the airport where their Trimotor awaited. Phifer undertook seven more fire jumps, six of which involved national forestland in Idaho. Most were small fires, triggered by lightning that had struck trees.[36]

One fire jump began on the evening of July 31, 1945. The men aboard the ancient Trimotor, piloted by Bob Johnson of the Johnson Flying Service of Missoula, detected several acres of fire close to a ridge top, as they looked for an ideal landing spot. Smoke wafted throughout the canyon. The hillside below the fire was covered with tall trees, while on the hillside across the way could be seen a rock slide containing giant boulders. Appearing as if out of the creek bottom were tall snags. In the woods below were eight smokejumpers, one with serious injuries. An eighty-foot snag had collapsed his parachute, causing him to fall to the ground.[37]

The Forest Service had ordered Phifer's crew to undertake the rescue mission. A number of the men had just come over from the Wind River, located in the Nez Perce National Forest. Streamer signals had indicated that a smokejumper was in distress. Thus, not even an hour after the injury had occurred, the rescue squad could be seen circling above. The smokejumpers, realizing that they were bound to land in tall timber, hoped to avoid snags and rocks. Phifer was one of the last to jump, after squadleader Jim Waite and four others. Then, spotter Frank Derry informed Phifer to get ready. As Phifer recalled,

> I quickly locked my static line to the cable above the door. A few — very few — directions from Derry to Johnson and the motors died. Our Trimotor dropped into a glide. One, two men gone, and my foot paused briefly on the step as I hopped into space.
>
> The wind rushed by as I hung briefly in the evening sunshine waiting to feel the tug on my risers as the chute opened. Moments later I felt my chute crack open. My canopy still pulsated from the opening shock ... as I glanced up to check my chute. No line over; all A O.K.
>
> Looking down, I quickly turned toward a little clearing from which someone flashed a tiny light. My chute came around quickly and easily as I gave thanks for the slots in my Derry Slotted Irvin parachute. I hung on my front risers, planing ... to increase forward speed. One thousand feet up ... five hundred feet ... still headed directly for my small but beautiful clearing.
>
> Then a hundred fifty feet up a dangerous down-canyon ground wind caught my chute and swept me swiftly toward the tall timber below the clearing. Luck as much as and probably more than skill guided me into a tiny opening between two tall trees, one barely wide enough for my inflated chute. I hit the ground moderately hard — typical at our higher altitudes — and got off my feet instantly.[38]

Once all of the men had completed their jumps, they met at the clearing, where they discovered that their injured colleague, Archie Keith, had already been carried out by rescuers. So, Phifer's team radioed regional fire control headquarters in Missoula about what had occurred. With the fire blazing "on the ridge top above us," Phifer related, the men searched for fire packs that had been parachuted to Keith's crew. After collecting all the fire packs, Phifer and his compatriots met in the small clearing at midnight. Working up the hillside with lighting from their headlamps, the men battled against "treacherous footing and thick underbrush" to build a fire line with their Pulaskis (firefighting tools that boast an axe-type head on one end, and a hoe-like head on the other) and shovels. This continued for hours, with only brief breaks taken. After K-rations were eaten around four in the morning, the crew slept for about 90 minutes. Awakening, they bolted down the K-rations and then resumed building the fire line.[39]

A Trimotor could be spotted overhead about nine A.M. Within an hour, the fire was burning hot. This went on until late in the afternoon. At different points, one or two trees "crowned out almost constantly." Phifer explained what this looked like: "If you have never seen a tall pine burn, it is truly awe-inspiring. First, the lower branches catch fire. Then, the fire spreads upward and in a moment the entire tree is a flaming torch." Such a crown fire can, of course, be quite deadly, possessing the ability to move rapidly through a fire line. Throughout the day, the men sported "five-gallon canvas backpacks of water" to be thrown on dangerous looking hot spots close to the fire line. Trees were "fire-proofed," with their lower limbs severed. The crew sought "to keep the fire on the ground." Once this happened, Phifer and the men knew, "we could lick this fire." On a couple of occasions, snags that dropped or rolling logs allowed the fire to move beyond the fire line, requiring the men to act more quickly to prevent it from spreading. Not surprisingly, sleep was in short supply that evening, with the crew taking shifts that offered about four hours of rest.[40]

Another day of firefighting, which proved largely uneventful, ensued. The men called on "dirt and water ... dirt and water ... twin allies of man in his battle against forest fires." At times, they resorted to a crosscut saw to knock down a tree or to split a log. That evening, the squadleader, Jim Waite, requested that the Forest Service send enough rations for three more days. The following morning, the Trimotor unloaded food and equipment, including stove and lanterns, for a fire camp. Fortunately, a packer and his mules arrived to carry out all the supplies. As Gerhard Smeiske and Phifer mopped up, sounds and sights alike startled them and the other smokejumpers.

> We heard a great roar and saw a tree just outside our fire line crown out. Our hearts sank even as we dashed to control the blaze. The other six jumpers heard the same roar we did and hastened up the steep slope.

Three more hours of hard work resulted in that spot fire being contained, which allowed the men to increase the fire line and extinguish the final ferocious fire.[41]

While two men watched the fire the next day, the others "closed camp and built trail." They hiked through breathtaking country, reaching Cooper Creek Trail, constructed by the CCC but little used for some time. By five in the afternoon on Saturday, they made it to the Forest Service cabin at Cooper's Flat, which was nine miles from the fire site. After eating and cleaning up in the creek, they rested until the following day, when they hiked another seven miles to Paradise. A Forest Service truck then carried them back to Missoula, with a couple of stops along the way. Referring to Cooper Creek, Phifer made the following telling observation.

> Don't look at Cooper Creek as a typical Smoke Jumper fire. There really are no "typical" jumper fires. All are different. We never found two fires exactly alike in jumping or fire fighting difficulty. We always saw differences in wind velocity or mountainous terrain, time of day, fuel conditions in the forest, acres covered by the blaze, difficulty of finding loose soil or water with which to fight the fire, availability of a good location for reaching the ground in our parachutes.[42]

Following his second fire season, Phifer returned to harvesting potatoes in Pocatello. He requested and eventually received a transfer to an
experimental unit of the Forest Service that the Brethren Service Committee operated in Olustee, Florida. After visiting his parents in Nashville, he
took a bus to Olustee. The experimental unit, part of CPS 149, was small
in scope. Along with the Rangers, the CPS men measured tree heights and
performed other tasks. On Sundays, many attended services at the
Methodist Church in Lake City. Suffering from a hernia that he had acquired
along the way, Phifer returned to Nashville for surgery. It was during his
recuperative period, as he lay flat on his back, that his discharge from the
CPS arrived.[43]

As Phifer saw it, he and his fellow conscientious objectors "had trans-
formed the Smoke Jumpers from a small experimental unit in 1942 to a
major force in regional fire control by 1944." Their experience had been a
"unique" one. At war's end, however, returning veterans prepared to replace
the COs in smokejumping units. Phifer declared, "FS needed us no longer
and sought the closure of CPS 103 ASAP."[44]

Phifer, boasting two degrees, a year of doctoral work, and experience
as a college instructor, had no difficulty in finding a job. Nor, he believed,
did other CPS men fortunate enough to have advanced degrees. Officials
of the Methodist Committee of World Peace, who sent his name and those
of similarly qualified individuals to a host of schools with which the church
was affiliated, came to his assistance. Phifer, in fact, received offers from a
series of academic institutions, before accepting a position — which paid
$3,000 a year — at Baldwin-Wallace College in Berea, Ohio, outside of
Cleveland. His responsibilities included teaching speech and journalism
classes, coaching the college debate team, and serving as adviser for the
campus newspaper.[45]

In 1948, Phifer returned to the University of Iowa, where he was still
enrolled as a doctoral student under A. Craig Baird, becoming an instructor in communications. The annual pay was $3,300. Before he completed
his dissertation, Phifer joined the faculty at Florida State University and
subsequently received his Ph.D. degree in the summer of 1949. While at
Florida State, Phifer met Betty Flory, who served as his debate assistant in
1954. After receiving her master's the following year, she remained at the
university as an instructor and debate assistant. They married on June 8,
1956, and subsequently had three daughters. Phifer moved up the academic
ladder at Florida State, becoming a full professor in 1959.[46]

CHAPTER 7

The Three-Timer

EARL SCHMIDT

The entrance of the United States into World War II had dramatically impacted Montana, as Earl Schmidt and other CPS men discovered. Prior to the attack on Pearl Harbor, the state's senior senator, Burton Wheeler, and Representative Jeannette Rankin had both opposed the Roosevelt administration's growing determination to assist the Allies. Wheeler's position shifted dramatically after December 7, 1941, while Rankin remained convinced that the president's policies had compelled Japan to act as it had. Her political viability plummeted accordingly, as Montana participated in the war drive. Once again, she was the lone member of Congress to cast a vote against a congressional declaration of war.

Residents of the state followed the wartime prowess of one of their own, Hubert Zemke, who had been a star football player at the University of Montana and now became an ace bomber pilot. Military bases cropped up across the state, and college students eagerly joined the Army Specialty Training Program housed at Montana's leading universities. Glasgow ran a "Scrap the Jap" campaign to collect metals for the war effort, while the Montana Education Association temporarily shut down all statewide championship contests involving sports like football and basketball. Just outside Missoula, Fort Missoula participated in the Federal Detention Center, housing more than 1,000 Japanese aliens and 1,000 Italian nationals. So-called "loyalty hearings" were conducted for the Japanese men who resided in the United States but had not become citizens. In many instances, families of the incarcerated Japanese were sent to internment camps, sometimes eventually joining the original detainee.[1]

* * * * *

Earl Schmidt was born on February 13, 1920, in Harper, Kansas, located in the southcentral portion of the state. His father, Samuel Schmidt, tended his own 160-acre farm and rented another 60 acres from a neighbor; Samuel cultivated wheat, barley, oats, and corn, and had Jersey cattle, chickens, sheep, and horses. Earl's mother, Alis Shupe Schmidt, was a housewife who took care of her two sons and three daughters. At the age of three, Earl was stricken with rheumatic fever, which confined him to bed for approximately two months. He could not walk for about three months and was left with a malformed right hip.[2]

The Schmidts regularly attended the local Mennonite Church, a source of inspiration and comfort during both good times and bad. Once the Great Depression pounded the Midwest, Schmidt participated in a lunch program that allowed for soup to be purchased for a nickel. "That made a lot of difference," Schmidt recalled, reflecting back on the tough times his family had experienced. He went through the local school system, which proved to be quite progressive. In addition to the church and school, Schmidt became fascinated with airplanes, particularly after one landed on the 220-acre family farm, which lacked electricity or running water, and he, then 14 years old, was given an opportunity to go up in it.[3]

Thanks to a program initiated by Montgomery Ward in the mid-thirties, which helped customers send their children to college, Schmidt enrolled at Goshen College. "I didn't excel as much as I might have," Schmidt admitted, and after one year in a liberal arts program, he dropped out. After wrestling with malaria, he got a job baling hay on a farm and another as a common laborer at a canning factory in Eureka, Illinois, pulling down 35 cents an hour. At one point, with the wages he had earned, Schmidt purchased a much-welcomed new sewing machine for his mother.[4]

After registering with the Selective Service in September 1941, Schmidt was called up the following January. Having filed as a conscientious objector—"If I tried to do what Jesus would do," he would live up to the ideals he had been schooled in, Schmidt reasoned—he was sent to CPS camp 22 in Henry, Illinois, to help out with a soil conservation project. The Mennonites ran that camp, which was situated 40 miles north of Peoria. While at Camp Henry, he also headed a topographic survey crew and teamed up to win the camp tennis doubles championship. Later, he transferred to CPS 67 in Downey, Idaho, where he led a crew that was primarily engaged in irrigation work. After writing a letter to Joseph M. Weber of the National Board for Religious Observers, Schmidt was one of first 60 men to be called

Earl Schmidt (courtesy National Smokejumpers Assn.).

on to join the smokejumper program in Montana. Both the notion of service and the danger involved appealed to him.[5]

Schmidt reached Missoula on April 23, 1943, and soon headed for Camp Paxson, located at Seeley Lake. A month later, he became the eleventh CPS volunteer and perhaps the seventieth man overall to undertake a series of practice jumps to learn about smokejumping. On June 20, Schmidt transferred to Basin Creek to build fences, a chore he performed for six weeks. Schmidt discovered that he "really enjoyed it."[6]

That first summer, he undertook seven practice jumps and one fire jump, which took place near Kalispell. Schmidt's initial jump, to his surprise, proved enjoyable and he experienced no sense of fear as it occurred. Only the fourth practice jump proved difficult, as he had to ward off some uncharacteristic nervousness, which probably resulted from the need to resort to an emergency chute. That jump also ended well and the anxiety passed. He hung up during his first fire jump, landing some 50 feet above the ground. Calling on his rope, Schmidt rather deftly eased his way down the yellow pine tree. On another jump, smokejumpers, including Schmidt, were dropped at Basin Creek for six weeks of project work. Schmidt helped to build a cable suspension bridge that ran for 172 feet. He also helped to construct cabin foot tents, and several miles of trail that led up to a ranger station.[7]

The winter months found him stationed in Clark Fork, Idaho, where he was involved with "blasting and building access roads," and in Lakeview, alongside Lake Pend O'Reille, where he helped to lay out a log bridge that, come spring, was submerged in water. When that fire season arrived, he trained at Nine Mile, using Remount Depot for practice. Schmidt worked for about two weeks at Big Salmon Lake in the Bob Marshall Wilderness, helping to maintain a trail. The summer was spent at Seeley Lake and saw Schmidt undertake one more fire jump. That one took place at 7,500-foot high Granite Ridge. Battling thirty-mile-an-hour winds, the crew witnessed a crown fire that expanded the field of operations. After working all night, the members of Schmidt's group welcomed a ground crew that arrived in the morning. With the wind having died down and heavier humidity in the area, the fire was brought under control. He missed the large Chelan fire, due to a sprained ankle.[8]

That winter, Schmidt could be found in northern Idaho and Metalline Falls, Washington. He was assigned to access road work, cut weed trees, and clear brush. While working at a fire station, Schmidt saw a memo about the Japanese balloon bombs. Instinctively, he reacted: "I knew it could happen." No opposition was expressed among the smokejumpers regarding the possible need to counter the effects of such bombs.[9]

During that winter season, Schmidt began to suffer a certain amount of anxiety about jumping again in the spring. But when the next fire season rolled around, he made three additional fire jumps. As matters turned out, 1945 proved to be the heaviest fire season yet, although Schmidt was saddled with a hip-joint injury induced by type-three rheumatism that made it increasingly difficult to jump. Concerns arose regarding a potential injury to his pelvis; in fact, he later acquired an artificial hip. A couple of rough landings had not helped matters. Nevertheless, while working in a parachute loft in Missoula in the late afternoon, he was called out on a fire. Reacting quickly, he grabbed a sandwich, an extra pair of socks, and some supplies, and took off, notwithstanding a raging headache. On the flight to the fire site near the Red River Ranger Station, some 90 miles from Missoula, Schmidt managed to sleep for about half an hour, which suppressed his headache. Approaching the spot from the air, the crew spotted a fire along Red River and another one near Sabe Creek River. Undoubtedly still feeling the effects of the earlier headache, Schmidt was, in his words, "a little chicken that day." Not wanting to land on the ground, he headed for timber and landed through trees in a pile of weeds. Schmidt "slammed into the trunk" of a 100-foot high pine tree, but sidled his way down to the ground. That evening, the smokejumpers bunked down but then moved to another spot. That proved fortuitous as "the dead top of a tree" landed precisely where they had originally planned to sleep. After about 24 hours, the fire was suppressed.[10]

To get back to Missoula required a mile hike uphill, followed by a seven-mile walk along a trail to a lookout and an additional 12½-mile push from the top of a ridge to the nearest road. Then, the men went by truck to the ranger station, before heading over to Dixie Landing Field for the flight to Missoula. The engine crank on the Trimotor that was to pick them up broke, leaving their pilot "very unhappy" and the men in need of a second plane, which soon arrived.[11]

To his dismay, problems with his hip joint brought an end to Schmidt's smokejumping career. Following the fire season, Schmidt cruised timber for about two months in White Sulphur Springs. Taking advantage of a furlough, he worked for a time at a sawmill in Oregon. Then, he was transferred to the Savenac nursery, before moving on to the CPS camp in Medaryville, Indiana, on January 1, 1946. He had just shown up when his separation order arrived; he had served in the CPS for four years and 13 days. But within three months, Schmidt boarded the *Pierre* Victory ship for Danzig, as part of the United Relief and Rehabilitation Administration program. Returning to the United States that summer, he bailed hay in the northeast sector of Colorado, before working at a feed store in Chappel, Nebraska. After that, Schmidt, who married Elizabeth Shue in 1950 and had two children, worked for the C. H. Musselman Canning factory in Biglerville, Pennsylvania, for 23 years. He also worked as an insurance agent for about two decades. He delighted in his short-lived co-ownership of a 146 two-place 65 horsepower Taylorcraft, which enabled him to fly solo for some 200 hours.[12]

From the distance of a near half-century, Schmidt looked back fondly on his CPS experiences: "CPS gave me a chance to re-evaluate life, people, circumstances, and provided the foundations for a fuller, more enjoyable life." It afforded "a kind of zest for living that I couldn't replace some other place," Schmidt acknowledged. Thus, the CPS experience was "quite a high point of my life." At the same time, he admitted that he might "have contributed more to humanity" working in a hospital setting or through some other kind of "direct service to mankind." As he turned seventy, Schmidt held onto the ideals that had propelled him into the CPS: "I still look forward to helping others, serving God, and enjoying life — not necessarily in that order."[13]

CHAPTER 8

A Man of God
LEE HEBEL

When the terrible tragedy at Mann Gulch occurred in early August 1949, which took the lives of a dozen young smokejumpers, Lee Hebel, by then a theological student, had little difficulty relating to that experience. As he later acknowledged, he believed "that could have happened to us on that eight-day fire on the Idaho-Montana border!" Hebel, seven other crewmen, and Earl Cooley, who was serving as their spotter, had taken off in a Ford Trimotor early in the morning. As they approached the fire, Cooley exclaimed, "Fellows, that's not all fog in the valley; there's a lot of fire down there!" Turning to Hebel, Cooley indicated, "You're the crew leader; we'll send more jumpers today."[1]

As they dropped from the sky, the men suffered no injuries. Also landing were cargo chutes, which contained a radio and water pumps. By the end of that first day, 16 more smokejumpers joined the initial crew, which had immediately surveyed the landscape, leading to the discovery that "fires, fires, fires" were spreading. As for Hebel, he never was able to completely "walk the burning mountainside." Along with his compatriots, he began at a stream, which was situated on the left side of the fire, in order to build a fire line. Dirt, found among the bounty of rocks, was tossed on hot spots. The men sawed and chopped wood, watering down as many spot fires as they could. The mornings, when it cooled off, were easier than the blistering afternoons when winds whirled about dangerously. "Sweat, work, struggle" characterized the enterprise.[2]

As they wrestled with steep terrain one afternoon, Hebel heard a worn-out Harold Graber pray as he fell to the ground, "Dear God, give us strength!" Somehow, the men continued to work the fires. When nightfall approached, they cleaned up as best they could in the cool stream, then cooked supper, before falling asleep in their goose down bedding. When the sun arose, so did the crews. After a quick breakfast, the men began fighting the fires once again. Day after day, mornings slipped by relatively smoothly, only to give way to the scorching, windy afternoons that proved so enervating. But notwithstanding their heroic efforts, the fire threatened to get out of hand. Hebel later recalled, "Every day that fire grew in spite of all we could do!" Finally, on the eighth day, they were ordered to hike out of the area, while smoke-chasers arrived to mop up the operation.[3]

Lee Hebel (courtesy Lee Hebel).

Later, Hebel admitted that he "wasn't particularly proud of that fire." He and his fellow crewmen had been unable to put it out, as it continued spreading until it became "an immense fire." Little helping matters had been the long afternoons and windy conditions. At the same time, he also considered himself and his fellow smokejumpers "fortunate." They had been instructed to remain apart from the top of the fire, working instead from the bottom and the sides, in an ultimately futile effort to suppress it. But he realized that "something could have happened there." After reading Norman Maclean's majestic account of the Mann Gulch fire, *Young Men and Fire*, Hebel well appreciated "that we were fortunate to be able to fight the fire from the flank — we all walked out!"[4]

*   *   *   *   *

When rapid modernization began unfolding in the United States during the latter stages of the 19th century, the nation experienced tremendous economic growth but severe dislocations too. As the processes of industrialization and urbanization proceeded apace, the American economy became a powerful force, with the gross domestic product skyrocketing thirty-three fold from 1859 to 1919. Some benefited enormously from the change in economic circumstances, as both giant corporations and a class of tremendously wealthy figures emerged. The middle class changed too, becoming more formally educated and more professional in nature, as its archetypal representatives were schooled in universities and became dedicated to the providing of services, rather than the production of goods. In the midst of this great flux, however, not all benefited. Many members of the working class, who included vast pools of new immigrants from southern and Eastern Europe, failed to share equitably in the economic bounty that seemingly characterized the new democratic state. Farmers too suffered grievously, caught up as they were in market scenarios that resulted in indebtedness, foreclosures, and reduction to sharecropper status, in numerous instances. Among those ill affected by the transformations wending their way through the national maelstrom were many people of color, including African Americans, Native Americans, and Asian immigrants.

As these sometimes happy, sometimes painful developments occurred, political movements rose and fell in response to the alterations that the United States continued to endure. Anarchists, socialists, and populists all sprang forth, offering different solutions for the ailments so clearly evidenced in both urban communities and throughout the countryside alike, particularly during hard economic times such as the 1890s when a severe depression wracked the nation. Among those insisting that new approaches be undertaken and attention be paid to the dispossessed and downtrodden were men of the cloth. Like other reformers and radicals during the period, they challenged the business ethic that propounded the doctrines of *laissez-faire*, with its insistence on hands-off economic practices by government entities, and social Darwinism, with its easy call for survival of the fittest. Preachers and ministers, especially drawn from Congregational, Episcopal, Baptist, Methodist, and Presbyterian churches, joined in the Social Gospel movement that heralded the Fatherhood of God and the Brotherhood of Man.[5]

In their own fashion, the Catholic Church and American Jews wrestled with social questions too. Edward McGlynn, the pastor of St. Stephen's Church in New York City, spoke of a "new crusade" that suggested "God has given an equality of essential rights to all His children just because they are His children." Father John A. Ryan, in keeping with an earlier papal encyclical by Leon XIII, demanded that wages "be sufficiently high to enable the laborer to live in a manner consistent with the dignity of a human being." The new Reform movement in America highlighted the need for "truth, justice and peace among all men." The Pittsburgh Platform of 1885 declared that Jews were obligated "to participate in the great task of modern times, to solve, on the basis of justice and righteousness, the problems presented by the contrasts and evils of the present organization of society." Rabbi Henry Berkowitz proclaimed that through its ancient injunctions, Judaism had "set up the highest ideal of society, as a human brotherhood under the care of a Divine Fatherhood." Rabbi Stephen S. Wise agreed that the nation's conscience demanded improved conditions for workers, particularly women and children, and the shaping of "completely free and self-determining, citizens."[6]

Participation by religious leaders in social and political campaigns was hardly unique to the Progressive era. Religious missionaries of various stripes had helped to establish many of the first English colonies established on the North American mainland. Calls for a reinvigoration of religiosity resulted in the Great Awakening of the early 18th century. Many American patriots purportedly hearkened to divine impulses, whether they were crafting the Declaration of Independence, writing the Constitution, or cementing a new nation-state. During the antebellum period, numerous reform efforts, including those involving abolitionism, women's rights, and peace, drew from religious tenets. As industrialization and urbanization with their attendant problems heightened in the United States, a new religious crusade appeared that also called on religious precepts, particularly the teachings and the life of Jesus Christ. Among the most noteworthy figures participating in the Social Gospel movement were figures like Washington Gladden, George Herron, and Walter Rauschenbusch. Some proved more radical than others, condemning capitalism altogether and underscoring the need for Social Christianity; W. D. P. Bliss considered Christian Socialism to involve "the application to society of the way of Christ."

But the Social Gospel in general sought to awaken one's "fellow citizens to the plight of others." That called for practicing the Golden Rule, at a bare minimum.[7]

Whether liberal or more radically inclined, Social Gospel ministers subscribed to the belief that the needs of the less fortunate had to be addressed. With their own churches situated in urban centers, they witnessed firsthand the corrosive effects that a loss of employment and pride could have on individuals, families, and entire communities. These ministers rejected the earlier pronouncements by some inside their own churches justifying the maldistribution of wealth and income that afflicted the United States during this era. They insisted that good Christians must be concerned about the entire populace, just as righteous ministers had to care for troubled and impoverished members of their flock. Francis Greenwood Peabody insisted that the church must grapple with "the age of the

social question," while Josiah Strong suggested that from a "new social consciousness is coming the new social conscience."

Christianity, Rauschenbusch pointed out, was "by its nature revolutionary," with Jesus standing as "the successor of the Old Testament
prophets," who in turn

> were the revolutionists of their age. They were dreamers of Utopias. They pictured
> an ideal state of society in which the poor should be judged with equity and the cry
> of the oppressed should no longer be heard; a time in which men would beat their
> idle swords into ploughshares and their spears into pruning hooks, for then the
> nations would learn war no more.

It was incumbent on the church to help mitigate "the crisis of society,"
Rauschenbusch affirmed: "The church, too, feels the incipient paralysis that
is creeping upon our splendid Christian civilization through the unjust absorp-
tion of wealth on one side and the poverty of the people on the other. It cannot thrive when society decays." Religious and political leaders could work
hand in hand "to transform humanity into the kingdom of God." This was "a
matter of life and death for both the church and the new social order," Shailer
Mathews exclaimed. The church, Gladden agreed, had to "Christianize society or society will de-christianize the church." The present capitalist system
required wholesale transformation, for "the Kingdom of God includes the economic life," Rauschenbusch argued. "We must change our economic system
in order to preserve the conscience and our religious faith." At the same time,
"we must renew and strengthen our religion in order to be able to change our
economic system." Rauschenbusch eloquently stated, "On the scroll of the
everlasting Gospel, God is today writing a flaming message of social righteousness, and you and I must learn to read it."

On December 9, 1912, the Methodist Episcopal Church adopted the
Social Creed of the Churches, which remained in effect for two full decades.
That manifesto avowed that churches must support "equal rights and complete justice for all men in all stations of life," "the abatement and preven-
tion of poverty," "a new emphasis on the application of Christian principles
to the acquisition and use of property, and for the most equitable division
of the product of industry that can ultimately be devised." All the while,
Rauschenbusch continued to believe that social engagement remained "the
most important ethical and spiritual movement in the modern world, and
the social gospel is the response of the Christian consciousness to it."[8]

The horrors of World War I seemed to give lie to the hopeful, somewhat utopian spirit that guided proponents of the Social Gospel. But a more
radical perspective also appeared, linked to such figures as Rauschenbush,
Norman Thomas, A. J. Muste, Harry F. Ward, and John Haynes Holmes.
The Social Gospel influenced organizations like the Fellowship of Reconcili-

ation, the American Union Against Militarism, the Women's Peace Party, and the People's Council. Writing in the Fellowship's publication, *The New World*, Willard Sperry condemned the "spirit of anti–Christ" that the bloodletting in Europe exemplified. Thomas came to believe that "War will not be eliminated from the world while the spirit of war remains in our economic and industrial systems." Social Gospel ideals increasingly influenced both the Quakers and the Brethren, although not the Mennonites, at this stage.[9]

The increasingly radical bent of some proponents of the Social Gospel caused it to be viewed with distrust in various circles. The movement was further weakened by the death of several of the most important proponents, including Rauschenbusch, Gladden, Lyman Abbott, and Josiah Strong. Nevertheless, mainstream Protestantism began to incorporate the Social Gospel. In 1921, the Fellowship for a Christian Order appeared, boasting such members as A. J. Muste, Reinhold Niebuhr, and Kirby Page. The Fellowship's manifesto bespoke Rauschenbusch's heritage.

> We believe that according to the life and teaching of Jesus, the supreme task of mankind is the creation of a social order, the Kingdom of God on earth, wherein the maximum opportunity shall be afforded for the development and enrichment of every personality; in which the supreme motive shall be love; wherein men shall cooperate in service for the common good and brotherhood shall be a reality in all of the daily relationships of life.[10]

Figures ranging from Shailer Mathews of the University of Chicago to E. Nicholas Comfort, founder of the Oklahoma School of Religion, attempted to keep the Social Gospel alive through the religious-education movement. Increasingly, however, the social ministry appeared on the defensive, particularly as proponents of militant fundamentalism damned modernist perspectives. Moreover, disillusionment, piqued by the terrors of war demonstrating man's inhumanity to his fellow man and by the onslaught of the Great Depression, led others to question the Social Gospel's optimistic tenor. Niebuhr, who had previously championed the Social Gospel and had served as chairman of the Fellowship of Reconciliation, now favored a supposedly more rationalist, less hopeful perspective. For a time, this also led him to demand more radical solutions to the nation's ailments.

Nevertheless, the Social Gospel continued to hold the allegiance of many within the faith community. In the mid–1930s, the General Assembly of the Presbyterian Church, U.S.A., spoke out against the economic ills still besetting so many Americans. The church's Permanent Committee on Moral and Social Welfare insisted that human rights were paramount to those involving property holdings; the committee urged the institution of better working conditions, the affording of security against the ravages of disease, unemployment, and old age; and the bringing of democracy into the economic realm. The northern branch's assembly criticized an industrial system that failed to provide security for the young, the widowed, the aged, and the victims of industrial accidents.

In 1937, the Central Conference of American Rabbis, a gathering of Reform leaders, declared through its Columbus Platform that

> Judaism seeks the attainment of a just society by the application of its teachings to the economic order, to industry and commerce, and to national and international affairs. It aims at the elimination of man-made misery and suffering, of poverty and degradation, of tyranny and slavery, of social inequality and prejudice, of ill-will and strife.... It champions the cause of all who work and of their right to an adequate standard of living, as prior to the rights of property. Judaism emphasizes the duty of charity, and strives for a social order which will protect men against the material disabilities of old age, sickness and unemployment.

As international events loomed larger and as the economic situation in the United States improved somewhat, socially engaged members of Protestant and Catholic churches and Jewish synagogues came to focus more on issues of war and peace. In contrast to Niebuhr, some adherents of the Social Gospel held fast to their belief in the Fatherhood of God and the Brotherhood of Man. But as had occurred during World War I, they concentrated more extensively on global events, with some remaining true to pacifist ideals and others determining that the threat posed by aggressive right-wing states had to be blunted. Pacifist ideals particularly resonated with the churches most closely identified with the Social Gospel: the Methodists, Disciples of Christ, and Congregationalists. Leading figures in the Fellowship of Reconciliation, including Norman Thomas and John Haynes Holmes, coupled their calls for the reformation of society with a condemnation of war. Through its Columbus Platform, the conclave of Reform Jews affirmed that Judaism, from ancient times, had

> proclaimed to mankind the ideal of universal peace. The spiritual and physical disarmament of all nations has been one of its essential teachings. It abhors all violence and relies upon moral education, love and sympathy to secure human progress. It regards justice as the foundation of the well-being of nations and the condition of enduring peace. It urges organized international action for disarmament, collective security and world peace.

Still more of the early "innocence" of the Social Gospel movement faded as the guns of war exploded yet again, haunting images of concentration camp victims arose, and mass slaughter reappeared on the world stage.

* * * * *

A future proponent of the Social Gospel, Lee Hebel was born on October 15, 1920, at the family farm in Hunters Valley, two miles from the

Susquehanna River and four miles outside Liverpool, Pennsylvania. His father, Lester, a general farmer, had Dutch and German Lutheran ancestors. His mother, whose maiden name was Martha Brown, had German and Scotch-Irish roots and was a homemaker who attended to the needs of her husband and four children until she died of cancer at the age of 42. Hebel received the first eight years of his formal education in a one-room schoolhouse, Charles School, where heat was provided by a large, pot-bellied stove, and drinking water gotten from the Charles family farm's spring. The children were transported to this classroom by a neighbor who had delivered the low bid to carry the students to Charles School. The vehicle in which the students rode lacked any kind of heating, other than that which the muffler provided.[11]

Liverpool High School was situated five miles away. It catered to 55 students, who received instructions in English, math, Latin, civics, chemistry, physics, and history from three or four teachers. The school also had a choir, a band, basketball, softball, and soccer. In addition to homework assignments, the students invariably had to tackle farm chores throughout the school year as they did during summer vacation. Lee, along with his brother and two sisters, assisted his father and grandfather with planting, cultivating, and harvesting; they also helped their mother and grandmother attend to gardening, lawn mowing, and the family washing, by way of tubs and washboards.[12]

The family church, Messiah Stone Church, was another one-room structure. It was an ecumenical enterprise, shared by Lutherans like the Hebels and by Evangelicals. Despite the congregation's small size, Lee was actually the fourth minister to emerge from the church.[13]

The Depression era proved difficult for the Hebel family, which had to struggle simply to cover the interest on the farm debt. Notwithstanding their financial difficulties, the Hebel children and their friends enjoyed themselves, playing ball, fishing, swimming, sledding, and skating. However, little money was available for family excursions, although one memorable trip to Watkins Glen, New York, was undertaken, shortly before Martha's death. She died in 1936, three years after breast surgery failed to eradicate the cancer that eventually took her life. She was heard to say, "I suppose that after I am gone, they will find a cure for cancer." Two years later, Lester married Kathryn Bell, who had two daughters of her own.[14]

Following his graduation from Liverpool High School in 1937, Hebel worked halftime for about a year at Weis Pure Food, a five-and-dime store in Harrisburg. The pay was $5.00 a week. The following year, he resided with his brother in Harrisburg. They worked for their Uncle John Lee, who ran his own five-and-dime store; the boys received $13.00 weekly.[15]

During that very period Hebel began to reflect "seriously about God's will for my life" and determined to become a pastor. He was inspired by such works as Charles Sheldon's novel, *In His Steps*, which appeared in 1896, at the height of the Social Gospel movement. The book posed the question of "What would Jesus do?" to grapple with contemporary life. Sheldon himself considered Christianity a living faith that had to address social ills, including providing for the needy and the disadvantaged. Motivated by such ideals, Hebel entered Susquehanna University in Selinsgrove, Pennsylvania, in 1940. Hebel informed the doubtful dean at Susquehanna that he was desirous of eventually studying for the ministry. Looking at the poor farm boy with an inadequate high school education, the college administrator responded, "Hebel, you'll never make it."[16]

After two years at Susquehanna, Lee had to contend with the draft. Hebel recognized that he could have obtained a 4-D, pre-ministerial deferment. He realized that he was opposed to killing, something that the teachings of Jesus Christ, as he understood them, demanded. "I was trying to be a follower of Jesus Christ and could not reconcile war and killing with the Master's example and teaching," Hebel later recalled. Furthermore, "I felt I was going to be honest about this." He knew that Martin Luther had championed the idea of Holy War, and that a leading American Lutheran cleric, in the midst of the Revolutionary War, had disrobed and donned a military uniform. But pacifism appeared truer to Hebel, who was well aware of the flourishing of right-wing aggression overseas. As he saw it, "Life was cheap, rather than being held sacred." By contrast, he "really believed in the long run in the Redemption."[17]

Fortunately, his family proved supportive. His father never said anything negative about his opposition to war, nor did his brother or his sister's husband, both of whom served in the military. The family "never appeared judgmental." During the war, in fact, Hebel corresponded with his brother-in-law, who was stationed in the Pacific.[18]

Consequently, when Hebel registered with the Selective Service, he filed as a conscientious objector. "I felt that God was to be obeyed above country, and yet acknowledged that our government had some stake in my life." Although only one of a mere 100 Lutherans to be deemed conscientious objectors by the Selective Service system during World War II, Hebel had no problems with his local draft board. He opted for the Civilian Public Service, rather than prison, as did absolute resisters. In December 1942, he was assigned to the CPS camp in Powellsville, Maryland, run by the Friends. Traveling alone by train and bus, he arrived at the Quaker-run camp. Making "many new supporting friends," Hebel "worked hard, discussed life issues continually, and survived on well-planned meals whose average cost was thirteen cents!" He helped out with soil conservation work while at Powellsville, striving to drain the river that had flooded thousands of acres of farmland.[19]

He remained there for ten months and then went to Brattleboro Retreat, Virginia, to work in a mental hospital that was also run by Quakers. While at Brattleboro, he noticed posters on bulletin boards regarding the smokejumper program, which Hebel came to view as "the most glamorous part of being a CO." He applied for the program in Missoula, Montana, and was accepted. At the time, the 5-foot 7-inch Hebel weighed 135 pounds; his size was considered ideal for a smokejumper. He was determined to prove "that folk with deep convictions could be about as courageous as those who went into the military and onto the battlefield." He remained with the smokejumpers for both the 1944 and 1945 fire seasons. His intensive six weeks of training, which began on May 1, 1944, took place at Nine Mile and Seeley Lake, spearheaded by Wag Dodge and Bill Wood. In contrast to the more charismatic Earl Cooley, Dodge, although a good crew leader, was no morale booster. At the same time, he provided Hebel with "quiet reassurance" that he could complete the tasks assigned to him. Still, certain parts of the program proved difficult for Hebel, who had a fear of heights. As he recalled, tree climbing was the most onerous, while "the tower was truly a torture tower" in his estimation. On the other hand, he had no problem with the rigorous regimen of calisthenics, which he was familiar with from his high school and college days.[20]

All in all, the practice jumps Hebel undertook proved far more difficult emotionally than would his fire jumps. As his first qualifying jump proceeded, he "was sort of numb." Undertaken from an altitude of 2,000 feet, it occurred only nine days after he arrived at Nine Mile. "Through no merits of my own, I hit the spot," Hebel remembered. After six additional qualifying jumps, he undertook four fire jumps the first year. The initial one took place on the Washington side of the Columbia River and was intended, he believed, to demonstrate to Forest Service personnel what the smokejumpers could accomplish.[21]

Along with Delbert Barley, Hebel was dropped from a Travelair to a fire located on a high ridge at Big Prairie. They landed on a giant flat rock spawning a ledge. As Hebel was falling easily from the sky, an updraft propelled him backward. As he approached a rather "massive rock area," he somehow managed to position his hips in the crotch of a tree. Only about eight or ten feet in the air, Hebel descended without having to resort to a letdown. The actual fire, which involved an old snag, proved quite small. The experience proved memorable, nevertheless, and included seeing a nanny goat and a pair of kids, at a distance of some 100–150 yards.[22]

Foreman Glenn Smith (left) and Wagner Dodge, 1943 (courtesy National Smoke-jumper Assn.).

When his initial fire season ended, Hebel and Clarence Quay were sent to Camp Remini, close by Helena, to help refurbish barracks that would be used as a transit point. Following the completion of that task, he remained at CPS headquarters in Missoula during the winter. He also joined with other smokejumpers in traveling to the Canadian border "to find the pine cone caches stowed by the squirrels under the banks of dry stream beds." Burlap bags filled with cones were later transported to Savenac Nursery, where the cones were dried and thrashed. The seeds were eventually planted at the nursery, while seedlings were sprinkled across the Forest Service, Region 1.[23]

The 1945 fire season proved far busier for Hebel, as it did for so many other smokejumpers with hundreds of jumps taking place. That year, Hebel undertook four practice jumps and seven fire jumps. The biggest and most enduring fire was the one situated on the border between Montana and Idaho, south of Missoula. When snow began to fall after his last fire jump, "we didn't worry about much, except to stuff ourselves on beef steak fried in butter."[24]

During his CPS days, Hebel experienced only a couple of scrapes, such as the time outside Coeur d'Alene when he was picked up while hitchhiking. When Hebel informed the driver, who had a couple of sons serving in the U.S. Armed Forces, that he was a conscientious objector, he was unceremoniously dumped out of the vehicle. Generally, however, he was able to avoid confrontations of that sort. As Hebel noted, "I tried not to be antagonistic."[25]

Altogether, Hebel considered his days with the smokejumpers to have been fruitful in many ways. He loved the Northwest, which he considered to be "the great frontier of God's creation." Happily, he acquired close friendships, many of which proved enduring. Important at that time too was the fact that "jumping on fires gave us status; besides, I suppose we all felt more secure from criticism and prejudice," Hebel wrote. "It would be difficult to judge a smokejumper cowardly or yellow; and just maybe, some of us had something to prove to ourselves." In fact, his smokejumping days afforded him with a considerable degree of "tenacity or stubbornness," a sense that "I can do it" and a feeling that any timidities and fears would be overcome. Indeed, as Hebel related, "It helped to make me a man and a better Christian."[26]

At the same time, he was not unmarred by his experiences as a smokejumper. While at Camp Rimini, situated near Helena, Hebel worked on a project that involved tearing down an old barracks building. Suffering from pain near the base of his spine that resulted from his spate of jumps and rolls, he was twice forced to go to a hospital for treatment. Once he was

Foreman Bill Wood (courtesy National Smokejumper Assn.).

released from the hospital, Hebel, feeling "pretty soft," hitchhiked to spend Christmas with his brother, a Navy man who was stationed close to San Diego. That adventure involved something of "a journey of faith," as he found himself, on at least one occasion, residing in a motor vehicle with a driver who was consuming alcohol. When he returned to Camp Rimini, he helped to build fences, maintain roads, and take care of telephone lines, all of which could be physically taxing as well. Then, during his time off and in an effort to pick up some pocket change, Hebel swept and cleaned a garage in Spokane. He also went over to the Fellowship Center, running into a group of Japanese Americans who had just been released from internment centers. At various points, Hebel joined with other CPS men to pick potatoes along the Snake River for a Mennonite man. Back in Missoula, where he resided at a fraternity house, he performed various chores.[27]

Following his two years as a smokejumper, Hebel was assigned to a CPS camp in Luray, Virginia, in the Shenandoah Valley, where "busy work," including shoveling snow by hand, awaited him. It must have been a relief when he was chosen to participate in the cattle boat shipments affiliated with the United Nations Relief and Rehabilitation Authority but run by the Brethren. He undertook three trips, which enabled him to "see some of the world"; two of his adventures involved the transfer of horses to Danzig, Poland. The middle assignment saw him travel to Trieste, Italy, on a boat loaded with cattle for Yugoslavia.[28]

Returning to the States in the summer of 1946, Hebel re-enrolled at Susquehanna University, receiving his undergraduate degree in 1948, having majored in sociology and minored in English. He had also remained a pre-ministerial student, "because of God's grace shown me in Jesus Christ." In September 1948, he began attending Lutheran Theological Seminary in Gettysburg, Pennsylvania. Hebel married Edith M. Wegner, a student at Susquehanna University, in New Brunswick, New Jersey, on May 29, 1949; the Hebels subsequently had three children, two sons and a daughter. In May 1951, Hebel received his degree in systematic theology, and shortly thereafter was ordained into the Gospel Ministry. A thirty-five-year career as a minister was about to begin.[29]

He received a call to serve the Karthaus Pastoral Charge in Clearfield County, Pennsylvania, where he would hold ministries on three different occasions. He also served as a minister in Bedford County, Pennsylvania; Hagerstown, Maryland; and Upper Bucks County, Pennsylvania. Throughout his ministries, Hebel sought "to relate with Christians of all denominations."[30]

By car, the Hebels traveled throughout the United States and into Canada; in 1977, they also made a trip to Israel, which proved to be "a very special experience." Into the period of Hebel's retirement from the ministry, he and Edith remained "strong proponents for Peace, Justice, and Care of God's Creation." Moreover, as Hebel reflected, "if we were called upon to make the choices again, we would be Christians, a Christian Pastoral family, and Christian pacifists: It's the way to go!"[31]

At a reunion for CPS 103 held at Bethel College, Hebel insisted that the smokejumpers' experience derived from the participants' patriotism and religious beliefs. Moreover, Hebel then explained, "There's a bond among the smokejumpers, to be sure, but there's a bigger bond before that — the peace bond. We all believed in reducing suffering, in suffering a wrong rather than doing a wrong."[32]

CHAPTER 9

The Flying Pastor
ALAN INGLIS

In the midst of an evening fire jump, as the wind swirled all about, Alan Inglis smacked into a large tree, some three feet in diameter, with his hands, feet, and face mask. Luckily, his whole body seemed to absorb the shock's impact and he emerged relatively unscathed. However, a colleague proved less fortunate. Calling out to this compatriot, Inglis was informed that he was hurt. The other CPS man had banged into a small tree and then fell onto a rock, breaking an ankle and chipping his hip. Inglis got to him quickly, sliding down his letdown rope. Inglis unfurled bright colored streamers to inform the spotter plane that a smokejumper had been injured. Having received powerful medication after an earlier jump had resulted in a banged up shoulder, Inglis passed some of it on to the uncomplaining man. "I also popped our reserve chutes to cover him and keep him as warm as possible during the night," Inglis later recalled.[1]

By the time darkness fell, the glow from the fire could be seen but no other smokejumpers had appeared. Inglis and his crew determined to sleep until additional support arrived. Exhausted, Inglis finally fell to sleep but was awakened when rescuers arrived with stretcher in hand. Subsequently, Inglis and other smokejumpers, some of whom were assigned to the rescue operation, carried out the injured man, which proved to be hard work. Four lifted the stretcher, while another smokejumper led the way, using an axe to help chart the course. The passage was difficult and seemed to take forever, but finally the trail was reached. Fortunately, a horse awaited the injured jumper. Placing him on the animal was no easy task, but imbibing alcohol at least partially anesthetized the young man. Eventually, "we had one of the drunkest, happiest injured Mennonites you ever saw," Inglis declared. Inglis was instructed to walk alongside the horse to ensure that limbs did not jostle his compatriot's foot. That entailed traversing the uneven and rocky portions of the trail, which at times required pulling the horse so that it would not slide down the cliff.[2]

The men had to walk several miles to get to the base fire camp. Inglis had marched out "like Superman," but "felt it later." He went to a nurse, received some aspirin, but begged not to be removed from the jump list. In fact, he received orders to continue down the trail on his own to undertake yet another fire jump, where he would meet up with a group of smokejumpers who were already on the ground. Inglis was allowed to take a pack mule but after a while, his legs cramped up. Unable to easily dismount the mule, Inglis deliberately fell off. Then, he had to contend with the fact that the mule, which was coming up behind him, threatened to step on his heels. Luckily, the mule was good-tempered, "so I survived and so did he," Inglis wrote.[3]

* * * * *

Alan Inglis was born on July 11, 1923, in Aurora, Nebraska. The parents of his father, Irving, were of Scottish ancestry and operated their own farms. At the same time, they instilled the value of education in their children. Irving volunteered for service in World War I, hoping to help "make the world safe for democracy." The experience, however, proved disillusioning. After the war, in fact, Irving's reservations about what he and so many others had endured resulted in his ouster from the American Legion. Irving subsequently graduated from the Chicago Divinity School and then headed Congregational ministries in Greeley, Colorado, and Groves, Missouri, where he resided for 26 years. Congregationalists like Inglis continued to adhere to a Social Gospel perspective. Alan's mother, whose maiden name was Laura Olds, was born in Mexico, the children of missionaries. She later informed her son, "We are descendants of the first woman of the *Mayflower*." After the death of her parents, Laura was adopted by an aunt who lived in Davenport, Iowa. Laura graduated from Grinnell College.[4]

As it appeared increasingly likely that the United States would get pulled into World War II, Alan and his three brothers had to decide what to do. He attempted to talk about the war with his buddies, who quadruple dated with their various girlfriends during high school. More and more, as war broke out in Europe, Alan wondered "what would this lead to?" Eventually, two of the Inglis boys opted for military service, while two filed as conscientious objectors. All the boys had listened to their own father deliver sermons in his church, where he attempted to impart lessons dating back to his wartime experiences. Although Irving had long adopted an antiwar posture, he presented his addresses "without hurting people's feeling." One of Alan's older brothers was the first to declare himself a conscientious objector and was accorded "a fairly rough time" by the local draft board. By the time Alan applied as a CO, however, the board "didn't even question me." As for his own experience as a CO, Alan later reflected, "I feel having been a yellowbelly was one of the best things that ever happened to me." He was sent to a CPS camp in Texarkana, Texas, where he "learned how the black people were treated."[5]

Inglis was hardly displeased when a transfer notice arrived, indicating that he would be stationed at the mental hospital in Lyons, New Jersey. Placed on the acute ward, Inglis— who weighed only 135 pounds but had been a successful high school wrestler — saw his shirt torn off by a patient at one point. But he stuck it out and was soon named runner-attendant, which resulted in his being called to situations where a physician was present but matters threatened to get out of control. The patients were veterans, including one former Golden Gloves boxer who insistently declared that he wanted to return home. When Inglis arrived on the scene, the patient grabbed a chair and belted the doctor with it. Inglis then knocked the chair aside and pushed the patient away from the doctor, enabling others to subdue the troubled veteran.[6]

The doctor informed the commander of the hospital about the incident, highlighting Inglis's role in preventing matters from escalating out of hand. Consequently, Inglis received a military citation, possibly the only one garnered by a CPS man during the war. As he later recalled, "I'm very proud of it." Eventually, however, Inglis was compelled to leave the hospital because of charges that he, along with others, had mistreated patients. Older attendants had taught him how to "wig out" patients. One of the COs, however, thought the patients were being mistreated. A government investigation took place, with only Inglis acknowledging what he had done. Thus, he became something of a scapegoat. Fortunately, by that point, he had already applied for the smokejumpers program.[7]

Inglis was delighted at the chance to join the smokejumpers. He considered it, in fact, "the elite opportunity for COs." It took some time for his application to be accepted, which Inglis attributed to the fact that he was "too lightweight." Earlier, Inglis had been turned down when he sought to participate in a starvation experiment. Now, he visited several camps in California, before heading for Missoula. He quickly discovered that there were problems with the operation of CPS camps where smokejumpers were stationed. It made little sense to him that Forest Service or ex-military men were placed in charge of a group of conscientious objectors. As Inglis saw it, "That doesn't work. COs are too independent ... too stubborn."[8]

But he came to enjoy flying, which smokejumping introduced him to, Inglis recalled. Owing to the fact that he had never been up in an airplane before, Inglis participated in several practice runs before actually attempting a landing. In his dreams, Inglis had fantasized that he "would take off and glide around the room and land easily." During one of his furloughs, his parents asked how he was able to jump from planes. Inglis indicated that he sang hymns. They wondered, "What did you sing?" He replied, "He Leadeth Me." Inglis was then told, "That is a good family hymn. They sang it at both your grandparents' funerals." In the midst of one jump, a number of the smokejumpers followed Inglis's lead in attempting to sing a hymn as they floated down from the sky. This proved unsuccessful, Inglis explained, "because there is no reverberation or reflection of sound to enhance hearing. The sound just disseminated through the air." Consequently, "after a few shouted notes, we gave up."[9]

The training at Nine Mile proved rigorous. In the morning, the men sat in classrooms, getting schooled in map reading, compasses, safety techniques, and fire dimensions. In the afternoon, they worked out "to get in shape." The fire line proved most memorable for Inglis.

> Eight of us would use the caterpillar technique on a fire line. The last man determined the speed of all eight men on the crew. He would determine when the line was secure against fire and say something to the effect of "up." Then each man would drop what he was doing and start on what the man ahead had been doing. Of course, the lead man often did little more than determine the direction the line would take. I remember when being in the lead taking just one or two whacks with my ax and then moving up three or four feet.

The honing of this technique, Inglis contended, "made us the best fire line builders," although the CPS men retained great respect for "professional Indian firefighters."[10]

As Inglis recalled, the CPS units, while in training, sported the equipment they would in the field.

> We carried a pack containing a mattock (ax on one end and heavy-duty hoe on the other), a shovel, a file to keep tools sharp, a down sleeping bag and K-Rations and any other personal gear we preferred. I always carried extra socks, both wool and cotton, wrapped around my belt.

They wore the cotton on the outside to prevent the more expensive wool from being worn down as it rubbed against boots.[11]

The men also took along necessary foodstuffs: "The K-Rations were little waxed boxes measuring about 8" × 4" × 2". We carried 6, or enough for 2 days, usually. They contained canned potted meats, cheese, biscuits and I especially remember the lemonade tablets that could be applied to water and make a drink." However, they were not told what type of container should be used to mix a drink. Consequently, during one of their outings, a smokejumper placed the tablet, which contained acid, in his aluminum canteen, causing both the tablet and part of the aluminum to dissolve. The smokejumper got sick, thereby imparting a lesson to his compatriots.[12]

Much of the training, of course, pertained to jumping. The men learned the Allen Roll, which was to be employed on landing.

> The Allen Roll consisted of landing with the knees slightly bent, using the legs as shock absorbers, twisting so that one fell on his hip and then rolled over backwards across the opposite shoulder. At best you could continue the roll so that as you rolled over on your shoulders, you could give a push with the hands, do a backward somersault and land on the feet.

This proved difficult for Inglis, notwithstanding his training as a wrestler and tumbler.[13]

Tower jumping was another major component of training at Nine Mile. The men, as Inglis related, had

> to jump off a high tower into space. It also involved feeling the shock of a chute opening. We wore our canvas pants and a jacket with the very high back collar. We wore the harness to which the chute was attached, only now it was attached to a heavy rope. The rope went to a pulley attached to a cross-arm which was attached to a telephone pole with the rope fastened to the bottom of the pole. I would suppose the tower was 40 feet high. After attaching the rope to the harness and putting on the football helmet with a wire cage across the front, we would jump off the tower. With arms folded, spine straight, we would look forward to the shock of coming to the end of our rope before having to hit the ground, or rather a flimsy net absorber other than the stretch of the rope.

At one point, Inglis attempted to jump without his helmet. "That was a mistake. The harness, or rope, or something, hit me in the jaw and made me feel as if I had been slugged. The helmet would have protected me." He never repeated that mistake.[14]

The CPS men also had to learn what to do as they dropped from the sky.

> Some other training we received was in how to let yourself down when hanging in a tree. The canvas pants we wore had a large pocket in the lower leg area. In it we carried red cloth streamers and a long rope — about 30 feet. The streamers were used to make a symbol on the ground to notify the airplane pilot that everything was or was not okay. (We had no radio on a 2-man jump.) With the rope in the pocket we were hoisted up into the air with block and tackle. Then the job was to thread the rope through rings in the harness and tie it on to what would be the ring on the parachute. Then all we had to do was chin ourselves and hold ourselves up with one hand so we could unhook the parachute from the harness with the other. It had to be done twice. Once for each shoulder.[15]

When the time arrived for his initial jump, Inglis and his crew were unable to suit up before they boarded the plane, an old Ford Trimotor. They dressed as the plane took off. This was Inglis's first jump and he "hardly had time to appreciate it." The plane contained no seats for the smokejumpers, just open floor space, and no door. Shortly before it was time to jump, the men checked each other's gear. Then, they were told to get ready, to stand and "fasten the clip on the end of our static line to the wire cable running the length of the cabin." The static line itself "was the strong 2-inch ... [webbing] attached to the top of the parachute canopy with a strong [cord] that would break when the parachute pack had been opened and the chute itself had been pulled out of the pack."[16]

Inglis was possibly the first man to jump.

> There was a small step about the size of the sole of your foot. The step was held in mid-air, out from the plane, by three rods. The idea was to put your heel on that step. Here you are, staring out into space, trying to put your foot out the door onto a little step. The first time I tried, my foot ended up a foot downstream from the step and off-balance, ready to fall out. So you pull your foot back and try again and still miss. By this time, you realize that with the "prop wash" you have to start your foot in front of the step so the wind carries it onto the step. Then all you have to do is watch all that wide open scenery go by while your wait for the spotter to tap you on the back. I always wished he would kick me so there would be no doubt that now was the time.[17]

There was a particular technique to the actual jump itself, as Inglis recorded.

> We were taught to jump out feet first with our ... arms crossed on top of the reserve chute on our stomachs. Why not fly out like Superman? Then you could follow the jumper in front of you very closely. Guess who had to try it? And I did follow the man in front very closely, so closely that I saw every crisscross of the ... [cover] and chute come out of the pack. But it was very hard on one arm when my chute opened, wrenching it rather severely. So that is why you jumped feet first with arms crossed![18]

Fires, large and small, could prove equally troublesome, albeit in different fashions. One fire, probably triggered by lightning, which Inglis was sent out to contain, proved so minuscule that he and his fellow smokejumpers worried they could not find it "unless we landed on it." Thus, a decision was made to drop Inglis and one other smokejumper from an altitude of only 600 feet. That required the men to be ready to land as soon as their parachutes opened up. That proved "no sweat," but Inglis "landed so close to the fire that I could see the smoke." Once they discarded their jumping gear, the pair built a fire line around the burning tree. A question arose about how to put out the smoldering smoke. As Inglis reflected, "Well, nature called, so that helped. In fact, it helped so much that we drank all the water we could and peed out the fire."[19]

Finding a way back to a trail proved more difficult. Inglis and the other smokejumper thought a ridge was close by, along with a fire lookout station. Thus, they reasoned they could easily take their gear to the trail and leave it to be picked up with pack animals. But first, they improvised. "We made a stretcher out of two boughs and threaded them through the arms of our jumping jackets and tied the rest of the gear on top of the jackets." Once they got on their way, however, they soon discovered how heavy the gear was. They opted to drop two emergency chutes and mark the spot. They then determined to discard all the equipment, except for water, K-Rations, and an axe to help carve out a path for the pack animals, soon to follow.[20]

Detecting the fire lookout tower from the trail, they proceeded to look for a phone. Having arrived there, they discovered that the lookout tower was unoccupied and the phone disconnected. As he fooled around with the phone, Inglis could get the ringer to work but he could hear a conversation occurring between two men on manned towers. Inglis broke in, indicated who he was and explained that he and his partner would be heading for the ranger station as quickly as possible. On arriving at the ranger station, they "were treated like royalty," because they had undertaken much of the firefighting themselves.[21]

Another fire, at first glance, also promised to be an easy one to contend with. That one was situated along the banks of a river. A crew of eight smokejumpers poured out of a Ford Trimotor. Once all the men were on the ground, they triggered the motor for a pump, with the crew chief attending to the nozzle. In typical fashion, non-COs, who received regular wages, not a pittance like the conscientious objectors, headed the crews. It appeared that the fire was quickly brought under control, so the men set up camp. As matters turned out, the fire camp was still smoldering. In fact, when the men awoke in the morning they encountered a "big SURPRISE!" with the fire "going strong again." Now, the crew was forced to build a fire line around the fire, no easy task. Dropping by a cargo plane, a crate, loaded with canned goods, provided lunch. Inglis was assigned to cook, not an unwelcome chore as he received "extra time off the fire line," a taxing enterprise under the circumstances. After the fire was brought under control, several smokejumpers headed for camp, while Inglis offered to remain behind until the fire was fully extinguished. When Inglis and the others who had stayed at the fire site finally walked back, a distance of some 18 miles, they went along the river, which afforded a panoramic view.[22]

A couple of other fire jumps Inglis made proved eventful, in their own fashion. On one, the spotter suggested that Inglis jump last and help drop gear on cargo chutes. This was the one occasion when he got airsick. Pushing the equipment out as the plane made its passes hardly helped. It was a relief when his actual jump took place, because once he landed, he tore off his face mask and threw up. After that, he could attend to his work. He was told to help retrieve a pair of parachutes that were in the path of the fire, but arrived too late to do so.[23]

Another jump saw Inglis take along an 8mm movie camera shipped to him by his parents. Inglis had worried about how he would carry the film out of the plane when he jumped.

> I sewed a pocket inside my jacket at chest level that would be closed when my jacket was closed. I also tied a nylon load line onto it in case it got away from me or was dropped. The spotter let me go in the last pass so I got some shots of jumpers in the Ford Trimotor. Someone even took a picture of men in the plane. Then I stuck the camera out a window and took pictures as jumpers stepped out the door. You could see the static lines pull out the chutes, the bouncing opening, and the chute and chutist becoming smaller behind the plane. When my turn came, I put the camera back in my specially made jacket pocket and jumped. After the chute opened, I pulled out my camera and started shooting, but nothing recorded since there was too much light.[24]

The largest fire Inglis had to contend with did not require him to jump. He and a group of 11 other smokejumpers had been out for about a week fighting fires. They were picked up by the Forest Service and then rode in a truck from the afternoon until midnight. When it turned dark, Inglis snuggled into his bedroll to fight off the cold. After the vehicle stopped, the men hiked "through several miles of Jack ... [pine] forest" to reach a large fire. They had only one flashlight to illuminate their way. "It was never darker in that forest. You could not even see what you were touching." Consequently, they latched onto each other's belts and relied on any warnings that the man immediately in front might convey so a message could be relayed to the man coming up the rear. Once they snaked their way to the fire, the thoroughly exhausted crew began constructing a fire line. As morning approached, the crew chief recognized that little was being accomplished. So, he told everyone to try and sleep until dawn. Now lacking his bedroll, Inglis "rolled over a burning log and scraped the burning ashes away also and lay down on the warm ground." When daylight appeared, Inglis spotted any number of small burn holes in his socks and in the rest of his clothes. "But what a wonderful sleep!" Inglis later recalled.[25]

Following the fire season, Inglis took advantage of a furlough and returned to the home base. Once back in Missoula, he discovered that the fire season had ended. The fraternity house the smokejumpers had used had been turned back over to students. Even Inglis's jumping boots were nowhere to be found. He soon transferred to the CPS camp at Glendora, California, which proved to be a difficult undertaking in its own way. While in Glendora, his camp went on strike. Like many of his fellow CPSers, Inglis was jailed. His time behind bars was brief, only two hours, and he was let out on his own recognizance. His case and that of his compatriots proved hopeless, for they were engaged in a strike against the U.S. government during wartime. As the sentencing took place, the judge induced Inglis and other defendants to agree to never again deliberately violate a government edict. Most, including Inglis, did so, with the lone Jew in the group the only one refusing the directive. Reflecting on his decision at the time, Inglis later acknowledged, "I'm ashamed of that." The judge handed out one-year sentences that he immediately suspended, while placing the men on probation for two years. Most important to Inglis, he did not lose his citizenship or his right to vote.[26]

Before he was released from CPS service, Inglis sought permission to visit Earlham College, which his younger brother was attending. Inglis told his brother to find him a wife. Amazingly enough, his brother proceeded to do exactly that, introducing Inglis to Margaret, whom he later married. Once Inglis completed his undergraduate studies at Earlham, Margaret helped to put him through Yale Divinity School.[27]

His first assignment on leaving New Haven was to lead a church in Wheatland, Wyoming. There, three children were born to Alan and Margaret, after they attended some of the first childbirth classes held in the region. There too, Inglis learned to fly, proving fascinated with his first landing. "It influenced the rest of my life," he declared. Later, Inglis took on the task of serving as a kind of "flying pastor" for five small churches in North Dakota. For three years, he flew from one spot to another, braving lightning, wires, and a dearth of landing fields. Instead, he relied on football fields, baseball diamonds, cornfields, and back-country roads to set off in his Piper Cub 11. In contrast to his predecessor, Inglis refused to carry a gun, even though he was skirting around what was considered potentially dangerous territory, the edge of an Indian reservation. One unfortunate moment involved his clipping of a plane and the receipt of a "nasty letter" from the Federal Aviation Agency. It was fortunate that his pilot's license was not revoked.[28]

Determining that he had been pushing his luck, Inglis chose to give up his flying ministry. Later, he was called to minister to a church in Waglina, Minnesota, affiliated with the Church of Christ. After eight years, he was forced out, due to his activist stances on civil rights and the Vietnam War, which demonstrated how Inglis followed the lead of his father in adhering to the social ministry. He had joined Clergy and Laymen Against the Vietnam War, marched in an antiwar demonstration in the nation's capital, and refused to pay his telephone tax, reasoning that the moneys were going to help conduct the war in Southeast Asia. The Internal Revenue Service came after him, but its agents proved to be "the nicest guys," affording Inglis three choices. They would confiscate his car and sell it to garner the necessary money to pay the tax, attach his salary, or take it out of his savings. Inglis told them to adopt the third strategy, but "the church couldn't handle it," encouraging him to submit his resignation.[29]

With only a month's severance, Inglis managed nevertheless to buy a used school bus for only $250. He removed most of the seats, converted the top of the bus into a carrier, and loaded up a piano. Alan and Margaret also owned a seven-passenger pallbearer's car that they had purchased for a trip to Mexico. The two vehicles transported the Inglis family and household goods to Colorado, where they settled in a cabin near Estes Park. As Inglis remembered, "We thought we would go where we wanted to be."[30]

He soon obtained a job in East Easton, Colorado, working for one of the War on Poverty programs. His clients were Mexican families, who possessed few material resources. One incident proved particularly harrowing, when a man phoned, indicating that he was drunk and could not find his car. When Inglis went to help him out, the caller pulled out a gun, put it against his head, and threatened to commit suicide. Inglis responded calmly, but the man then changed his tune and declared, "I'm not going to kill myself. I'm going to kill a gringo." Inglis was taken to the drunkard's home but managed to escape. In fact, Inglis's wife was on the phone with the man, when Inglis slipped out the back door and returned to his own house. When he arrived, his wife told the man, "Well, he's here, so goodbye."

CHAPTER 10

The Carpenter
WILMER CARLSEN

Wilmer Carlsen thought about the new draft law, the first peacetime conscription measure in the nation's history, which had just been enacted. He concluded, "I'm not going to shoot somebody on somebody's order. If I'm going to shoot somebody, I want to decide to do it." He reasoned, "'The Authority' could shoot me if they willed, but I would not shoot another man because of an order to do so." Moreover, "I didn't really trust my government," he later acknowledged. At the same time, "I didn't know anybody who expressed the same thought I did about the war." Then, he came across an article by A. J. Muste, America's foremost pacifist, discussing conscientious objection. Carlsen now knew "that people like me were called Conscientious Objectors."[1] That hardly cleared up everything for Carlsen, who failed to receive any support from either family members or friends. A pair of his uncles viewed him as "a disgrace to the family." One asked Carlsen, "Do you have to go that way?" A number of his friends and acquaintances were entering the U.S. armed forces. Coupled with his dealings with the Selective Service, Carlsen endured "a traumatic and lonely" period.[2]

He considered filing for I-A-O status, and becoming a medic. "I thought I could do that," he said. As matters turned out, his draft board in Lancaster, California, denied such a request. Carlsen reasoned to himself, "I thought they considered me mentally unfit for any kind of military service." Then, by the time he showed up for his physical examination, Carlsen had heard about the CPS camps. His draft board clerk took little liking to the young conscientious objector. "When I first heard you were a CO, I could have taken a knife to you," the clerk told Carlsen. However, that same clerk subsequently asked him if he wanted a drink as a send-off. To Carlsen's astonishment, the clerk also declared, "I kiss all my boys goodbye."[3]

* * * * *

Wilmer Carlsen was born on February 3, 1917, in a farming community outside Harlan, Iowa. During high school, Carlsen earned a pair of football letters and also threw the discus for the track team. After graduation, he remained at the family farm for about a year, helping out with chores. The Great Depression was in full force, and Carlsen and his brother Ad soon chose "to strike out on our own." The pair hopped on a freight train that was heading for Minneapolis. Before they were outside their home state, they got separated when Ad jumped onto another train, but Wilmer was unable to do so. In Laurel, Montana, Wilmer managed to get on a slow-moving train. By chance, he spotted his brother walking along the highway, located next to the train tracks.[4]

The now reunited brothers went to Hamilton, Montana, situated in the Bitterroot Valley, hoping to find jobs picking potatoes. No work was available there, however, so they continued riding the rails of the Northern Pacific and Milwaukee railroads. They finally found work in Omak, Washington, picking apples in an orchard for twenty-five cents an hour. The work was welcomed, for "jobs were something you wanted," especially during the hard times of the Great Depression, Carlsen later recalled. The two brothers resided in a new A-frame shed that had been built to house pigs; at least it contained straw for bedding. Once the picking season ended, the two young men stayed on to move tree props for a while.

As they had saved a little money, the Carlsen brothers returned to hopping on freight trains. They traveled to Seattle, where, in a show of "frugality," they slept in a flophouse that charged 10 cents per night for a bed. As Carlsen looked around, he estimated that approximately 50 men were camped out in the same room. For 10–15 cents, the brothers received their meals in an area known as Skid Row. Next, the two went down to southern California, where one of their uncles lived. They rode trains down the coast, stopping off in Canby, Oregon. In the midst of their quest for an inexpensive place to sleep for the night, they ended up in the local jail, courtesy of the night watchman who had taken them there. The watchman returned at 9:00 the next morning to ensure their release. Going through northern California, they "sawed firewood and pulled some weeds for our first income there," Carlsen recollected. They rode more rails until arriving in Stockton, where they resided "in hobo jungles" and "had meals in a skid row café operated by a Japanese." It was November 1936, with the Depression still enveloping the national landscape.[5]

Aware that cops in the area were pretty rough, the Carlsen brothers took a bus to Pasadena and then another to Los Angeles to stay with their

Wilmer "Bill" Carlsen (courtesy Bill Carlsen).

uncle and his wife, who ran a fruit stand. Their uncle helped them obtain jobs with a local dairy, where, for the next year, they herded cows. Occasionally, they also helped at the fruit stand. Continuing their adventures, they went to Lancaster, California, where they baled hay during the summer months and then helped to prepare the ground for hay fields. Eventually, Carlsen's brother left for a job with the American Potash and Chemical Company, situated in Trona, California, while Wilmer remained behind working on hay ranches.[6]

Prior to 1940, Carlsen neglected to give much thought to events overseas that threatened to pull the United States into war. But that would change following the introduction of the Selective Service System that year. In the meantime, Carlsen used a small Farmall tractor in a manner that pleased his employer. "I was the only man that he had ever hired who could plow a straight furrow," Carlsen remembered. Finally, he had to contend with the draft. By now, Carlsen, who received his draft notice in January 1941, had found out what a conscientious objector was and something about the CPS camps. Not involvement in one of the peace churches but rather his opposition to war led to Carlsen's decision to apply for conscientious objector status. One of his uncles, a veteran of World War I, unsuccessfully attempted to dissuade him from doing so. The day he was ordered shipped off to camp, Carlsen, having submitted his papers to be declared a conscientious objector, went to the draft board early in the evening, as requested. The clerk passed him over to a physician for a physical examination, which largely involved the simple question of whether he had suffered any injury or illness during the past several months. Having responded no, "I was cleared for travel to Cascade Locks 21," Carlsen later reflected.[7]

To his amazement, Carlsen found himself on a Pullman headed for the camp. With a government voucher, he obtained breakfast the next morning and then started back to the Pullman. On the way, four men, who also appeared to be in their early twenties and were, like Carlsen, attired in civilian garb, asked where he was headed. They had spotted him using the voucher to cover the costs of his meal. When he responded to their query, "To Cascade Locks, Oregon," they in turn indicated, "That's where we are going. We are conscientious objectors." As Carlsen recalled, "These were the first real live C.O.'s that I had ever seen. It was a relief to find that I wasn't the only 'screw-ball' in the world and to know that whatever fate had in store, I would at least have some company." At the same time, given the war-like atmosphere that was beginning to take hold, he wondered how advisable it was to state "to all who could hear, that they were C.O.'s."[8]

At Cascade Locks, Carlsen joined in a series of projects, including the building of a lookout post, the setting up of fire hose boxes, and the cutting of firewood. He also shared KP duties with other CPS men. From time to time, they were sent to help reroof Forest Service stations in Portland, Oregon. Before the CPS volunteers arrived, various community folk had asked the superintendent of the Forest Service project if they should pack guns "to maintain law and order." When informed of this, the CPS men "thought that was kind of funny."[9]

During his stay at Cascade Locks, Carlsen spotted a notice about the smokejumpers program on a bulletin board. He recalled having witnessed various air shows back in Iowa where jumpers leaped from their planes. More-over, he considered smokejumping "a kind of daring thing to do." Carlsen, who had fought forest fires earlier in Oregon along the Deschutes River and on the Olympic Peninsula, immediately volunteered and was accepted as one of the first CPS smokejumpers. In May 1943, he arrived in Missoula, accom-panied by another CPS man, Bert Olin. They were sent to the U.S. Forest Ser-vice Region I headquarters, located in the federal building. Ralph Hand informed them how to get to Seeley Lake. First, however, they went to get breakfast at Jim's No. 1 Café, a kind of "Greasy Greasy Spoon," located on East Main Street. Next, they took the Seeley Lake Stage, which dropped them off near the ranger's station at Seeley Lake. Along with 15 other future smoke-jumpers, they were assigned to beds at the ranger's station bunkhouse.[10]

Within two weeks, another 60 men had arrived. At that point, all the prospective jumpers took a boat across the lake to Camp Paxson, which had recently been set up by the U.S. Forest Service as a Boy Scout camp. Some of the men were assigned to put the finishing touches on the campsite, including the building of two bathhouses. Training took place in April, May, and June, and then men were farmed out to various side camps. Among their instructors, who schooled them in how to build fire lines and put out blazes, were Frank Derry, Art Cochran, Wag Dodge, and, of course, Earl Cooley. At one point, Dodge, to his credit, reined in a Forest Service employee who was ragging on the CPS men. For his part, Carlsen was instructed to remain at Seeley Lake, where he would again reside in the bunkhouse. During this same period, the U.S. Coast Guard had sent 10 of its men to Seeley Lake to be tutored in Forest Service techniques, includ-ing parachuting, to assist them in rescue operations. The two groups of men got along well. On a few occasions, Carlsen actually wrestled a Coast Guardsman, albeit unsuccessfully.[11]

Carlsen spent two additional summers at Nine Mile, making him one of the few CPS smokejumpers to serve during three fire seasons. Altogether, he made 29 jumps, approximately 10–15 of which were fire jumps. The training went pretty smoothly for Carlsen, who certainly came to hold "a little respect" for what the smokejumpers went through. At the same time, as he remembered, "I didn't feel it was particularly difficult to jump out of a plane." During his second jump, he did land pretty hard, bruising his right foot. However, "I pretended that it didn't show, I hoped anyway. Cause I didn't think it was enough to quit jumping anyhow," he recalled. Carlsen, who relied on both Ervin and Eagle parachutes, also pointed to two or three occasions when the Eagle opened so quickly "as to make me see stars.... Whether the risers hit my head or whether it snapped my back or neck or whatever, but it gave me a jolt, I tell you."[12]

At one point during his second or third year, Carlsen joined with a group of other CPS men to offer "exhibition jumps" for Forest Service managers who had come from Washington, D.C. The area selected for the demonstration was a Remount pasture, situated west of the camp. After a few men had already leaped, Harry Burks and Carlsen prepared to go next. They were flying on a Travelair, which dropped a drift parachute. Burks jumped first, virtually coming down on the spot that had been selected. Unfortunately, the wind picked up as the plane readied for Carlsen's jump. He bolted out the plane and the parachute unfurled. However, as Carlsen later related,

> I discovered that I was sailing cross-country so fast that I doubt slipping the 'chute would have been of much help. The wind was blowing toward camp so I just turned 180 degrees and went as far as I could — over the hill, over a gully, and half way up the next slope — and out of sight.

Normally, the other smokejumpers were willing to help draw out the parachute, pull in its lines, and pack the materials in a bag. However, "This time I got to do it myself."[13]

On August 6, 1944, Carlsen was waiting in the parachute loft in Missoula, along with another dozen men or so. They had received word about a fire on a mountaintop in the Salmon River country, located near Riggins, Idaho. The territory was inauspiciously referred to as the "Land of No Return." While a group of men had just arrived from the camp at Nine Mile, the men at the top of the jumping list received the call. Tossing their equipment onto a truck, the men got on board and headed for the airport at Hale Field. Those not selected, in typical fashion, remained back at the base, getting ready "and praying for more fires." Having suited up before getting on the Ford Trimotor, the men placed their fire equipment and parachutes into the plane's cabin, and flew out. Bob Johnson piloted the plane, while Vic Carter, the Parachute Project administrative officer, served as spotter. The relatively smooth trip lasted two hours and carried the crew over rugged Idaho mountain ranges. Typical horseplay broke out, with "fellows pugnaciously inviting each other to step outside, pretending to vomit, and other delicate touches of humor." Some 20 minutes from their intended destination, the men readied their backpacks and emergency chutes.[14]

The fire was soon spotted, with a good deal of smoke wafting along a high mountain ridge. When they arrived, the crew discovered that the fire was situated "near the end and top of the ridge, about two or three thousand feet above the notorious Salmon river, a silver ribbon in the afternoon sunlight." Circling, they looked for clear areas in the grass. Carter called on a pair of drift chutes to check the direction of the wind. Although not strong, the wind was gusting toward the river. The first two jumpers were

Wilmer and Ad Carlsen, both experienced parachuters. Carter signaled for Johnson to cut his motors and ease the plane into a glide, and then tapped Ad on the back. He jumped, followed almost immediately by his brother. As Murray Braden recalled, "We could hear the chutes crack viciously." As the plane conducted a second pass, the remaining smokejumpers spotted Wilmer's parachute caught up in a high tree. George Robinson and Walt Reimer were the next to jump, followed by Braden and Gregg Phifer. Al Thiessen and George Leavitt made up the last pair. Before he leapt, Braden heard Carter warn, "And for God's sake stay out of the river!" To avoid gliding over the ridge-top, the men had to maneuver their chutes deftly.[15]

Johnson made a number of passes to drop cargo, including firepacks, a saw, and other vital equipment, before flying back to Missoula. The men were ready to begin battling the fire, a mere three hours after they had received the call back at the loft in Missoula. To their surprise, they encountered Homer Chance and Merle Hoover, whom they had not seen since early June, when the two had departed for McCall, Idaho. In addition, Eldon Whitesitt and Gordon Miller had also jumped from the McCall Travelair earlier that afternoon. A quarter mile away, the men were able to get "a good look at our fire. It was narrow, two or three hundred feet wide, and ... extended down the slope almost half a mile." Whitesitt and Miller had determined that the fire was "burning merrily, advancing steadily up the forty-five degree slope." Luckily, plenty of loose mineral soil could be found, which the two used to cool the fire down a bit, enabling them to build a fire line around its top.[16]

Another jump took Carlsen and a CPS crew to Madison Plateau, located in the majestic Yellowstone National Park. Excited that they were about to tackle "a real fire," the men tossed their gear onto a Ford Trimotor piloted by Dick Johnson and headed for West Yellowstone. After arriving there, they suited up and took off once more, soon reaching the Madison Plateau. The smokejumpers landed about a halfmile from the fire, onto a plateau perched around 8,500 feet. Many landed in relatively small trees, but quickly eased themselves to the ground. They immediately headed for the fire, but Carlsen was soon instructed to obtain water. The lake was situated at least two miles from the site of the fire and required negotiating a rather steep mountainside. Carlsen noticed a mountain lion track and then discovered that the water in the lake was stagnant and would have to be boiled before the men could drink it. Leaving the spot of the fire entailed another chore, an 18-mile hike, about a third of it along mountainous terrain. When a trail was discovered, Carlsen and the crew leader engaged in something of a foot race back into West Yellowstone.[17]

In addition to a series of fire jumps, Carlsen pitched in with various work projects. One involved constructing a lookout tower on Ashley Mountain near Whitefish. Another called for building a bridge at St. Regis. Carlsen also helped to clear roads at Clark's Fork, Idaho, taking out brush and timber along the way. At the same time, "I perfected my carpentry skills a little bit during my smokejumping days." On other occasions, he could be found toiling in a sign shop or serving as a camp cook, where he was forced to split his own firewood, hang meat in a shed, and wash dishes. KP duty sometimes came his way for having violated camp edicts. Although the men generally got along together, Carlsen admitted that he "probably was more of the obstreperous type than most of them." That resulted in Carlsen's acquiring "a few marks against my career" that might have precluded him from continuing in the smokejumpers project even if the government had afforded CPS men such an opportunity.[18]

For Carlsen, his service as a smokejumper proved "exciting.... Certainly, I don't have any regrets for having participated." Furthermore, it "probably was a beneficial experience, broadening my scope a little." After all, camp sessions resulted in a commingling of men of different faiths.[19]

In 1946, Carlsen obtained his discharge and subsequently applied for admission to the Carpenters Union in Missoula. He was accepted and soon initiated a career as a carpenter and cabinetmaker. Later, he moved to Polson, worked part-time, and enjoyed living in a cabin, situated next to a home owned by Phil Stanley, along Flathead Lake. Carlsen also made use of a boat — one he built himself — on the water.[20]

CHAPTER 11

The Actor:
JOE COFFIN

In July 1942, Audine Coffin drove her husband Joe at 6:00 in the morning to the bus station in Los Angeles, where he readied for a 440-mile ride to Coleville, in eastern California. Just outside Coleville was CPS 37, located on a former CCC camp, in high desert country in the Mono National Forest. Morale at CPS 37 was low, with a number of CPS men present from camps in Petersham, Buck Creek, and Patapsco, among other sites back east. The men had been told they would help to open a new camp out west that would be involved in fighting forest fires. The actual location of CPS 37 was barren; firefighting too seldom appeared on the horizon, and the tasks the CPS men were assigned—"fence building and sheep trail clearing"—hardly appeared to involve "work of national importance."[1]

Serving as a truck mechanic, Coffin did, on one occasion, help to save a rancher's home, which was threatened by fire. Standing on a log beside the house, Coffin chopped wood, resulting in the very soles of his shoes becoming charred. Nevertheless, an increasingly frustrated

Joe Coffin (courtesy Joe Coffin)

Coffin, like a number of his fellow campmates, seriously considered walking out of CPS 37. They "were very bitter" about not being allowed to engage in meaningful work. Coffin, for his part, could not handle being forced to participate in makeshift work of an "absurd sort." He did a good deal of soul-searching, and knew that leaving the camp might well result in a prison sentence. All the while, the situation at Coleville failed to improve, which Audine immediately discovered during her visit to the camp. The wooden barracks where the men resided were "dirty," and the campsite as a whole seemed "terrible," in her estimation. She, like the CPS men, watched as Stubby Hayes, a terribly overweight individual, struggled to keep up, to no avail. Fortunately for all parties concerned, the 380-pound Hayes was eventually released.[2]

The possibility of Joe's walking out of the camp worried Audine, who was all of twenty years old herself and teaching a group of Mexican students at a segregated school. "I thought that we would be detained" as a consequence, she later revealed. By this point, over 100,000 Japanese Americans and Japanese aliens resided in internment camps, as did a much smaller number of Italian and German Americans. Although misplaced, Audine's concerns were understandable, given the temper of the times. Joe never had to make the decision to walk out of camp because of the arrival of Dr. Conway, who served as superintendent of Eastern State Hospital, located near Spokane, Washington. Conway was seeking 25 men who would join him at Medical Lake at CPS Camp 75. Now, Coffin decided to "stick it out in CPS a little bit longer." He was not only selected to go, but was also appointed camp director. First, Coffin took a leave and returned to Whittier, where he picked up a touring car he had built, a Model-A Ford, with a funnel-like ventilation system. Along with Audine, Coffin drove to Medical Lake, arriving on December 24, 1942, despite a leaking radiator hose and losing a generator along the way.[3]

*　*　*　*　*

Coffin was born on November 15, 1919, in Richmond, Indiana. His father, Joseph Herschel Coffin, was raised in Indiana and became a professor of philosophy and psychology at Earlham College. His mother, Pearl Dean, came from Ohio and Iowa farm stock, before attending Penn College, where she met Herschel. In 1923, Herschel was appointed dean of Whittier College, a Quaker institution, in southern California. There, he was involved with the Whittier Plan for Core Curriculum College Education. Herschel helped to plan state curriculum, putting together a coordinated design for community colleges, which blended science, literature, history, and other disciplines, in a holistic manner. Whittier College was located in a Quaker community, Quakertown, where Coffin grew up. The Coffin family was involved in both university functions and affairs associated with the First Friends Church of Whittier. This was in keeping with family tradition, for the Coffins had longstanding Quaker roots, with relatives having participated in the Underground Railroad that steered slaves out of the American South. Not surprisingly, a felt need to become socially active was imparted. "I grew up with general contributions I saw as the normal way to do it," Joe Coffin later recalled.[4]

At the same time, young Joe was a typical child, albeit one who was growing up as the Great Depression swept across California. He and his friends industriously made their own way, devising "an interesting juvenile economy of lunch money, allowances and odd job earnings." They experienced "a world of 5 cent malts, 10 cent movies, summer camp, crystal sets, kites and stripped down bikes."[5]

His family moved to the East Coast when Coffin was twelve. Herschel agreed to serve as resident director of Pendle Hill, a retreat center run by Quakers, and to teach at Swarthmore College, outside Philadelphia. One selling point was the promise of a scholarship for Joe to attend Westtown School. A Quaker boarding school that dated back to the late eighteenth century, Westtown resided on a large farm situated in Chester County. Coffin was now introduced "to scholastic excellence and upscale eastern culture." As he later recalled, "I had some difficulty adjusting to the academics— Latin in the 8th Grade, coat and tie in all weather, tea time, etc., but I loved it."[6]

After two years, the Coffins moved back to Whittier. Entering the ninth grade, Coffin called on his "new found social skills to plunge into everything. Sports, Yearbook, Christian Endeavor, clubs, dances, the works." Having failed a Latin course back east, he took French at Whittier Union College. That class contained mostly upperclassmen who were student leaders. Like Coffin, a number were involved in the Friends Church Christian Endeavor. Consequently, "my social status was established early." His athleticism, demonstrated by Coffin's lettering in swimming during both his freshman and sophomore years, also helped to ensure his popularity. Overall, "life at Whittier High and First Friends was just fine," and even saw Coffin purchase his first automobile, a 1923 Dodge Roadster for which he paid $12.[7]

Nevertheless, he eagerly accepted the opportunity to return to Westtown School when a scholarship was forthcoming. Along with a friend, he boarded the Santa Fe Chief for Philadelphia. His second stop at Westtown proved "wonderful," with Coffin easily fitting in socially, athletically, and academically. His senior year, in particular, proved a delight, with Coffin garnering "honors in scholarship, sports, theatre, student affairs." Romance appeared too, along with "a deepening religious life fed by my introduction to the blessings of the unprogrammed meeting for worship." For him, the Quaker admonition to "be still and know that I am God" dug deep roots.[8]

During two summers back at Westtown, Coffin worked at the farm affiliated with the school. This too proved "a wonderful experience," with Coffin putting in five-and-a-half days for $12 a week. His room and board, in turn, cost $7 weekly. Enjoying himself immensely, Coffin "learned to pick and pack apples and peaches, trim the roadway with a scythe, mow acres of campus grass ... clean water grasses out of the lake, and help to install fire sprinklers and new floors in the boys' dorm." In Westtown, Coffin was virtually adopted by the family of Bill Pile, a fellow swimmer and his roommate.[9]

Following the summer after his graduation from Westtown, Coffin enrolled at Whittier College, taking advantage of a faculty family scholarship and a work-study job that paid 25 cents an hour. The academic training he had received at Westtown served him well, while he easily reestablished old friendships connected with Whittier High School and First Friends Church. His involvement with theater back at Westtown also afforded a jump start as he moved right into performances at Whittier College.[10]

Pearl Dean Coffin played no small part in encouraging her son's involvement in the dramatic arts. As Coffin remembered, "She was a dilettante. She was smothered in Whittier" and hardly relished her role as a faculty spouse. Consequently, Pearl spent considerable time in Los Angeles where she acquired friends in the movie industry. She spoke to George Brand, a self-employed drama coach, about her son. "She told him I was so wonderful," Coffin recalled. Brand agreed to take on Coffin as a student, declaring, "No charge, unless you earn the money for motion picture work." This proved "both a blessing and a bane." Brand got Coffin a spot with Bliss-Hayden, where he could learn to be in the movies. During a rehearsal, Coffin met Mitch Gertz, a Hollywood agent, who wanted to sign him to a contract. Gertz began to garner bit parts for Coffin at Warner Brothers, where he showed up in a number of Boston Blackie movies, beginning in September 1938. As he appeared in these B movies, Coffin also acquired a screen name: Joel Dean. In October, Columbia Studios hired Coffin for a part in *Blondie Meets the Boss*. He also appeared in *Cheers for Miss Bishop*. The pay was "twenty times" what he had received for his summer job in Westtown. Moreover, "the movie work was glamorous and exciting." He was on hand for a preview at the Hollywood Pantages Theatre.[11]

Increasingly, however, Coffin began to feel conflicted about his new experiences. By his junior year at Whittier College, he "became withdrawn." As he later reflected, "I had a kind of searching program going along in my life." Little helping matters was the fact that he suffered "a failed romance and ... conflict at home." Perhaps not surprisingly, "Gradually, I just quit going to class." Instead, he devoted his time and attention to tinkering with "my 'hot rod,' a souped up Model A Ford Roadster."[12]

In the springtime of 1939, Coffin left Whittier, tossing his tools, including welding tanks, in his car, and he drove to Philadelphia to visit the Pile family. He stopped at farmhouses along the way, seeking to swap work for food. He also saw his older brother Tom, who was staying in New York City. His old roommate got him a job at a gas station in Philadelphia. He was paid $15 for a 60-hour work week, and soon was promoted to assistant manager, which resulted in a $3 weekly pay increase.[13]

His depression having lifted by the early fall, Coffin sold his car and returned to Los Angeles on the Santa Fe Railroad. He re-enrolled at Whittier College, soon meeting the lovely Audine Meyer, whom he married on October 2, 1941. Active at Whittier Friends Church, the Coffins became involved with a series of peace organizations. Given his background, it was hardly surprising that Coffin registered as a conscientious objector. As he later reflected, "I came to it naturally." Coffin was classified 4-E but his induction was postponed until he, like Audine, garnered a teaching credential: his in secondary education and hers in elementary education. During her graduation ceremony, he sat in the audience with his induction notice in hand.[14]

Coffin's early experiences in CPS were difficult, involving the unhappy time spent at CPS camp 37 in Coleville. The time spent at Medical Lake was also mixed, to say the least. Both Joe and Audine quickly recognized that the local community folk were quite hostile to the CPS men. As she remembered, "These guys were really taking a beating." Coffin indicated that the people in the surrounding environs refused to speak to the CPS men, as did the hospital employees. Coffin worked in a receiving ward and there too the attendants refused to talk to him. The other employees, Audine remembered, "tried to run us down" while even the switchboard operator was "very nasty." In addition, the living circumstances once again were hardly ideal, with the men forced to dwell above an epileptic ward, having to make do on their $5 monthly stipend, and being compelled to work even on Christmas day. They also received room and board and a uniform for completing twelve-hour shifts, six days a week. Many of the buildings at the hospital seemed antiquated, while 52 patients had to be attended to. For a time, Joe shaved all the patients with a straight razor. Audine became a psychiatric social worker at the hospital, receiving $25 a month pay. She was the first to see patients, and then encountered their families. Both Audine and Joe tried to improve conditions for the patients, with Joe proceeding to remove restraints. One patient, an elderly gentleman around 80 years old, thought Coffin was Jesus and bowed down to him. Later, the patient indicated to Coffin, "I know you aren't Jesus but you are the prettiest man I've ever seen."[15]

Fortunately, a support group emerged in Spokane, drawn from the ranks of the Fellowship of Reconciliation and various church organizations interested in helping out the CPS unit. Many CPS men met up with the group during their time off, when they were free to go into the city. Eventually, Audine found an old, three-story mansion that was on the market for $5,000. It was located near the hospital, and Audine and Joe reasoned that it could serve as a home of sorts for the CPS unit. Consequently, Joe was able to convince his father to borrow enough money on his life insurance to pay for the mansion, which was converted into an International Fellowship Center. Bunkhouses were set up for men coming over from Missoula. The International House became a temporary waystation for both Nissei, first-generation Americans of Japanese ancestry, and their Issei parents. Among those staying there for a time was Gordon Hirabayashi, a conscientious objector who was soon to end up in an internment camp; the U.S. Supreme Court would hear his challenge to a government evacuation order. Joe and Audine began residing at the mansion too, which became something of a social center. Most important, it allowed for the creation of "a real support group for the CPS men," including George Case and Ad Carlsen, while their arrival in Seattle introduced the Coffins to the smokejumpers program. Both Case and Carlsen suggested that Coffin consider transferring to Nine Mile.[16]

Despite the getaway in Seattle, circumstances remained difficult at Eastern State Hospital. Relations with other employees never seemed to improve, nor did those with town folk. The rigidity with which the CPS unit was met never dissipated. Furthermore, a Methodist minister who befriended them paid the price for having done so. After inviting CPS men to his church, he lost his pulpit. As for Audine, who had become head of the hospital's Psychiatric Division of Social Services, she too suffered because of intolerance. "I lost my job because I refused to buy war bonds," she declared. Two co-workers also were fired for the same reason.[17]

Consequently, Coffin was delighted when the opportunity arose to join the smokejumpers. At the same time, as he later wrote, "After over 3 years of indoor work I was soft and very concerned about succeeding at training for the demanding role of smokejumping." As matters turned out, Coffin was accepted into the program, which he considered "a lifesaver." In April, he and Audine drove to Nine Mile, where, after "really walk[ing] the streets to get a job," she obtained work as a housecleaner and as a care provider for a crippled woman. Eventually, she was hired as the assistant director of the YMCA in Missoula. In the meantime, Joe completed his training, although he never managed to climb the rope, which left him "panic-stricken" that he would be unable to qualify as a smokejumper.[18]

Nevertheless, Coffin convinced the instructors that he had devised a technique of his own that worked at least equally well and he readied for his first practice jump. Audine, who was tending to the needs of their first child, five-month-old Jerry, was asked by the trainers if she cared to witness that event. A local church offered baby-sitting services so she left Jerry there and rushed over to the airfield. As the plane began to take off, Audine informed the truck driver who had driven her to the site, "Joe has never been in an airplane before." Perhaps because that was so, an "excited" Coffin opted to be the first man to jump. His confidence level nevertheless was high due to the quality of training, which included both reinforcement of the need to remain alert and a series of leaps from the tower. "I felt I knew what I was doing," Coffin remembered. And on that first occasion, as he related, "I nailed it. I came right in on the spot" and rolled perfectly. Audine remembered, "It was glorious."[19]

Overall, he "experienced a truly wonderful summer" as a smoke-jumper. Thus, he and Audine "were able to share the excitement and the fellowship," including stories of his adventures or misadventures in the CPS. On one occasion, the Forest Service readied to fly Coffin, who had some medical training, to help out an injured man at a fire site. However, when a call was made to the Coffin household, Audine informed them that Joe was already out on a fire, which turned out to be "blistering." As he returned from that fire, it was discovered that Coffin's boots had been burned and efforts were undertaken to repair them quickly. That proved impossible and a physician was sent to assist the injured smokejumper.[20]

Coffin joined another crew in tackling a mid-sized fire that proved difficult to subdue. Finally, one of his compatriots suggested the need to sacrifice one of the Mennonite smokejumpers to the fire gods. Not surprisingly, no volunteers were forthcoming so the fire had to be reined in through dint of hard work. Still another fire, which Coffin remembered quite fondly, saw crewmembers being dropped on different passes. The ground appeared to contain lovely green hillside but was actually heavily forested. Coffin proved lucky enough to slip through an entire group of older trees to make a nice, soft landing, but others were temporarily stuck several feet above the ground. Nighttime witnessed chipmunks on the ground gnawing on bootlaces, thereby forcing the smokejumpers to use whatever means they could concoct in the morning to hold their boots together.[21]

The toughest fire that Coffin encountered occurred up a small valley and initially appeared under control. Suddenly, the men realized that the fire was racing toward them. The air got "hotter and hotter," while bushes exploded in the midst of a small glade. As Coffin related, "We were getting extremely hot," and they leapt onto a small island surrounded by a stream. When the bushes on the island began erupting in flames, the crew chief ordered the men to jump into the water. They did so and the fire soon passed over. When the men arrived back at camp, the blackened, muddied men discovered that their fellow smokejumpers had feared the worst. Coffin and his team were received like "recovered ghosts." Looking back, he considered this "a bonding experience" that involved "participation and excitement and satisfaction. The total experience was a great one."[22]

That fire season was a busy one. "I was being called out nearly as fast as I was coming in," Coffin reflected. Altogether, he undertook seven practice jumps, a single refresher jump, and eight fire jumps. The overall experience had proven quite memorable.[23]

Following the 1945 fire season, Coffin was transferred to the San Dimas Camp, where he was placed on hardship leave. His discharge enabled him to return to Whittier College, where he received an M.A. in history. He went on to teach auto shop in high schools in Montebello. He thrived on the assignment, enjoying the start of each academic year when "fresh ... new ideas" could be exchanged with a group of new students.[24]

Additional opportunities developed that Joe and Audine eagerly accepted. As the decade of the 1940s neared an end, they actually "invented a new Television Program Rating service." They also set up a survey company that later was taken over by the American Research Bureau. Following the merger, Coffin helped to establish a research department for a local television station. As a consequence, he took a leave of absence from the teaching profession for about a dozen years. Then, in the summer of 1964, he agreed to teach for the Covina Valley Unified School District. He had two assignments: to help establish a pair of new auto mechanics programs for local high schools and to teach at one of those institutions. In 1982, he retired from Covina High.[25]

From the time he left CPS, Joe and Audine both remained actively engaged with the Friends Church and in Quaker programs. Simply put, as Coffin wrote, "Peace and working for peace have been central to our family activities." Increasingly, the Coffins also helped to provide for the needs of the elderly, something Friends Church was deeply concerned about. Eventually, they helped to establish a life care retirement facility that attended to over 300 individuals and was sponsored by the Southwest Yearly Meeting of Friends Churches. Coffin was named to the initial board of trustees — Audine joined later — and served as chairman when a subsidized rental facility was constructed in Whittier. "This labor of love has been one of the most satisfying activities of my life," Coffin reported.[26]

In addition to his focus on "good works," in Quaker-like fashion, Coffin simply enjoyed retirement. By way of a trailer, he and Audine had traversed the United States and Canada, while having even more time for various causes, including serving as officers for the California Retired Teachers Association. Most exciting of all, he had devised a means "to turn scrap auto tires into 6 foot lengths of ¾" × 6' steel reinforced construction material." This enterprise began in the early 1970s in Coffin's auto shop, and in 1994, he applied for "a patent on 'laminated' structures made from pieces of scrap pneumatic tires." He set up a shop to construct "samples of these steel belted rubber 'planks' which can be fabricated into a great variety of useful structures." As he saw it, "the environment is one of the next great theaters of progress for our world." His planks, Coffin hoped, "represent a solution that can use a large portion of the 240 million tires being fed into the solid waste stream each year." He planned to carry out these enterprises through J. H. Coffin & Co., a "developer of a great new national resource."[27]

Throughout it all, he, like many other CPS veterans, retained the bonds that had united the smokejumpers. As he told the audience at the CPS Smokejumpers Reunion in Hungry Horse, Montana, in mid–July 2002, "This is a place I've felt comfortable with since my first days with CPS."[28]

CHAPTER 12

From the Disciples of Christ to Non-Belief

GEORGE S. LEAVITT

His own mother called him "a coward" on hearing that he would prefer prison rather than to serve in the U.S. armed forces. Respectability was important to her and consequently, she was infuriated by his decision. George S. Leavitt's local draft board turned down his request to be classified 4-E, labeling him 1-A instead. His initial appeal was also refused, as was a second one to the state board, which did offer to consider delivering a 1-A-O classification. Waving his right to a hearing, Leavitt received an "extremely violent letter" from the appeal board at the national level. The FBI conducted a field check into his background, undoubtedly seeking to determine if he were some kind of subversive.[1]

After months of haggling, Leavitt was instructed to take part in an interview before a final determination would be rendered. He heard from other would-be conscientious objectors who had been grilled in such a manner that trick questions came their way. One query might involve how an individual would respond if afforded the opportunity to act as a Good Samaritan, which could involve the use of force. A favorite in such an instance involved the conundrum for absolute pacifists, "What kind of a Christian are you?," if the young man declared he was unwilling to act to assist another. Leavitt's own record was "kind of Simon Pure," including regular church attendance, but that seemed to make no difference to the Selective Service. Leavitt waived his right to appear before the board, a decision that resulted in another letter from the appeal board. Now, Leavitt was warned that he had better carefully consider what he was doing. However, after he again declined to exercise his right to a hearing, the national board reconsidered and labeled him 4-E in September 1943.[2]

When the opportunity arose to serve as a smokejumper, the admonitions of his mother still burned in his memory. Undoubtedly, her condemnation of George influenced his decision to join the ranks of the CPS smokejumpers who served with the U.S. Forest Service during World War II. Indeed, Leavitt later acknowledged as much and also indicated that he thought of how his own children might view his wartime service. If he became a smokejumper, Leavitt reasoned, they would be "more proud of me than if they just knew that I was a conscientious objector."[3]

* * * * *

Born on March 30, 1922, Leavitt was brought up in initially comfortable surroundings in St. Paul, Minnesota. His father, Jessie Samuel Leavitt, had English roots, while his mother, Ethel Morris Leavitt, had Dutch and Irish ancestors. Jessie did well during the 1920s, a generally prosperous time for many Americans, working as a salesman in a music store, but he lost his job as the Great Depression continued. Throughout that dire period, Jessie struggled financially, as he was forced to eke out a precarious living through commissions earned by selling insurance policies. Notwithstanding their personal misfortunes, the Leavitts remained "pillars of the First Christian Church" and rock-ribbed Republicans, refusing to support Franklin Delano Roosevelt. One daughter was able to complete her undergraduate education, but another could not attend college due to financial considerations.[4]

As Leavitt was growing up, his family was deeply involved in the First Christian Church in St. Paul. For much of that time, his father served as the superintendent of the Sunday school while his mother taught the adult women's Sunday school class. Leavitt was "pretty much forced to attend" both Sunday school and weekly church services, while each summer he frequented a church summer camp, in which his parents also actively participated. He did experience one religious moment, never to be repeated.

> I experienced a period of "ecstasy that came unbidden" ... which I recognized from extensive reading was identical to "mystical experiences" usually interpreted as "coming from God." I knew that it occurred as a result of the release of long pent-up inhibitions.

However, generally speaking, the more Leavitt was involved with the church, as he recalled, "the less I liked it."[5]

The women at First Christian Church devised a "Junior Church" that would be held during the same time regular services were offered. On one

George Leavitt (courtesy George Leavitt).

occasion, the women leaders beseeched the children who were present to sign a pledge promising to abstain from smoking or drinking alcohol. Leavitt "couldn't see why" he should have to commit to this, given that he could hardly foresee the future. To their credit, his parents did not compel him to sign the pledge.[6]

While at St. Paul Central High School, Leavitt was approached by a teacher in English History, a young woman who asked if "my rapid growth had been a problem for me." Leavitt, who had shot up to 6 feet 3½ inches, managed to reply, "I don't think so." The history instructor's obvious concern meant something as only one other teacher displayed any interest in him during his high school years. That was his physics teacher, who suggested Leavitt play tennis his senior year. Leavitt opted instead for track, considering it a more masculine sport, but failed to make a mark at that point. That changed when he attended Manchester College, where he competed in the 220-yard low hurdles and occasionally ran a leg for the mile relay team.[7]

A small Presbyterian school at the time, Manchester College had only 700–800 students, along with a limited budget and restricted course schedule. The college, established by the founder of the Encyclopedia Brittanica, was located only five or six blocks from the Leavitt family home. Leavitt was able to attend, thanks to a $50 scholarship and a work-study job at the college. Uncertain of what he wanted to do, Leavitt was interested in psychology but the professor of that discipline at Manchester was "not his ideal," somewhat ineptly using his own personal experiences to impart lessons. Consequently, Leavitt opted for a special joint economics–political science program that allowed him to major in both subjects by taking only a few extra courses in each discipline. An indifferent student at the time, he failed to study much but read widely and randomly. As he recalled, "I spread myself thin," adding minors in speech, Spanish, and philosophy, a subject he "really did like." A girlfriend, who was "very intellectually stimulating," introduced him to Aldous Huxley and mysticism. When he criticized Plato's *Republic* in one class, drawing on his newfound interest in mysticism, the professor praised him, declaring, "You're the only one thinking." Thanks to a sociology course, Leavitt became fascinated with Thorstein Veblen's *Theory of the Leisure Class.*[8]

During the period when Leavitt first enrolled at Manchester College, World War II broke out. As the horrific realities of war continued, young men at the First Christian Church in St. Paul discussed the possibility of becoming conscientious objectors. Leavitt became involved with the Fellowship of Reconciliation, had several contacts with the famed pacifist A. J. Muste, and conversed with Bayard Rustin, the African-American activist who would be jailed during the war because of his opposition to the Selective Service System. Leavitt also met David White, the FOR traveling secretary who became a professor of philosophy at Manchester. By now an active member of the FOR's local chapter, Leavitt participated in a daily group meditation that lasted for an hour during the workweek. This indicated a certain level of dedication on his part and demonstrated his appreciation for the pacifist organization, which appeared to provide the level of "social support" lacking from his own church.[9]

Leavitt's interest in conscientious objection strengthened, no easy matter during this "very difficult era." As draft notices arrived, for example, Leavitt was the only one from his church to file as a CO. He received no encouragement from his church, although one young man who had become a paratrooper believed that Leavitt "had more courage" than did those who went into the military. At least that was what the paratrooper's mother told Ethel Leavitt, who, nevertheless, viewed with askance her own son's refusal to serve in the U.S. armed forces. The local minister of the First Christian Church, notwithstanding his disagreement with Leavitt's stand, did write a reference letter to the local draft board, attesting to his congregant's sincerity.[10]

Before being drafted, Leavitt served for several weeks during the summer of 1942 in a work camp, run by the Quakers, near Torreon. The experience proved "disappointing," with work camp participants believing that the Mexican laborers "did not want to do work"; most of the work was performed instead by labor unions. As Leavitt later wrote, "The failure to achieve the stated goal of U.S. youth working alongside Mexicans on a project for them contributed to my skeptical attitude toward poorly executed 'do-gooding.'" While at the camp, Leavitt spent a month or two simply carrying bricks. When his stay at the camp ended, Leavitt decided to hitchhike to California. However, he was picked up the Laredo police, who conducted a "good cop, bad cop" interrogation of him. Eventually, he was released and boarded a bus back to St. Paul.[11]

After battling with the Selective Service, Leavitt finally received his hard-fought 4-E classification. He checked with the National Service Board for Religious Objectors, soon receiving a hoped-for assignment in California. Leavitt took his physical in San Francisco, where he heard grunts about "One of those!" Leavitt was aware that Ralph Penny, a neighbor back in St. Paul, had been assigned to Civilian Public Service Camp 76 at Chileo, situated near Pasadena. The CPS men at the Chileo camp, which was run by Quakers and associated with the U.S. Forest Service, tended to be well educated and could take advantage of a program in Latin American studies that was offered.[12]

All of this appealed to Leavitt, who hitchhiked out west to check up on the camp and visit Penny. Leavitt soon discovered, however, that he could not be drafted into the Chileo camp because his actual induction was to take place at least 200 miles away. That occurred in northern California on December 28, 1943. As his physical examination was given, Leavitt was forced to carry around a folder that had the words "conscientious objector" displayed all over it. This amounted to a "subtle" form of harassment, in his estimation. In Berkeley, Leavitt obtained a temporary job at an old Quaker camp. He also visited the Pacific School of Religion, a seminary situated in the Berkeley Hills, which helped to provide relief and rehabilitation for individuals following the war. Leavitt in fact temporarily entered that program before his service in the CPS officially began.[13]

Soon, Leavitt returned to Chileo, where he helped to clear brush. At that CPS station, Leavitt occupied a bunk bed situated between one sporting "a socialist of the Norman Thomas variety" and another one featuring a man who boasted about how he scouted out left-wing organizations in Los Angeles in order to pick up women. However, not all was levity at the Chileo camp, where Forest Service personnel clearly favored the use of convicts over conscientious objectors. Indeed, the Forest Service men appeared determined to discard CPS volunteers altogether. It turned out that a band of "aggressive homosexuals" could be found in the camp, which displeased and appalled Forest Service representatives. Leavitt had his own run-in with a Forest Service worker who, he later indicated, "looked me up-and-down. He did not smile at all. 'They'll break you in half,'" he told Leavitt, before walking away without further comment.[14]

All of this may have contributed to Leavitt's decision to apply for the smokejumpers program. Leavitt did so, in the winter of 1944, when he was residing in a so-called "Bunk House" in Pasadena that the Forest Service had allocated for CPS men. This station, ironically enough, was frequently visited by the FBI, attempting to ferret out any signs of disloyalty from the anti-warriors in their midst. Weekends often found Leavitt working, in order to pick up some spending money.[15]

Arriving in Montana, Leavitt was part of the last training group of the season. Training was uneventful although it proved difficult to properly fit the tall, gangly Leavitt. On one occasion, his feet, which required size 11½ shoes, were saddled with blisters after he received a pair of ill-fitting, mountain-type boots. "I was too shy or overly impressed with authority" to request another pair, Leavitt remembered. In the midst of a practice run, he discarded the boots, opting to go barefoot instead. By that point, the broken blisters on his feet bloodied his socks.[16]

During his training, Leavitt dealt with one civilian, "a macho, ex–navy man" who worked for the Forest Service and "obviously had doubts about the courage" of CPS volunteers. That instructor became enraged when the one non–conscientious objector in the training group suffered a sore neck from jumping and could not continue the program. As Leavitt recalled, the foreman was "out-of-his-mind with anger" that the CPS men were the ones still in camp. They also suffered from the shock that their bodies received from the training jumps, leading a number, including Leavitt, to turn to chiropractors for assistance. Notwithstanding his own physical discomfort, Leavitt completed his required seven training jumps and then undertook four or five fire jumps.[17]

In between fighting fires, Leavitt helped to unload hay. His most memorable jumps involved one that occurred on rocky terrain and another that called for the clearance of a very steep slope and large log. His most distant jump took place in Idaho. In each instance, he experienced the sensation of being treated like "the elite" when a mop-up crew came in to clean up the fire. Yet another occasion saw Leavitt fly into north central Washington, where a fire was blazing in the Washington Alps alongside Lake Chelan. After being dropped into the northwest sector around the lake, the men fought the fire before another group arrived from Cave Junction, aboard a Marine Corps DC-3, which temporarily replaced a malfunctioning Trimotor.[18]

Near the close of the fire season, Leavitt applied to be sent back to the camp in Glendora, but his papers got mislaid. Consequently, he was left burning trash in the wet snow in the woods, with leaky boots, before being assigned to drive a dump truck. At last, his transfer was located and Leavitt returned to reside in southern California, where he got bored washing dishes through the late fall and early winter of 1945.[19]

After his smokejumping days, Leavitt volunteered for an experiment, the Philadelphia Jaundice Project, which involving the drinking of 2,000 cc of water that had been infected with the hepatitis virus. Leavitt was the only member of a control group of five who failed to come down with infectious hepatitis, which was transmitted through sewage-laden water and proved pandemic during the war. An earlier bout of hepatitis, resulting from his stay in Mexico, evidently had afforded him immunity. As Leavitt saw matters, hepatitis, although less sexy, did more damage to the CPS men affected than had smokejumping."[20]

After working for a time at the Trenton State Hospital, which catered to mental patients, Leavitt was transferred to Chicago during the early winter of 1946. At that point, he decided to participate in cattle runs to Eastern Europe sponsored by the United Nations. The overcoming of earlier congressional disapproval enabled CPS men like Leavitt to undertake the journey. He went on two UNRAA expeditions, the first to Trieste, Italy, and the second to Gdansk, Poland.[21]

Once released from the CPS, Leavitt met with the former personnel director at Manchester College who had left the school to become a partner in a clinical psychology group. Recognizing that the young man sitting in front of him "had a high I.Q.," the director told Leavitt that if he were interested in the field, "You've got a job." Leavitt opted to work at the Lincoln State School in Lincoln, Illinois, which housed over 500 mentally challenged girls. During this same period, he met Marjorie, a social work graduate; they married on August 31, 1946.[22]

Soon determining that the work he was engaged in hardly suited him, Leavitt decided to return to school. He applied to a number of graduate programs in psychology around the country, was accepted by all, and chose to attend the University of California at Berkeley. Returning to the classroom in the fall of 1947, Leavitt was joined by hordes of World War II veterans with similar hopes and aspirations. Not having majored in psychology as an undergraduate, Leavitt was compelled to take a number of preparatory courses, along with intermediate algebra, which provided a foundation for the study of statistics. Marjorie obtained a job at the Alameda County jail for women, while he "worked at all kinds of things," including helping out in a kindergarten.[23]

The graduate program in Berkeley was the largest in the country, featuring some 300 graduate students. Leavitt "really studied hard" for the first time in his life as he prepared for his doctoral examinations. While many students failed their comps, he skated through in April 1955, receiving his Ph.D. as a consequence. Having the choice of a number of academic positions, Leavitt selected Fresno State, where he remained for the next three and a half decades.[24]

He came to consider himself a non-believer, even an atheist, in sharp contrast to his smokejumper compatriots. Nevertheless, he felt bonded to his fellow CPS participants.

CHAPTER 13

A Kindred Spirit
TEDFORD LEWIS

His smokejumping experience, to Tedford Lewis's delight, enabled him to become involved with people of "kindred spirits." He remembered participating in a spate of "fantastic bull sessions." He also recalled jumping with Phil Stanley, which resulted in an embarrassing moment that each promised never to reveal. At the 1978 reunion of CPS smokejumpers, however, Stanley told the story of a fire that broke out in Pierce, Idaho, one summer 35 years previously. When the two landed at the targeted spot, they discovered that a boy and his dog had already brought the fire under control. With nothing to do and darkness fast approaching, Stanley and Lewis began seeking out water, which could be found three-quarters of a mile away in a stationary truck. Along the route, the two talked about issues of war and peace, along with various social concerns, before discovering that they were lost. They agreed to remain within sight of one another, as the temperature began to drop. After gathering firewood, "We spent a rather miserable night," Lewis reported.[1]

The next morning, they searched for a way out of their predicament. Finally, they spotted a ridge, which enabled them to discover a route to a nearby town that boasted wooden sidewalks. They came upon a combination drugstore–filling station–hotel, run by a mother-and-daughter team, which loggers favored. There, Stanley and Lewis awaited orders, while a series of lightning strikes and ground fires spread across the area. Eventually, they were sent out to a ground fire on land occupied by Nez Perce Indians. When they met up with a Native American guide, Lewis, as he later admitted, displayed "white man's arrogance." While the Indian indicated that he knew a shortcut, Lewis asked if there were any possibility of getting lost. Consequently, they remained on the trail, finally found and put

148

out the fire, and later passed a mountain that Lewis named "Sourdough." At that point, the guide, referring to the terrain filled with heavy underbrush, asked if the men were going to get lost this time. The CPS men now discovered that the Indian had been right all along about the passage he had suggested they take earlier.[2]

∗   ∗   ∗   ∗   ∗

Tedford Lewis was born in Webster Grove, Missouri, on March 1, 1919, the third son of Emily Woods and Charles Reed Lewis III. His mother died when he was seven years old and Charles married Emily's sister Helen. The family relied on housekeepers to help take care of Ted and his two older brothers, Leonard and Charles. Some of the care providers were quite helpful, while others seemingly desired only to sweep the children off the front porch with a broom. On one occasion, as dinner conversation revolved around the watering of stock by Wall Street operators, the Lewis housekeeper piped up with the observation, "We do too down on the farm." The family favorite was probably Ardella Dukes, a black woman whom Charles later helped set up in her own business enterprise.[3]

In many different ways, Lewis's stepmother, Helen, played a large role in his life. As a YMCA worker in Europe during World War I, she had witnessed what could result from man's inhumanity to his fellow man. She later recalled reflecting to herself on the boat ride home, "I've just helped fight the war to end all wars," now "I'm going to help prevent future ones." Adhering to that promise, she became an ardent pacifist, regularly attending Quaker meetings in St. Louis, taking Tedford along on occasion. He attended local public schools, including Webster Grove High School.[4]

The family frequently attended the First Congregational Church in Webster Grove, where an outspoken pacifist, George Gipson, served as pastor. Two other church ministers, Dwight Bradley and Irving Inglis, also adopted pacifist perspectives, although Bradley abandoned his stance once World War II began. Along with four other members of a Boy Scout troop, Lewis, undoubtedly influenced by the clergymen, took the Oxford Pledge, which he had heard about through his stepmother and the peace movement in general.[5]

During that same period, Lewis continued to work alongside his brother Leonard at a children's camp. Three years earlier, Leonard had received permission from the local school board to make use of a forty-acre tract of land that featured a building where crafts could be performed and various games conducted. The young students who came to the camp participated in sports events, swam, and hiked, with weekly overnight excursions offered. Lewis

Tedford Lewis (courtesy National Smokejumper Assn.).

served as a junior counselor until Leonard decided to take on a job as a camp counselor in Colorado. At that point, Lewis went to the school superintendent, who agreed to make him caretaker of both the property and the 100–150 kids who attended the camp during the school year. When summer arrived, the camp was turned over to Lewis for his personal enjoyment.[6]

On completing high school, Lewis attended Grinnell College for a year, but was "scared to death" after being propositioned by a gay professor. He went to Westminster College for another year, but was troubled by the overt presence of a strong ROTC program there. For his junior year, Lewis transferred to Washington University in St. Louis, where he graduated in 1940.[7]

Having run the children's camp in Webster Grove for three years, Lewis was hired by the owner of the Ivanhoe Lodge to work for him, with the proviso that Lewis could maintain his own operation. Lewis continued to do so as the United States entered World War II, but controversy began to brew about his serving as the lodge's project director. One woman, who was working with the Rossman School, a fine, private school in the area, was seemingly jealous that Lewis had attracted so many young people to his camp. Subsequently, she began complaining about his belief in conscientious objection. The man who had hired Lewis indicated that he was going to have to let him go. Seeking to stave this off, Lewis went to visit the woman to discover what was driving her complaint. She had been an ardent pacifist before the war and had a six-year-old enrolled at Ivanhoe Lodge. "We don't think it's right that he associate with a conscientious objector," she told Lewis. But after they spoke, she declared, "I don't agree with you but I respect what you have to do 100 percent." Her son remained in Lewis's program.[8]

Once the war began, other problems beset Lewis. After the United States entered the fight, he went home, staying holed up in his room for nearly a month. When it was time to eat, he only picked at his food. Uncertain about what to do, he phoned his old minister George Gibson, who was now residing in Chicago. Gibson offered, "What you are doesn't change because of external circumstances." Dwight Bradley felt differently, affirming, "In times of war you have to support your nation." By contrast, Irving Inglis also supported Lewis's decision to file with the Selective Service as a conscientious objector.[9]

In the process, he was following the lead of his brother Leonard, while Charles had opted for military service. By now, Lewis was working on his master's degree in education at Washington University. But his battles with the Selective Service had only just begun. His local draft board, which had accorded Charles conscientious objector classification, refused to do the same for Lewis. When he met with the local board, just days before the deadline for submitting an appeal, Lewis was told, "Our religious adviser had said he doesn't believe you're sincere." In characteristic fashion, Lewis asked what the name of the adviser was so he might go to speak with him. One board member indicated that he was unwilling to release that information but said, "I'm not going to watch while you look at the file on the desk." There, Lewis spotted the name in question.[10]

On arriving at the minister's home, he was told, "Well, Lewis. My judgment is you're not sincere because your brother filed with the Department of Justice as a conscientious objector. You had the same opportunity. So I think you're copping out." A stunned Lewis, who was several years younger than his brother, composed himself enough to ask, "What kind of fourteen-year-old is going to take this matter that seriously?" That was how old he was when Leonard had filed as a conscientious objector. The minister refused to budge.[11]

Lewis sought out advice from Irving Inglis. "What do I do here?" Lewis queried. Inglis offered to set up a meeting for the next evening with a host of local luminaries, including members of the city council, attorneys, and other people of stature in the community. "I wound up with about 20 letters from people attesting to my sincerity," Lewis recalled. Along with his father, he then went to visit the director of the state Selective Service Board. He was told, "Lewis, I'm glad you're here. Do me a favor. Why don't you just forget this whole thing and ask the president for a ruling." When Lewis asked why he should do that, the director stated, "You have the thickest file in the state of Missouri and anybody with such a file should get the classification."[12]

In the meantime, Lewis discovered that the Federal Bureau of Investigation was investigating him. He jauntily stated to one acquaintance, "I hope you didn't tell them anything too bad." One day, Lewis noticed a car with Illinois license plates carrying a pair of men sporting black fedoras, white shirts, and pressed suits. They showed up at Ivanhoe Lodge, asking where a Mr. Coombs could be found. Recognizing that these were FBI agents, Lewis informed others in the room, "Because they're from the FBI, I'll excuse myself."[13]

Nevertheless, a new draft notice bearing Selective Service director Lewis Hersey's signature and a 4-E classification eventually arrived. Lewis had been attending meetings of the local chapter of the Fellowship of Reconciliation and was influenced by Theodore F. Lentz, a professor of Education at Washington University, later known as the father of peace research. Lewis was also continuing his graduate studies at Washington University, where he conducted field work for his master's thesis. But the Selective Service ordered, "March on," drafting him on May 15, 1942. Initially, Lewis was assigned to Camp Coshocton in Ohio, which conducted soil research and tackled water run-off. Then, he was sent to Camp Chilao, outside St. Dimas, California. Lewis helped out with roadwork, fought forest fires, and also cooked. That latter assignment came his way after he told a story about "a horrible camp-out" in which he had forgotten to toss in salt for the hunter's stew. His somewhat rapt audience responded with the pronouncement, "Well, he knows how to put salt on stew, so we'll use him for a cook." As matters turned out, Lewis thoroughly enjoyed cooking.[14]

On a less happy note, he soon discovered that anywhere from one-third to one-half of the men at Camp Chilao were apparently engaged in homosexual activity. The American Friends Service Committee, which operated the camp, became disturbed after receiving reports to that effect. A friend, whom Lewis had earlier found out was gay, was booted out of the camp, and received a discharge for "mental reasons," not because of his sexual preferences. When word got out that this individual and his lover were going to depart from the camp, a party was held for those "very well-regarded" men. Unfortunately, Lewis's friend, who had served as a college instructor, subsequently lost his academic post.[15]

While at Camp Chilao, Lewis noticed a call for CPS men to volunteer for the smokejumpers project. He later recalled his response and that of those closest to him: "I knew how to fight fire. I wanted to make a parachute jump. My parents didn't want me to, my family didn't want me to, but they were not the kind that put strings on you and said, 'Don't do this, don't do that.' They let me go my way and so I did." Soon, he took a physical and received full backing from the AFSC. In contrast to so many of his compatriots, the smokejumping endeavor was somewhat disappointing for Lewis. As he later acknowledged, "I'm sorry that it was not as big a thrill to me as to many, many people. I liked it. I thoroughly enjoyed it. But it wasn't the biggest thing I'd ever done." On the other hand, "CPS as a whole," Lewis reflected, "was one of the biggest things I ever did."[16]

Lewis trained at Seeley Lake, which he immediately considered to be a "beautiful campsite," situated in "beautiful countryside." He also was greatly impressed with the group of men working there. There were in good physical shape and not given to complaining about every little ailment. Rather, "this was a group of people that were eager and enthusiastic to be involved in what was going on." That made for a different atmosphere than would have otherwise existed. During the 1945 fire season, Lewis made three fire jumps, one that led to a fire that was a mere 8 feet × 11 feet in size. With winter approaching, Lewis, who was lacking warm clothing, put in for a transfer to sunny California. As matters turned out, however, the same day his transfer orders arrived, two large trucks filled with World War I army surplus materials, including wool shirts and pants, did likewise. But "it was too late" and Lewis returned to Chilao. Lewis hoped to be allowed to work in one of the relocation centers, where Japanese Americans and Japanese aliens were held under military control. It was determined, however, that "conscientious objectors, yellow on the inside, shouldn't mix with Japanese, yellow on the outside." Nevertheless, a number of CPS men, including Lewis, did visit relocation centers. They would take letters that had arrived at the office of the American Friends Service Committee office in Los Angeles to the internees.[17]

Later, Lewis ended up at Pennhurst in Spring City, Pennsylvania, which proved to be "a major experience." Twenty-nine CPS men were assigned there, all but two possessing college degrees and about half with graduate training too. Lewis, who had studied psychometrics at Washington University, was slated to head a division where his educational training would prove fruitful. As matters turned out, a woman boasting only an eighth-grade education was in charge of that unit. She complained about Lewis replacing her and was retained, while he got assigned to the library. Soon, he was asked to head laundry operations but eventually served as overseer of the dormitory that housed 200 severely handicapped people. Uncertain how to handle the situation, Lewis informed the camp administrator, "I've got to get out of here." That was "better than a blight on my mind," he reasoned.[18]

Dissatisfied with conditions at Pennhurst, the CPS men produced a report that caused the director to be fired. The story was later told in a book, *Turning Point*, the publication of which helped lead to the founding of the Institute of Mental Health. As for Lewis, he was transferred to Elmira where he remained until his discharge in February 1946. That summer, Lewis, who had completed his master's degree at Washington University, was asked to go teach in Beirut. He departed in August, remaining in the Middle East until July 4, 1948. The experience was "fantastic," with Lewis teaching secondary school classes. After returning home, he met his future wife, Margi. Eventually, Lewis worked as both an engineer and a contractor, even constructing church-run schools on Pacific islands.[19]

CHAPTER 14

The Rebel
Looking Northward

ROY PIEPENBURG

His first fire jump occurred at Meadow Creek in the Nez Perce National Forest, situated in the northern sector of Idaho. Roy Piepenburg recalled "vividly the pillars of billowing, gray-black smoke, the occasional leaping orange fingers of flames, and the aroma of acrid, hot gases as we got within jumping range." The CPS men, stationed around the fire, "could see through the patches of smoke a silvery thread deep in the valley" known as Meadow Creek. Piepenburg felt pained on watching "towering Douglas firs being torched on the steep mountain sides below." Eight smokejumpers, two at a time, leaped from their "pitching, banking 'Tin Goose.'" After landing, some of the men were instructed to build fire lines on the slopes. Others moved to set up camp. Consequently, "the sound of pulaskis slashing through the brush and the occasional pinging, ringing as they tapped hidden rocks, filled the air."[1]

In the afternoon, the temperature rose and the situation became more precarious as winds swirled about. To the dismay of the crew, which watched "with silent resignation," the fire began to get out of control. It "exploded and crowned up a steep mountain side," with "red-hot embers" coursing to the other side of the beautiful canyon and spot fires cropping up all around. A command could be heard, "It's going to the ridge top. We can't hold it! Drop your tools and packs and run to the valley! There's water down there." Quickly reacting, the men left their equipment behind and began to "flee for safety close to Meadow Creek." There, the "grimy and hot" smokejumpers took a break, fearfully uncertain of what might be next.[2]

Roy Piepenburg (courtesy National Smokejumper Assn.).

Somewhat characteristically, Piepenburg got into trouble at Meadow Creek when he "did an unpardonable thing." He met a group of German internees, previously held in South America but shipped to the United States to help fight fires in the American West. Having heard about these men and wondering what their experiences were like, Piepenburg left the fire line at one point to go over and talk with them. That decision, along with other problems that occurred, led to Piepenburg being placed "on the USFS list of campers to be transferred at the end of the season."[3]

The crew left the scene of the fire, having battled it for over a week. They walked to a ranger station and then were taken by truck over rough roads to an airstrip in Dixie. The dusty street in the center of that town contained a general store that looked like something out of a Hollywood movie: "the board porch facing the street, a creaky floor with a few protruding nails, an antique, rusty pot-bellied stove that had seen its best days and, especially, the hard as rock Halloween candy that had been on display 'x' number of years." Down the main street, a woman repeatedly raced her horse, to the amazement of the band of smokejumpers. Finally, they arrived at the airstrip where a plane transported them back to Missoula.[4]

*   *   *   *   *

The placement of the training camp for smokejumpers during World War II was perhaps fitting, given Montana's history during the previous three-quarters of a century and the rebellious makeup of many of the CPS men. Beginning in the 1870s, the Knights of Labor, which called for the carving out of a cooperative commonwealth, appeared in various assemblies in Montana. In 1878, silver miners in Butte battled against a proposed cut in wages. Three years later, the Butte Miners' Union emerged and soon became a potent force out West. In the mid–1890s, workers formed the Butte Trades and Labor Council. During that same period, miners in Montana influenced other labor activists in the region, including those in the Coeur d'Alene district in Idaho who conducted a heated strike that resulted in the imprisonment of many labor leaders. A number of those union men gathered in Butte with other representatives from across the region to discuss organizing millers and miners. They determined, in mid–May 1893, to establish the Western Federation of Miners (WFM). That organization insisted on wages befitting the work performed by miners, safety measures, an end to child labor, and a prohibition on the employment of private security guards by mining companies. The WFM, along with the United Mine Workers and various labor organizations, pushed for passage of an eight-hour day, achieving that goal in 1901. For a brief period, the WFM joined ranks with the American Federation of Labor, but withdrew from that organization after the AF of L failed to back striking miners in Leadville, Colorado, and other workers elsewhere.[5]

The hard times of the 1890s, when a severe depression swept across the national landscape, had crippled communities like Butte, whose production of ores had made it appear as if it were "the richest hill in the world." While Jacob Coxey of Ohio guided an army of the unemployed for a march on Washington in 1894, William Hogan brought together his own contingent of 500 down-and-outers who planned to offer President Grover Cleveland a "petition with boots on." Hogan's men went so far as to steer a train eastward, garnering support along the way in places like Bozeman and Livingston. However, in Billings, a battle with local police officials ensued, resulting in one death. Governor John Rickards requested that Cleveland send federal troops. Those soldiers met Hogan's contingent in Forsyth, where Hogan was jailed, but his band of the discontented continued their trek, arriving in Missouri, before the campaign dissipated.[6]

The depression of 1893–1897 helped to strengthen the Populist movement in Montana; like the Knights, the Populists envisioned the shaping of a cooperative commonwealth. In 1894, a number of Populists won state assembly spots, while two years later, a fusion ticket joining Populists with Democrats helped propel Robert B. Smith into the governor's mansion and took control of the lower house. But fusion, along with improved economic circumstances resulting in part from the amassing of "free silver," helped to lessen Populism's appeal.[7]

Early in the twentieth century, Butte was riddled with tremendous contradictions that were complementary in their own fashion. Big Bill Haywood of the WFM delivered a scathing indictment of Butte:

> There was no verdure of any kind; it had all been killed by the fumes and smoke of the burning ore. The noxious gases came from the sulphur that was allowed to burn out of the ore before it was sent to the smelter. It was so poisonous that it not only killed trees, shrubs, grass, and flowers, but cats and dogs could not live in the city of Butte. Housewives complained that the fumes settling on the clothes rotted the fiber.... The city of the dead, mostly young miners, was almost as large as the living population.[8]

At the same time, Butte was referred to as "the strongest union town on earth" and something of a closed shop. An early push for the eight-hour day unfolded. For a brief period, the WFM affiliated with the new Industrial Workers of the World (IWW), which was headed by Haywood and condemned the refusal of the American Federation of Labor (AF of L) to support industrial unionism. Nevertheless, the IWW's radical thrust, including its support of direct action and anarcho-syndicalism, quickly alienated many involved with the WFM, resulting in the WFM's eventual determination to reaffiliate with the AF of L. Agitating among miners and migratory workers alike, the IWW—whose members were known as the Wobblies—remained a force to be reckoned with in Butte and other pockets throughout Montana.[9]

Tough economic times, including the depression of 1907, resulted in attempts to reduce wages and subsequent labor unrest. That year witnessed strikes breaking out among workers ranging from telephone operators to machinists, while printers in both Butte and Anaconda also walked off the job. Another major strike occurred during the winter of 1909-1910, with the Great Northern Railway compelled to discard plans to shut down operations in Butte. In 1911, the WFM linked up with the AF of L once again. Within a year, radicals battled against more conservative elements, headed by President Charles H. Moyer, for control of the union, with many angered by the firing of hundreds of miners who considered themselves socialists. The IWW became a force to be reckoned with in various communities, moving to organize miners and migratory laborers.[10]

This proved true in Butte, which remained a staunchly pro-labor community and possessed an extended radical heritage. In 1913, socialists, who had performed well in the state during the previous year's gubernatorial race and in Eugene V. Debs's presidential bids, came to dominate municipal governance. Miners continued to believe in industrial unionism, allowing a group like the IWW to make inroads. However, union activists who challenged conservative union forces, which appeared to operate in league with mine operators, were accused of being socialists, Wobblies, or anarchists. Blacklisting of malcontented workers often occurred. Discontent mounted, resulting in the decision by miners in 1914 to condemn WFM chieftain Moyer and to pull out of the organization altogether; they subsequently formed the Butte Mine Workers' Union. Violence erupted, which led to injuries suffered by both the mayor and policemen, and the apparent call by Moyer for the deployment of state troops. Tensions failed to abate, with the Butte Mine Workers' Union attempting to ensure that all miners held union cards. Dynamite ripped through Union Hall, leading to the speedy departure of Moyer and his cronies. As a miners' court gathered and a mine employment office was ransacked, mine operators demanded the institution of martial law and closed the mines. Buttressed by the presence of troops, the operators ushered in the open shop, while the leaders of the Mine Workers' Union received lengthy jail sentences. With the union crushed and martial law declared, the labor movement in Butte appeared decimated. Nevertheless, the leading labor activists in Butte were now Wobblies or those sympathetic to the IWW, and a pair of unions, one independent and the other an IWW local, soon emerged.[11]

As the labor movement struggled to survive in Butte, a terrible tragedy occurred there shortly after the United States entered World War I. By April 1917, the open shop had come to prevail in Butte, where mine owners relied on a "rustling card" system that saw company-run employment offices dole out cards allowing recipients to "rustle" for jobs in the mines. Pinkerton detectives and company police also helped to ensure that the labor force remained in check. But on June 8, 1917, fire spread through the Speculator Mine in Butte, taking 164 lives. Enraged miners, guided by Wobblies, established the Metal Mine Workers' Union and carried out a strike, demanding improved working conditions, a hefty wage increase, recognition of their union, and the abandonment of rustling cards. For a time, craft unionists joined in, but became convinced by their own unions and AF of L national boss Samuel Gompers to return to work. Both sides sought support from Washington, while mine operators moved to crush the new union, denouncing it as a byproduct of the IWW. Eventually, federal troops appeared, having received orders to keep the mines open. Vigilantism, encouraged by hysterical reports cropping up in local newspapers, flourished, as miners and their supporters were targeted. W. A. Clark, one of Butte's leading copper magnates, exclaimed that he would flood his mines before recognizing "the anarchistic leaders of the Union." When the workers returned to their jobs, malingering resulted.[12]

As unrest continued in Butte, vigilantism led to one of the most horrific incidents of the period. On August 1, 1917, a ring of gun-toting, self-proclaimed patriots tore into the room where one-eyed Frank Little, an ailing organizer from the IWW, could be found. Unlike many other Wobblies in Montana, Little had repeatedly condemned American participation in World War I, claiming that it was guided by imperialistic and capitalistic designs. Moreover, Little had referred to the soldiers who were policing Butte as "scabs in uniform." Now, at three o'clock in the morning, half a dozen vigilantes grabbed Little, pulled him outside, tied him with a rope to an automobile, and dragged him through the streets. Later, they hung his broken body from a railroad trestle, leaving behind a vigilante sign, "3-7-7," thereby hearkening back to an earlier generation of vigilantes. A newspaper editor in Helena declared, "Good work: Let them continue to hang every I.W.W. in the state." Not all shared that sentiment, for some 3,000 gathered for Little's funeral procession, where they sang, "La Marseillaise." Burton K. Wheeler, then serving as a U.S. district attorney, decried the lynching as "a damnable outrage, a blot on the state and country."[13]

The workers had been seeking a wage increase from $4.75 to $6 a day,

and the operators had offered to deliver a 50-cent hike. But the mine owners refused to relinquish their "rustling card" system. By late August,
smeltermen in Anaconda left their jobs, and the mines in Butte and the
reduction works in Great Falls also soon experienced walkouts. Still, martial law remained in effect for over a year.[14]

In the meantime, the IWW continued to haunt the Montana landscape, at least from the vantage point of employers, local officials, and the
federal government. In 1917, lumber workers, encouraged by Wobblies in
their midst, agitated for improved conditions in Eureka, situated in the
state's northwestern sector. They sought higher wages, an eight-hour day,
a six-day workweek, and sanitary kitchens and bedding. Wobblies also
could be found in Montana's central and eastern regions, where they joined
with agricultural workers to battle against 15-hour workdays. While the
involvement of IWW men often produced scurrilous accusations, it also
resulted in salary increases and the adoption of 10-hour days in many farming communities.[15]

Like Wheeler, who soon was compelled to resign as a district attorney,
federal Judge George Bourquin expressed displeasure with the resort to
lynch law. By contrast, Governor Sam Stewart insisted that the "free air of
Montana" was "too pure; too sacred, and too precious a heritage ... to be
used as a medium by the vicious, the traitorous and the treasonable to
breathe forth sentiments of disloyalty against our cause and to extend comfort to the enemies of the country." The IWW remained an easy target of
local, state, and federal operatives. An unsuccessful strike in Butte in February 1919 proved costly to the organization, which got involved after a
wage cut was ordered by the Anaconda and Great Falls reduction plants
when prices for copper plummeted at the end of the war. Once again, troops
and special deputies policed the streets of Butte, undoubtedly having been
ordered to ferret out any laboring men who held little red cards signifying
that they were Wobblies. The next year saw another strike involving Anaconda, which concluded shortly after two men were killed and nearly a
score injured following the peppering of a picket line with gunshots. Prosecutors went after the IWW in other ways, while damning them as unpa-
triotic German agents. Government operatives conducted raids against
Wobbly headquarters, jailed leading IWW figures, seemingly encouraged
vigilantes determined to mete out violence to the radical labor activists, and
compelled others to depart the state altogether. The Montana legislature
impeached Judge Crum, who was assigned to the District Court in Forsyth.
His crime? He was said to have demanded that Wobblies be accorded due
process of the law.[16]

The implementation of criminal syndicalism laws and the wholesale assault on the IWW, which also experienced federal conspiracy trials involving its top leaders, led to a waning of labor activism in the state. Labor unions remained in existence in communities like Butte but carried little weight. Open-shop campaigns prevailed, while industrial accidents and diseases related to work conditions increased. All sorts of ailments afflicted miners, including pneumonia, tuberculosis, and "miners' consumption" or silicosis. Eventually, improvements in working conditions did help somewhat, but work in mines and shafts remained dangerous. The institution of the National Recovery Administration in 1933 brought about various changes involving wages, hours, safety, sanitation, and labor organizing.[17]

Nevertheless, strikes remained the weapon of ultimate resort by disgruntled workers. In May 1934, Butte, Anaconda, and Great Falls again experienced walkouts, this time conducted by the International Union of Mine, Mill and Smelter Workers. The strike actions resulted in a closed shop, a wage increase, and a 40-hour workweek. Later that year, striking printers also received a wage bump following a strike. These successful job actions helped to revitalize the labor movement throughout Montana. Unions thrived in Butte, Missoula, and Kalispell, among other locales. The International Sheep Shearers' Union began achieving gains of its own. Thanks to reliance on the National Labor Relations Act, passed in 1935, and the setting up of the National Labor Relations Board, the Committee for Industrial Organization (CIO) began making headway in the state. Unions particularly appeared potent in western Montana, while in the eastern sector of the state, the United Cannery, Agricultural, Packing, and Allied Workers moved to organize field workers.[18]

* * * * *

Roy Piepenburg's father, Reinhold, toiled as a teamster in a logging camp in northern Wisconsin, before obtaining a Ford dealership in 1908, where he sold Ford tractors, trucks, and automobiles for the next 35 years. His wife, the former Esther Otto, was a schoolteacher before they married. Later, she served as a part-time journalist for newspapers in Wisconsin, focusing on human-interest stories. She also became very involved in civic affairs and women's clubs, while Reinhold stood as one of the trustees of the village community, Readsville — by Lake Michigan, where they dwelled — even becoming president at one point. However, after discovering that embezzling had occurred, Reinhold withdrew from politics.[19]

Due to Esther's health problems, the Piepenburgs packed their three sons, including the youngest, Roy, born on February 12, 1926, in Alberta, Canada, and moved to San Antonio. For Roy, attending a segregated school during the 1935-1936 academic year was eye-opening. The socially conscious Esther was deeply disturbed by the ghettoes that peppered the Texas city and the menial work she saw blacks performing. Moreover, blacks delivering prescriptions to white homes were referred to as "pink niggers." The Piepenburgs attended a Baptist Church in an African American district, where they were welcomed without hesitation. But developments in San Antonio, including the presence of a red-light district frequented by military officers, offended Esther.[20]

Happily returning to Wisconsin, Roy continued to be involved with the Boy Scouts, attending summer camps run by the organization. Once again, however, his mother was disapproving, believing that the camps were orchestrated in "para-military" fashion. Nevertheless, reasoning that the good qualities in the Boy Scouts outweighed the bad, she allowed Roy to remain a Scout.[21]

The Piepenburgs, like many other German American families, watched carefully as events overseas increasingly darkened. Both Roy's parents and grandparents were quite embittered about the Treaty of Versailles, which had proved so crippling to Germany. The community they dwelled in contained any number of individuals whose ancestors were Irish Catholic, Czech Catholic, and German Protestant. As Germany began making demands on Austria and Czechoslovakia in 1938 and 1939, a good deal of anti–German sentiment cropped up in the rural sector of Wisconsin where the Piepenburgs resided.[22]

With war looming in Europe, Reinhold and Esther Piepenburg decided to leave the fundamentalist Evangelical Church of their youth to join the Quakers. Esther told her three sons, "We, as a family, had not been evangelized; we had become Quakers by convincement." She was impressed with the Quakers' devotion to the cause of peace. They "did not accept philosophically that there would always be 'war and rumors of war,'" as the Bible suggested. Undoubtedly influenced by the Nye Committee hearings and the accounts by popular historians regarding the causes of U.S. entrance into World War I, Esther reasoned that "the only beneficiaries of war [were] the munitions makers." Referring to grieving mothers who had lost their sons in battle, she stated, "If men had the babies, they wouldn't send their sons off to war." She also indicated forthrightly that eighteen-year-olds should not be conscripted as they were "too immature to recognize the horror and folly of war." Nor did she think well of farmers who obtained deferments for their own children while accepting the economic bounty that came their way during wartime.[23]

Esther's insistence that the family move to Madison, the home of the famed University of Wisconsin, again demonstrated the influence she wielded in the Piepenburg household. She wanted her boys to be close to the university, which she hoped they could attend at nominal cost. Her oldest son, Lyle, had been stationed in the U.S. Foreign Service in Rome when war had been declared, resulting in his internment at the Vatican for approximately nine months. On his release, Lyle headed for Portugal. Brother Roy was experiencing his own difficulties, dropping out of high school during his senior year. A series of incidents led to that decision, a number piqued by his refusal to go along with a school program involving the promotion and sale of war bonds. "I had no inclination to buy any," Piepenburg remembered, referring to the bonds that were sold in homerooms at his school. Lists of those who had purchased bonds could be found in classrooms. Thus, as Piepenburg saw it, "In a way, I was blacklisted in reverse."[24]

He regularly attended Quaker meetings in Wisconsin, where he witnessed faculty and students from the university, along with others, bear witness to their opposition to war. He felt disappointed one Sunday when a Quaker leader, a professor from the University of Wisconsin, showed up wearing the uniform of an officer in the U.S. armed forces. The professor purportedly intended to help ensure that the German people, with defeat approaching, received "just treatment." This confounded Piepenburg, who failed to appreciate "the 'altruistic connection.'"[25]

With the date when he would become eligible for the draft fast approaching, Piepenburg "went through a lot of turmoil" due "to peer pressure." Most of his friends were going into the military, with some choosing to become 1-A-O, which enabled them to perform alternative service of the kind that Piepenburg would not accept. He was also disturbed by the presence of military recruiters at his high school, who were eager to sign up the young men about to graduate. Compelled to attend recruitment sessions, Piepenburg refused to take a pledge that he would soon join the U.S. military. As a consequence, "other students wondered why I hadn't signed," Piepenburg recalled. Deeply upset about the ridicule and pressure he was enduring, Piepenburg escaped from Madison, heading back to the village where his grandparents and an old girlfriend lived. As he related, "I tried to cope with the emotional turmoil that results from going against the grain of society," having experienced "various kinds of harassment." Piepenburg stayed there for two weeks, but his parents insisted that he return to finish school. "Under duress," he did so and managed to graduate, even ending up in the top quarter of his class.[26]

He discussed with his parents what his options were, including filing as a conscientious objector unwilling to perform non-combatant service for the U.S. military. Once more, Esther Piepenburg's influence proved considerable as she guided Roy through the process of seeking 4-E classification from his local draft board. By this point, his middle brother, Willard, had already filed as a conscientious objector, joined the Civilian Public Service, and ended up at Hill City, South Dakota, where he was handed a shovel to help out on a reclamation project. Willard "always resented that," desiring more meaningful work. Thus, while stationed at New York Harbor, he jumped at the chance to volunteer as a guinea pig involving a test of what diets best suited men flying B-17s at high altitude. Then, Willard transferred to Byberry Hospital in Philadelphia, a facility for the mentally ill, where he served as a musical therapist but came to deplore the conditions that patients endured. For Willard, it was as bleak as the Hollywood film *The Snake Pit* would graphically demonstrate.[27]

In late 1944, Roy joined Willard in the CPS, and was assigned to Camp 94 in Trenton, North Dakota. This was the first time he had ventured west of the Mississippi River. Piepenburg was now afforded, as he later admitted, "ample time to ponder over the wisdom of my choice to stay clear of the military establishment." Furthermore, "I enjoyed the comraderie [sic] of dozens of other young men like myself who were 'disciples of peace' and away from home for the first time." The work itself he enjoyed, as he joined a land survey crew involved with an irrigation project on the Missouri River. He also was pleased to befriend landless Chipa Indians who lacked even the resources that a reservation might offer. "I really got good rapport with those people," Piepenburg later fondly recalled. Other CPS men had similar experiences. Perhaps, he reasoned, "a bond developed between oppressed segments of society."[28]

On the other hand, he thoroughly disliked the camp environment, although the project administrator, who lived in Williston, proved quite helpful in providing needed medical care and in finding the right kind of job for each of the conscientious objectors under his tutelage. The food was of poor quality and most striking of all, many of the men assigned there seemed terribly frustrated, particularly married men who had been separated from their wives and children and had no way to support them financially. Piepenburg's own social life, like that of other single men at Camp 94, was limited at best. On occasion, young women from nearby Williston, 18 miles away, came out to the camp and "seemed to have some understanding of our peace testimony." While dating occurred on the sly, those young women could not openly go out with the CPS men for fear of enduring the wrath of their parents. Those folk "definitely had prejudices toward COs." Even the congregants at Williston's Methodist Church, which some of the CPS men attended one time, indicated their displeasure with that appearance. The men failed to return to the church, instead holding their own services at the camp.[29]

Another unhappy incident occurred when Piepenburg was returning to camp one evening abroad a Great Northway Railway train. As the train arrived at Trenton, it only slowed down. The conductor, as Piepenburg recalled all too vividly, "contemptuously pushed me from the platform between two cars." Moreover, "after I got to my feet, I knew for the first time in my life what it meant to be an outcast." Still, notwithstanding the difficulties encountered in Williston, Piepenburg and other CPS men went there as often as possible, taking in a movie or grabbing a beer at the Silver Dollar Bar. One night, due to a blizzard, he got stranded in town. Worried about becoming AWOL, Piepenburg started to walk back to camp. Luckily, Pat Allard Sr. from the Landless Indian Commission happened by and gave him a ride to Camp 94. Piepenburg always felt that Allard had saved his life.[30]

Accepted into the smokejumpers program, Piepenburg set off in May 1945 for one month of training at Nine Mile. He had been attracted by the possibilities that the program seemingly offered: "better food and higher pay; high adventure; a chance to do something unusual in the conservation realm and, hopefully, better acceptance by the population-at-large." In addition, Piepenburg possessed "an insatiable desire to see and feel the Rocky Mountains." It appeared as though "the 'go west young man, go west' spirit had gripped me," he later recalled.[31]

As matters turned out, Piepenburg proved to be a "kind of maverick in the smokejumpers." His disdain for the CPS system only mounted, but he never seriously considered walking away from the new camp and either being sent to prison or placed in a non-combatant role in the U.S. armed forces. Nevertheless, to demonstrate his displeasure with "the entire 'internment' system," he "did anti-social things, including failing to co-operate fully." Piepenburg did not much care for Vic Carter, "a failed smokejumper" himself who was spearheading the Parachute Fire-fighting Training Branch. With the backdrop of majestic Ponderosa pines, Carter spoke to the latest recruits near the start of their training session. As Piepenburg saw it, Carter proved determined "not so much to motivate us as to ride us." Hardly endearing himself to the men, Carter opened by declaring, "Oh, you guys. You have two strikes on you already. Don't strike out."[32]

Although he tried his best to succeed, Piepenburg resented Carter's verbal assault that lasted all summer long; he was little happier with the ineptitude displayed by various camp officials. As soon as the project manager delivered his warning, Piepenburg wondered yet again how severely his civil liberties would be violated. On top of all that, in the midst of his training session, officials triggered a "training fire" that began racing "madly through a large stand of diseased pines," to Piepenburg's considerable dismay.[33]

Altogether, Piepenburg undertook eight training jumps and six fire jumps that summer. Afterward, he was transferred to CPS 128 in Lapine, Oregon, situated in the Deschutes National Forest. Piepenburg was taken with "the awe-inspiring Cascades." Affiliated with the U.S. Bureau of Reclamations, Camp 128 was involved with the Wickiup Dam Project. Piepenburg arrived with a back injury, suffered from a tower jump at Nine Mile, about which he had informed no one. At Lapine, he did apprise camp officials of his physical ailment. He was offered jobs as a weather observer, a dam tender, and an office worker. After about three months of this relatively menial work, Piepenburg suggested to the camp administrator that he should receive a medical discharge. When he appeared before a three-person medical review board in Bend, Oregon, in April 1946, one of the physicians informed him, "You have a congenital back defect and should never have been inducted." Moreover, his training program in Montana, particularly the tower jumps, had exacerbated that disability.[34]

Returning home resulted in "one negative experience after another." As he traveled on a bus to get back to Madison, Piepenburg met up with soldiers who were themselves coming back from overseas. They "demanded to know why I was not in uniform," he related. "When they found out I was a 'conchie,' they threatened to put me off the bus." He found a position as a map draftsman, but was displeased by the low rate of pay and decided, with his parents' encouragement, to attend the University of Wisconsin to study civil engineering. At the time, freshmen male students were required to enroll in the ROTC program, something, of course, that Piepenburg was not comfortable with. Forced to go to the officers who ran the program to obtain an exemption, he suffered a "dreadful experience." After hearing his story, Piepenburg reported, "They ridiculed me and chastised me," before granting the desired exemption.[35]

By contrast, he never had any difficulties with the vast bulk of students who were studying under the G.I. Bill. The only exceptions were some old high school buddies who were "cool" toward him, so he had to make new friends. Lacking any savings, Piepenburg worked summers for the U.S. Geological Survey in Wisconsin and Iowa, and was involved with additional projects in South Dakota, Nebraska, and Oklahoma. While in South Dakota, Piepenburg related, "I really had a chance to observe exploitation and discrimination toward the Sioux people." Some from the Pine Ridge reservation attempted to integrate into Rapid City, but were reduced to living in tents year-round. Piepenburg joined in a project run by the American Friends Service Committee, which sought to integrate the Sioux into mainstream society. To his disgust, Piepenburg encountered a bootlegger, perched at the edge of the Pine Ridge, selling whisky for $10 a gallon to the Sioux.[36]

Oklahoma proved to be the last place where he worked for the Geological Survey. He became friends with Ralph Wormy, a Comanche who had been a Golden Gloves boxer. The two coursed through the segregated streets of Anadarko, which had separate restaurants and drinking fountains for blacks. Nobody messed with Wormy, Piepenburg soon realized. While in Anadarko, Piepenburg got interested in snooker, playing in a commercial establishment on Main Street that catered to blacks.[37]

Returning to the University of Wisconsin, Piepenburg, who had tried his hand at geology, now got interested in sociology. As he continued his undergraduate studies, the Korean War began. To his chagrin, his friend Wormy ended up in a combat unit. The two corresponded regularly while Wormy was stationed overseas, and the soldier indicated "unreservedly how much he detested the horror of war." In his own way, Wormy "strengthened my convictions about what kind of society we should have," Piepenburg noted.[38]

In addition, he had long come to appreciate, Piepenburg acknowledged, "the rare wisdom of my parents' advice to resist wars" and "not only so-called 'just war,' but all wars against humanity." As he recalled,

> After I had learned to live with the ridicule that is so freely dispensed against pacifists, and all constructive non-conformists, an idea caught fire in my mind. I planned to dedicate my life to social reform along avenues that would aid the poor and oppressed in American society.[39]

In the midst of the Korean conflict, Piepenburg had to battle with the U.S. Selective Service once again. His draft board was hardly impressed with the 20 months he had worked for the Civilian Public Service or with the medical release that he had eventually obtained. But for the most part, Piepenburg had no time for political activity as he continued his studies at the University of Wisconsin. In addition to his summer work, he bartended and set pins in a bowling alley at the Student Union. At the same time, he was hardly ignorant of the furor that was unfolding as Joseph McCarthy, the junior senator from the state of Wisconsin, began ranting and raving about the presence of communists in U.S. government service. Hardly surprisingly, Piepenburg's mother closely monitored McCarthy.[40]

On October 2, 1951, Piepenburg married Beatrice Randall, a Chippewa from northern Wisconsin who was six years younger than he. Beatrice was a distant relative of both Theodore Roosevelt and John Humphrey Noyes, the founder of the utopian community in Onedia, New York. After completing his undergraduate degree in Madison, Piepenburg obtained his first professional job, teaching at an Indian reservation, beginning in September 1952. In fact, he served as school principal, recreation director, and basketball coach for a three-teacher school in northwestern Wisconsin. As matters turned out, Piepenburg remembered, "Things happened there that sort of turned me upside down but also strengthened my convictions." He was troubled about the county's mediocre school administration and by the fact that jobs on the reservations were filled by whites from outside, while most Indians were compelled to get by on relief vouchers. The school itself was ill equipped, lacking up-to-date textbooks or library books, despite being located in a new building.[41]

His experiences at another Indian school, located outside a reservation, proved little happier. Consequently, Piepenburg admitted, "I became a thorn in the side of the school board." In addition, "things started to come out there." As the McCarthy hysteria continued, word got out that there was "a teacher who ... might have been a communist." With such rumors occurring, an official with the Wisconsin Department of Education, who happened to be a former naval commander, confronted Piepenburg. "If you don't like the way we run things in this country, pack up your bags and get out," he told the CPS veteran. Later, Piepenburg believed that the official must have discovered that one of his teachers was a former CO. Piepenburg resigned before being fired, but still received a good recommendation letter from the county administration.[42]

Thanks to a friend who worked for the Bureau of Indian Affairs, Piepenburg got a job with that agency. Eventually, he worked "in numerous Indian communities and boarding schools all the way from the Navajo reservation in Arizona to Yellowknife on the shores of Great Slave Lake in the North West Territories of Canada." In 1961, enamored with the liberal Canadian prime minister, John Diefenbaker, Roy and Beatrice Piepenburg, along with their three young children, headed north of the border. His middle brother, another ex–CPSer, had moved to Ontario nine years earlier.[43]

Piepenburg had come to view himself as both a socialist and a pacifist. His socialist ideas led to his belief that "social and economic injustice breeds civil and international war." He was determined to "work against forces that humiliate, exploit and deprive the downtrodden peoples of the world." His pacifist beliefs convinced him that one "must struggle unrelentingly for peace that can only evolve from sanity in international relations." In Canada, he supported the national Project Ploughshares and the Canadian Peace Alliance, while maintaining an affiliation with the Mount Diablo Peace Center found in Walnut Creek, California.[44]

Refusing to give way to cynicism, Piepenburg explained his beliefs in an autobiographical sketch he produced in 1990.

> In my heart is a strong feeling that the Great Creator loves all his/her children, and we are duty bound to emulate that love in all our human relationships, both domestic and foreign.

What is my vision for the future of humanity? I've never been a cynic, and I will not be in the future. Pacifists, although small in numbers, will link up with staunch environmentalists in a powerful struggle to save our planet. As our survival becomes more precarious, our intellect, natural resources and monies will have to be diverted for wholly constructive uses. The military-industrial complex that has held us as hostages for many generations will be rejected universally. Peace will break out, the air, land and waters will be pure and safe, and happiness will prevail on Earth.[45]

CHAPTER 15

The Resister
NORMAN MOODY

He served, albeit not always happily, with CPS units during World War II. But when the U.S. government reinstated the draft in 1949, Norman McClure Moody, then a twenty-five-year-old student at the University of Kentucky, refused to register. Moody, a conscientious objector who had toiled in CPS camps during World War II, recognized what this meant. He would possibly be subjected to indictment for violating the Selective Service, trial in a federal court, and incarceration in a federal penitentiary. It would have been far easier, he knew, to register and be accorded conscientious objector status once again. As Moody recalled, however, at this point "I thought I couldn't go along" with the Selective Service System.[1]

On January 10, 1949, Moody, with the full support of his mother and sister, appeared in Judge H. Church Ford's courtroom at the federal courthouse in Lexington, Kentucky. Charged with having failed to register with the draft, Moody pled guilty. Judge Ford responded by admonishing the defendant, "You can't make yourself the law of this country." Moody acknowledged having registered for the wartime draft and Ford questioned whether the young man was "simply determined not to register" this time around. Moody responded with a simple, "Yes," and then declared that he felt "responsible to a higher being."[2]

Ford moved to cut him off, exclaiming that he was not about to engage in "arguing religion." Then, the judge stated, "You are doing yourself and your intelligence a great injustice." The United States government, Ford admonished Moody, "is simply asking you to register," after which point the issue of conscientious objection could be explored. Moody responded that it was "a system of registration which leads to war." Then he offered, "If I thought it would help the United States and her people and the world

Norm Moody (right) with spotter (courtesy Norman Moody).

and her people," he would register with the Selective Service one more time. However, he refused to do so now "because of conscience."[3]

A week later, Ford again asked Moody if he had failed to register for the draft or if he intended to do so. The federal judge had received a note from Moody indicating that he would refuse to register. Now, Moody calmly and directly responded to the judge's query, "That's right." Ford informed the defendant that the court had "given you an opportunity to comply with the law." Then, Judge Ford proceeded to deliver a sentence of a year-and-a-day, with Moody to be incarcerated in a federal penitentiary.[4]

"Two Friends" delivered a note to the *Lexington Leader*, which appeared in the newspaper shortly following the announcement of Moody's sentencing. Moody, in their estimation, "isn't just a draft dodger, but is standing up for what he believes." They continued, "We think he's more of a man for standing up for what he believes than the newsmen are for making an ugly story out of a good boy's reputation." The *Leader* responded with an editorial regarding the Moody case.

> No reporter and probably few other people doubt the sincerity of Norman Moody in opposing the draft. He has his own reasons, which deserve respect. But the fact remains that registration for selective service is required by a law enacted by Congress as the representative of the people of the United States. If Moody had obeyed this law, and then set forth his conscientious objection, he would have stayed out of court. He defied the law, and if everybody did that this country would be in a heck of a fix.[5]

Moody's fellow inmates mostly included moonshiners, individuals convicted of postal fraud, and those who had committed manslaughter. He was paroled from prison after serving about seven months of his sentence.[6]

Perhaps Moody adopted the stance of an absolute resister because of a belief that he should have done so during the war. Others, about 5,000 in all, had refused to go along with the Selective Service apparatus in any fashion. As a result, those absolutists had been jailed, remaining behind bars for the duration of the conflict and even beyond. Fewer chose this approach as the Cold War unfolded, but Moody was never one to go along with the crowd, but chose to carve out his own path.

*   *   *   *   *

That path had hardly been typical from the very beginning. Moody spent many of his early years outside the United States, due to the missionary work his parents engaged in. His father, Joseph Edger Moody, had been born in Estrella, California, in 1880, while his mother, Emma Louise Daughtery, was raised in Grants Lick, Kentucky, in 1885. Joseph's family was of German ancestry, while Emma's was Scotch. Both attended Transylvania

College in Lexington. After Joseph received his B.A. degree, they traveled to India in 1909 to serve at the behest of the United Christ Missions sponsored by the Disciples of Christ. Joseph completed his B.D. degree in 1921 from the College of the Bible, located in Lexington, while on furlough.[7]

The Moodys' youngest boy, Norman, was born on February 9, 1923, in Mungeli. Growing up, he attended the Woodstock School, which was located at an altitude of 7,000 feet in the Himalayas. The school was very strictly run, with mostly missionary children attending, and a strict code of ethics emphasized. Children of all backgrounds could be found at Woodstock, including Parsis and Indians, among others. Later, Moody reflected, "I began to feel early on there wasn't much difference in religions." At the age of seven, Moody came to the United States for the first time, when his parents took a furlough. Although he returned to India for several more years, he did not graduate from Woodstock as his parents elected to send 12-year-old Norman back to America. His father, only 57 years old at the time, died in an automobile accident when Moody was but 12.[8]

Among his seven siblings, the argumentative Moody was viewed as "kind of the fly in the ointment." He was, in his own words, "a troublemaker." At the same time, he was a curious soul; not surprisingly then, he became very well read, devouring the writings of Mahatma Gandhi, Jawaharlal Nehru, and others, particularly those who espoused non-violent ideas. While in his teens and before the war began, Moody became acquainted with a Quaker, Morris Mitchell, who had been gassed during World War I, subsequently became a pacifist, and now resided at the Macedonia Cooperative Community in Georgia. One of Moody's brothers went to live in Macedonia and took over the dairy farming in the community. Before he was drafted, Norman went to help out his brother and eventually relieved him.[9]

In February 1941, however, Moody had to register for the draft in Lexington, Kentucky. Both his minister and the church youth director back home attempted to dissuade him from filing as a conscientious objector. Believing that he was receiving no support from those leaders, Moody asked to be taken off the church roster. When church officials said they could not do that, Moody retorted, "Yes, they could." He now "had a kind of feeling about the Christian religion, which professedly believed in non-violence" but whose practitioners objected to a pacifist stance.[10]

When Moody attempted to file as a CO, he was sent to a judge in Atlanta who had to determine his draft status. Rather than relying on Christian ideals in the manner of most successful applicants for conscientious objector status, Moody selected a different approach. "I said I was more of a follower of Gandhi and did not believe in war and killing people."

When asked which church he wanted to be placed under the tutelage of, Moody said he preferred the Quakers but he was sent to a Mennonite camp in Luray, Virginia, instead. There, he volunteered to serve as a kind of guinea pig in a medical experimental project before becoming a smoke-jumper.[11]

In the fashion of other smokejumpers, Moody underwent a rigorous training program. Parachute jumping proved to be one of "the most thrilling" and nerve-wracking parts of the training. Prior to his practice jumps, Moody suited up, making certain that his harness and chutes were in order. Having received his jumping order, he awaited his turn aboard a Ford Trimotor. After attempting to kneel on the plane's floor, Moody and his fellow jumpers attempted to sit before settling in as best they could. The plane headed for an altitude of approximately 2,000 feet before the spotter pointed to the prospective landing spot. Along the way, the men checked out both wind direction and velocity. After undertaking a wide loop, the plane headed for the ideal spot yet again and the first men to jump readied by the door, with their static lines hooked to the cable. They checked their harnesses and bunched up close together. The spotter, whose head was perched outside the window, signaled with his left hand to the pilot. When he dropped his palm, the pilot cut the plane's engine. The first jumper received a slap on the back and leaped. Shortly thereafter, his compatriots did likewise. Those remaining on board watched the white canopies diminish in size.[12]

Nicholas Helburn related what the experience was like for smoke-jumpers such as Moody.

> Now it is your turn and the tenseness in your stomach begins in earnest. Your mouth is dry. You hook your static line, making sure the snap is locked. You put your foot out on the step; the wind pushes it off and you have to try again. You grip the sides of the doorway, get your bearings. Your mind goes something like this: no need to worry ... you've done this before ... lots of others have too ... keep your eyes on the horizon or you'll get your neck snapped ... there's a peak to concentrate on ... it must be about time ... there's the spotter waving ... the tap on the back ... here we go ... oh I'm turning onto my left shoulder ... when is that chute going to open ... ahh an easy opening even if I was on my side ... boy doesn't it feel good to have that chute above you ... now where is that spot and which way is the wind carrying me?[13]

After targeting the spot, Moody would work his chute in that direction.

> Guide lines controlling two slots in the rear of the canopy will turn you to right or left. Planing, pulling down the front of the chute, increases your forward speed. Slipping, or increasing downward speed by decreasing the area of the canopy, is used to keep from being carried too far by the wind. For a slip, two or three load lines are pulled down, very hard work....[14]

Besides jumping from the plane, the landing proved "the most exciting part and actually the most dangerous part" of the operation. One tended not to appreciate that the ground was fast approaching until it was only a hundred feet or so away. The jumper had to work to stop oscillating, while avoiding logs and rocks. Moody would bend his knees and ready to spring to his feet after completing his roll. Then, he would deflate his parachute and begin to take off his gear.[15]

During the 1944 and 1945 fire seasons, Moody operated out of McCall, Idaho. Afterward, he was assigned to a CPS camp in Trenton, North Dakota, and then to the mental hospital in Lyons, New Jersey. There, he initially worked on the violent ward, before transferring to the suicide ward. Following his release from CPS in 1947, Moody returned to the University of Kentucky, where, in 1949, he completed his B.S. degree in agriculture.[16]

That was a truly formative year for Moody. He refused to register for the draft, was sentenced to federal prison, and served seven months before being paroled. He also married Martha McClary from Elmira, New York. Norman and Martha then volunteered to work overseas through the American Friends Service Committee. In 1950 and 1951, they resided in Israel, where, with the permission of the Israeli government, they helped out on an agricultural and commodity project.[17]

After their return from overseas, Norman completed his M.S. in agronomy from the University of Kentucky. Then, they became involved with the Macedonia Cooperative Community, where Norman had worked before being drafted. For the next two years, he assisted with both dairy and field crops. The Moodys never progressed past the so-called "helper" stage, and thus never became full members of the community, which would have required the relinquishment of all their material assets.[18]

The Macedonia colony, which welcomed individuals of all religious persuasions, contained within its midst one Southern Baptist and a number of Quakers. There were also some agnostics and atheists present. The families of several former conscientious objectors effectively ran the colony, which worked through consensus. As helpers, the Moodys were not allowed to attend general meetings, but Moody, due to his communitywide responsibilities, did frequent business sessions.[19]

However, with the passage of time, Martha became increasingly disenchanted with the operations at Macedonia. Consequently, the Moodys, along with one other couple, decided to move to Florida to form their own community. They reasoned that perhaps a smaller number of people operating in communitarian fashion would be able to succeed. Pooling their assets, which amounted to approximately $4,500, the two couples went to Seville, Florida, in the central portion of the state, where they ran a combination store–gas station. Seville, however, proved to be "a real redneck town," and the business operations proved insufficient for the two families, both soon adding small children to the mix.[20]

Norman and Martha, whose three children were born in Seville, next opted to go to West Palm Beach, where he began running an auto electrical shop that rented for about $50 a month. After a couple of years, finances remained tight so Norman began working as a salesman for World Book. That lasted for another two years or so, but proved no more lucrative. Consequently, he agreed to serve as an agronomist for a garden supply and grass company. During that period, he sought and obtained a pardon from the Kennedy administration, which enabled him to vote once again.[21]

Within two years, Moody again moved on, starting work with the school board of Palm Beach County. Eventually, he became assistant director of operations, attending to the needs of 100 schools throughout the county. Moody's responsibilities including supervising custodians and ensuring the maintenance of school grounds, landscapes, irrigation systems, and playing fields. He retired in 1984, while three years later, Martha followed suit. The Moodys lived on a five-acre plot of tropical land that they called "The Jungle," appropriately enough. It contained a lake, along with various sorts of tropical fruits and plants, especially palms, from all over the world.[22]

In the June 2002 issue of the *Palm and Cycad Times*, Moody discussed "The Jungle" and his political icons. When asked whom he admired, Moody responded, "Mahandas Gandhi and ... Jules Horowitz. His outspoken honesty and concern for mankind make him a real jewel. He is a worker for peace in a war-torn world."[23]

CHAPTER 16

The Quaker
ROBERT H. PAINTER

Danger lurked from more than the fires with which the smokejumpers had to contend. Flying out of Cave Junction, Oregon, for example, was an interesting proposition. The airstrip there was "a primitive dirt runway," while the plane used by the smokejumpers was a single-engine Fairchild 700. At one point, Robert Painter was one of four CPS men in line for firefighting duty when a call was received about a lightning strike. The men suited up, readied their chutes, and, along with their spotter from the Forest Service, departed from the airstrip. However, as the plane reached 300 feet, its engine began to give way. Painter remembered what happened next: "All of us instinctively threw our weight forward in the plane," while the pilot steered the plane onto a field next to the airstrip. There was, of course, no room to jump out and, as Painter remembered, "My heart skipped a few beats." After the pilot labored over the motor for about half an hour, he declared, "Okay, we are ready to go." The now-leery foreman, Jack Heintzelman, from the Forest Service, responded, "No, you take it up for a test." The reluctant pilot did so and again the plane, once it hit about 300 or 400 feet, began to fail. The pilot, unable to land as he had earlier, crashed into the airport close by the waiting unit with the Fairchild 700 bursting into flames. Although shocked by the tragedy, as were the others who witnessed the incident, Painter knew he would fly again.[1]

* * * * *

The Quaker heritage of Robert Painter's family was old and rich. Ancestors on his father's side were among those called on by William Penn to settle in the New World before the seventeenth century came to a close. John Painter took his family to New Jersey and then to Virginia, before set-

178

tling in Paintersville, Ohio. The Hardins and Tests, his mother's relatives, also traveled to America during the late 1600s. The Hardins set up farms near Spiceland, Indiana, where a Friends Academy could be found. While at the Friends Academy, Levinus Painter met Margaret Hardin, whose brother became a secretary of agriculture; both went on to graduate from Earlham College in Richmond, Indiana. Subsequently, Levinus completed his studies at Hartford Theological Seminary. He then married Margaret and took her to rural New York and northern Vermont, where he served as pastor of a small Friends congregation in South Starksboro.[2]

Robert Painter (courtesy Bob Painter).

There, Robert Henry Painter was born on May 12, 1922. With his reputation as a peacemaker, Levinus was instructed to go to Putney, Vermont, to establish a Federated Church that would be drawn from Baptist, Congregational, and Methodist congregations. In addition to creating the Putney Federated Church, Levinus also served as a scout leader. His son Robert proved enamored with the outdoors, becoming a hiker, camper, and nature lover. He also skated, skied, swam, and played tennis.[3]

Painter attended a small country school in Putney, where he had such noteworthy mentors as George Aiken, a fine horticulturist and naturalist and later the highly regarded governor and U.S. senator from the state of Vermont. When Painter was 12, his mother died. Like his sister Mary Emma, he went on to attend boarding schools, including Westtown School, a coeducational Quaker institution located outside Philadelphia. As Painter recalled, "Prep school was highly regimented, strict, and academically excellent." The students who attended Westtown came from throughout the United States; many of their families were affluent. Virtually all of the Westtown students later went on to college. Together for the full four years of high school, the students "developed a family feeling." To Painter's delight, Westtown was a powerhouse in both soccer and tennis; he played both sports, ran track, and swam.[4]

By the time Painter graduated from Westtown, he was imbued with the Quaker ethos. He believed firmly in the non-violent precepts of the Friends, and had developed "a strong social consciousness." While at West-town, he spent his summers "at Quaker work camps in depressed soft coal fields and on family farms in Indiana." He also appeared regularly at anti-war gatherings. Painter was influenced too by his father, who had his own well-developed sense of social consciousness and had been a conscientious objector during World War I. Levinus actively participated in the opera-tions of the American Friends Service Committee and helped out with a rehabilitation housing unit in Pennsylvania coal districts. Later, Levinus participated in the United Nations' campaign in the Middle East, joined in Quaker missions in Africa, and supported Native American causes. Either with his father or on his own, Painter did a good deal of traveling, often visiting family members. He learned how to hitchhike and became quite self-sufficient.[5]

Following completion of his studies at Westtown in 1940, Painter attended Earlham College. In high school, he had participated in peace marches and now he wrote a series of articles and papers on the issue of war and peace. Painter ran into Phyllis Greene, who was from Dayton, Ohio, on the tennis court, during his first week on campus. The two began dating almost immediately. Earlham proved a happy fit for Painter in other ways too. His prowess as a soccer player served him well on the college football team. Interested in science, guided by "humanistic ideals," and influenced by an uncle who was a physician, Painter undertook a regimen of pre-med courses. In the typical fashion of the war years, he attended school year-round, to complete his undergraduate studies early. For three years, he also drove a newspaper truck in the early morning hours, from 2:00 to 7:00.[6]

During the summer of 1942, only months after the United States had officially entered the war, Painter encountered a group of conscientious objectors who stayed in Richmond to train for their alternative service with an ambulance unit in China. That batch of young men certainly had an impact on the young Quaker, who became still more determined to adopt a pacifist stance. He was certainly conscious of worldwide events, but his Quaker-honed beliefs were firmly entrenched. "I felt Hitler was wrong, but I didn't believe war was the way to go about it," Painter recalled. "I didn't condemn people. I wouldn't take a life." He soon registered as a conscien-tious objector and received a 4-E classification without any difficulty. Painter had been accepted into the Western Reserve Medical School, but was compelled to relinquish the spot because of his draft status.[7]

He had his degree from Earlham College in hand when his induction notice arrived. He was assigned to work at a soil conservation nursery, run by the U.S. Forest Service, located in Big Flats, New York. Like other conscientious objectors performing alternative service, Painter was obliged to complete "work of social significance under civilian direction." At this stage, that amounted to "thinning trees in a forest!," as he later noted. After six months at Big Flats, Painter was transferred to a CPS camp in Elkton, Oregon. At one point, Painter was part of a crew that was sent into the edge of redwood country in northern California to confront "a very hot fire." That one "crowned out on us," Painter recalled. The men were forced to run through the fire, with trees falling all around. As he admitted many years later, "I still get shivers" thinking about that one.[8]

Like many other COs, he was on the receiving end of "various kinds of harassment," the stance of a conscientious objector hardly proving popular during the early period of American involvement in World War II. That very harassment undoubtedly influenced Painter's decision to apply for the smokejumpers program. Again, like any number of other conscientious objectors, he was happy to demonstrate that he was "not a 'yellow-belly.'" As Painter later indicated, "I wanted something that was active. I was not a coward and [wanted] to prove and do something constructive. And probably prove to myself." Having played high school soccer and college football for several years, he was in good shape, one reason, he assumed, that the Forest Service readily accepted him. His training took place in Missoula, with the CPS camp run by Brethren, Mennonites, and Quakers. The morale seemed quite good, although the training itself proved highly rigorous. To Painter, the experience was "exciting and *esprit-de-corps* was great."[9]

Later, Painter characterized the first week or week and a half of training at Nine Mile as involving "the most intense and rigorous conditioning any forest fire-fighter experiences." The training session, he recognized, had developed over the course of the past five years and was intended "to make smoke jumping safer and more efficient." Consequently, new techniques were added each season, while older ones were tossed aside. The new men approached their initial ground training "hesitatingly." Having arrived at the parachute loft, they encountered either Frank Derry or Jim Waite discussing the intricacies of parachutes, including how they were devised and should be handled. Afterward, Painter joined with a group of seven or eight CPS men to follow the lead of an experienced smokejumper or squad leader. There might be as many as five squads, or there might only be one.[10]

Painter, who was "very enthused" about his experience, had played football every year growing up, loved physical exercise, including hiking, and was not fearful about jumping. Rather, "it was just a challenge," but being in good shape like Painter certainly helped. The morning session opened with a quick run around the campgrounds, followed by calisthenics designed "to strengthen the legs, arms, neck, and back." Next on the agenda was the obstacle course. There, the squad encountered quite a sight: "a motley collection of ropes, ramps, nets, stakes, and tubes." In succession, the men were compelled to "run up the first steeply-inclined ramp, grasp the edge, drop seven feet to the ground, and roll under the watchful eye of the squad leader." They then climbed up a rope to a wooden platform, from which they would "turn a flip into a rope net."[11]

Matters certainly did not get any easier after that. As Painter noted, "Then they run along the two ankle strengtheners, three planks arranged in concave and convex shapes," before moving onto the horizontal ladder. Invariably, "each squad leader vies in thinking up new and torturing methods for its use." Painter continued:

> Dropping from the horizontal ladder, the neophyte runs uphill toward a series of alternate shallow holes. Like a football halfback he criscrosses [sic] his feet as he stumbles past this obstacle. Then comes the tight squeeze, a pair of corrugated tubes through one of which he must wriggle on elbows and knees. Final item on the Nine Mile obstacle course is another, lower ramp designed for more intensive "hit and roll" practice.[12]

One innocuous-seeming item placed in the center of the obstacle course could pose particular difficulties.

> This "tank trap" consists of a number of paired stakes, each with a strap near the top. The candidate straps his legs to the stakes, folds his hands on his stomach, arches his back as far as he can, and attempt a back bend. Some accomplish this exercise with comparative ease; others find it impossible to return to an erect position even if they do touch their heads to the ground before collapsing. A final obstacle course tantalizer is a twenty-five foot rope to be climbed, arms only.[13]

After completing that assignment, the novice smokejumper, sporting full gear, dangled from a "let-down cable," as if ensnared by a tree. Then, he was taught how to suit up on the plane and was informed about spotter signals, the static line, and how to jump from the plane. The last task required jumping from a training tower, which was the most difficult part of the training and led to his seeing "stars" as he landed. This was designed to ready one "for stepping off into space and absorbing the opening shock of the parachute." The reasoning went that "if the recruit can take this body kinker, he can jump a chute." Afternoons saw the new smokejumper hike, climb trees, conduct "skull practice on jumper-to-plane signals," and gather wood.[14]

Recognizing that most injuries occurred during landing, the instructors during the 1944 training program compelled the men to practice that aspect of smokejumping. Repeatedly, veteran paratroopers from the U.S. Army and Marine Corps barked out orders to the smokejumpers: "Get off your feet! Faster! When you jump off the ramp, don't hesitate as you hit the ground; you won't be able to get ready to roll after you hit the ground in a parachute jump. It's one motion — hit and roll!"[15]

Following this "torture chamber," which produced "kinks and sore muscles," the first jump, Painter stated, was "almost a relief." His own initial practice jump proved "unforgettable." In fact, as he reflected, "No experience in my life has been comparable to my first parachute jump, not even my first football game or my first high dive." As he recalled, "the thrill was so great, I looked forward enthusiastically to each jump." Other CPS men experienced different emotions. Gordon Miller reported, "My teeth were chattering and my knees knocking." Charles Stucker declared, "We were getting our final instructions for the jump when everything in me seemed to tighten. There were five to jump before me.... As each one went out, I seemed to tighten up one more notch." Jim Spangler, who was making his first trip in an airplane, admitted, "I chewed my gum about 2500 times a minute. My throat had a sort of almost choked feeling and the pit of my stomach felt queer." Bill Laughlin, on the other hand, strove to "invariably remember the finding of J. B. Watson that the fear of falling is fundamental. Considering and questioning this serves to dissipate my nervousness." By contrast, Winston Stucky stated, "Things happen so fast that you don't have time to fear the things that actually do happen." Allen Moyer admitted, "If you stop to think, you may turn back. You just jump."[16]

The toughest moment during Painter's training sessions occurred during a practice jump when he reached the 200-foot mark and his chute became entangled. Following the instructions he had received earlier, Painter moved to grab hold of the silk chute and "made a hard backward landing." His supervisor, Frank Derry, told him that he "did everything right." Other landings undertaken with his Eagle chute resulted in Painter seeing "stars every time." He also suffered whiplash from the jarring impact of the landings, including twice when he ended up in trees and had to let himself down, relying on 120-foot ropes.[17]

In the midst of the training, which continued to prove "very demanding," Painter was chosen by a group of smokejumpers who had been stationed at the CPS camp in Cave Junction, Oregon, to serve as director of their side camp. At the time, Painter was little aware of the ongoing problems that existed between some of the conscientious objectors and members of the Forest Service. The smokejumpers had been on the receiving end of "a lot of animosity" from Forest Service administrators. The smokejumpers thought Painter could make peace between the groups, which he sought to do, relying in part on Roy Wenger. All in all, relations, although difficult on occasion, proved peaceful under Painter's tutelage.[18]

While at Cave Junction, Painter was kicked out of a church and beaten up by a gang. Others smokejumpers suffered similar indignities but such actions only strengthened his outlook. He was most upset by the fact that churches in the area refused to welcome the CPS men.[19]

That first year was a busy one for Painter, who undertook 15 fire jumps. The most noteworthy occurred when a full crew of 20 men took a military DC-3 out of Medford, Oregon, to an area north of Lake Chelan in Washington state, where a big fire was spreading over "very rugged terrain." They fought the fire for over a week, soon joined by smokejumpers from Montana and a ground crew of miners from the Holden Mining Camp, who came to mop up.[20]

During the winter of 1944-1945, Painter and the other CPS men were stationed at a remote spot some 50 miles outside Roseburgh, Oregon, where they surveyed timber. Following the completion of refresher training sessions in Missoula, Painter traveled to Ohio to marry Phyllis Greene, later bringing her back to McCall, Idaho. She saw him jump once, when he ran into thermal air and began drifting from the intended landing spot. "I was just hung up there," some 1,500 feet in the air, Painter related. But after his chute oscillated, he descended in the typical fashion of the smokejumpers, although he landed in the next field, not the one Painter — who was highly competitive — was shooting for, causing some consternation for his wife. In McCall, she worked in a resort, while Painter undertook an additional 15 jumps in the vicinity of the Salmon River in Wyoming and Montana.[21]

Having completed his service as a smokejumper, Painter went on to serve as an attendant at the Philadelphia State Hospital for about five months. He was assigned to "the most violent ward" there. Once again, Painter applied for admission to medical school and was accepted at Jefferson Medical College before he was discharged. Prior to entering medical school, he joined with a group of other conscientious objectors who traveled on a cattle boat carrying horses to Poland. While in Europe, he hitchhiked through Poland and Scandinavia. Returning to the United States, he received his discharge from the CPS in September 1946.[22]

Like other CPS veterans, Painter was not entitled to the G.I. Bill to assist with his studies. His wife obtained a teaching position and he worked as a medical researcher during the summers he attended Jefferson Medical College. While in medical school, Painter and Phyllis lived with Clarence Pickett of the American Friends Service for about two years. In 1950, Painter received his M.D., subsequently interning in Buffalo, New York, before serving as a preceptor in a mission hospital in Colburn, Colorado. He then linked up with a classmate from medical school to work in a hospital in Two Harbors, Minnesota, which relied on a cooperative health plan. The hospital employed "a pre-paid medical system" that was bitterly opposed by the American Medical Association. "Consistent with my life, I was again a non-conformist," Painter wrote. He also "loved medicine," which he eventually practiced for half a century. He was committed "to take care of human life, to take on the healing process." Once more explaining why he had refused to participate in World War II, Painter declared, "Killing did not go along with this."[23]

During the midst of his stay in Two Harbors, Painter received another draft notice from the Selective Service. Although he had served as a smoke-jumper in World War II, a succession of draft boards refused to grant him conscientious objector status a second time. For three years, Painter undertook a series of appeals, culminating with one directed at the president of the United States. "They couldn't see why I couldn't go into military service as a doctor," Painter remarked. But he just could not do it. In the end, his case was closed because of his age. "The experience," Painter reported, "gave me another chance to evaluate and express my own pacifist views, which had become stronger."[24]

After completing a residency in internal medicine in Danville, Pennsylvania, at the Geisinger Hospital–Foss Clinic, Painter worked in a combination medical clinic–hospital in Grant, Michigan, a rural area. He toiled long hours, 80–90 a week, while also serving as a local community leader. For a time, he was a member of the city council and eventually became mayor of Grant. After a decade and a half at Geisinger, Painter determined to specialize in anesthesiology. He also moved with his family to nearby Lakeview, where the Painters constructed a new home along the lake and he joined a new medical group, which enabled him to practice both general medicine and anesthesiology. He became a member of the board of director at Montcalm Community College and, believing firmly in the worth of educational rehabilitation, taught in a prison program.[25]

During the Vietnam era, Painter, who remained "very proud" of the stance he had taken during World War II, participated in a series of protest marches against the war. At the same time, he was perhaps less dogmatic regarding the position he had held. Nevertheless, he readily became involved with Physicians for Social Responsibility. He also continued to feel quite close to his cohorts from the CPS, whom he viewed as a highly "dedicated" group of men. They had experienced "a great sense of purpose," and Painter felt "a stronger kinship" with them, derived from their dedication and purpose, which amounted to love and brotherhood. He emphasized that those who stood against war were not just "a bunch of slackers and yellowbellies."

For Painter, his CPS experience profoundly influenced his life and only reinforced already strongly held beliefs about war and violence. "It's part of my philosophy of the dignity of life, the preservation of life.... My philosophy that there's something of God in everyman."[26]

In the mid–1980s, pressures induced by three malpractice suits helped to drive him from the practice of medicine. Nevertheless, he remained devoted to the field of medicine, strongly supporting holistic approaches and offering workshops on both stress management and preventive medicine. During the period of his semi-retirement, Painter remained active in many other ways as well. Along with his wife, Phyllis, he traveled widely, bicycled regularly, and continued playing tennis. He also served as medical advisor for the National Ski Patrol. He maintained his love of the out-of-doors, which led him to the start of a Christmas tree planting business that eventually covered 400–500 acres and resulted in the harvesting of 120,000 trees.[27]

At a get-together with fellow smokejump veterans, Painter again explained what the CPS experience had been like for him.

> I felt like I had to do something so I wouldn't be called a yellowbelly, a coward. We took quite a bit of harassment from our peers. It was pretty important to build up our self-esteem, and I think we did go on to demonstrate that there are socially conscious ways to serve our country other than going out and taking a life.[28]

CHAPTER 17

The Mennonite
JAMES R. BRUNK

Having discovered a valley full of dead wood, which could be likened to a "matchbox," the spotter admitted to the crew, "I hate to drop you fellows in there." Smokejumpers Jim Brunk, Archie Keith, and their six compatriots darted into a small valley containing a host of snags, beneath a fire that was scorching a ridge. Only Brunk managed his jump easily enough, with the others all getting hung up in snags. Worst of all, Keith, who followed after Brunk, landed at the top of a snag some 80 feet high. Unfortunately, the snag broke and Keith was hurtled into brush and rocks. As Brunk recalled, Keith "hit the ground so fast, out of my sight, that I thought almost certainly he was killed." While he attempted to unhook his harness, however, Brunk heard Keith cry out. Brunk raced over to the fallen Keith, discovering that the smokejumper had broken his leg. Along with other smokejumpers, Brunk put a splint on Keith's leg and constructed a stretcher, using poles and jump jackets. The closest road was a good 16 miles away, and was situated in a valley filled with "dead falls and tall snags." The men also had to contend with head-high brush and the fast-approaching nightfall.[1]

One smokejumper, younger and considerably lighter than the others, remained with the fire to ensure that it did not spread. The other six men undertook the arduous task of carrying out their injured comrade. The path proved "so rough" that Brunk and Al Theisen went ahead, armed with Pulaskis, which enabled them to cut a swath through the brush and dead falls. They did this for approximately 100 yards and then returned to help carry Keith to the end of the cleared space. After a short break, they began anew. They continued making slow progress throughout the night and into the early morning hours. By about seven o'clock, having toiled for a good dozen hours, the men had advanced only two miles and encountered "more open woods."[2]

Coming to an unkempt trail, strewn with dead falls, "the going was very tough." By about 10 A.M., they ran into two men from the Forest Service who had come out to meet them. Along the way, the Forest Service representatives had blazed a trail using crosscut saws, which eased the passage considerably. Within a couple of hours, Keith had been carried some seven miles from the original campsite. Relief came in the form of a physician, who attended to Keith with pain medication, and a new ten-man crew, which had been dropped into the small wilderness area that had been cleared. The new crew took Keith the rest of the way, while the original band of six was "only expected to keep up" as the last nine miles were traversed.[3]

*   *   *   *   *

Jim Brunk was born in Harrisonburg, Virginia, on May 25, 1926. His father, Harry A. Brunk, taught history at Eastern Mennonite College in Harrisonburg, while his mother, the former Lena Berkholder, was a home-maker. In addition, Harry served as superintendent of the Mennonite Church's Sunday school program and as adviser to the Young People's Christian Association. Just before Jim turned one, the Brunks moved from Lena's family home to a house they constructed close to the college. It was situated in Park View, a small Mennonite community.[4]

When Brunk and his three younger brothers were growing up, their parents determined to instruct them in the ways of the Bible and the Mennonite Church. Initially, Lena read stories based on the Bible to her children; then she began reading the Bible itself to them. Especially emphasized was the need to "love our enemies" and to heed the lessons in the Sermon on the Mount. Brunk particularly came to hold dear the pronouncement, "Blessed are the peacemakers for they shall be called the children of God."[5]

Brunk attended Eastern Mennonite School, located in a three-room building only a half-mile from home. Teachers at the school were trained in conjunction with a junior college program. Slow in developing physically, Brunk was barely five feet tall and weighed only 100 pounds when he graduated from high school, having just turned 16. His father believed that Jim should wait until he was 19 before attending college, just as he had. Perhaps his son's small stature also contributed to that decision.[6]

For the next two and a half years, Brunk worked in a family enterprise, which involved cultivating flower plants, cutting flowers, and tending to vegetable plants. Lena ran the operation, which required caring for both greenhouses and outdoor beds with transplanted plants. While Harry taught

Opposite: Jim Brunk (courtesy National Smokejumper Assn.).

full-time at Eastern Mennonite College, he also helped out with the family business.[7]

When the United States entered World War II, Brunk was still in high school. He believed that the war would likely end before he turned 18 and became eligible for the draft. His father had nearly faced a similar dilemma during the World War I era, when he had received notification about his impending induction into the U.S. military. Undoubtedly, Harry would have refused to serve but the war ended before he was ordered to report.[8]

In 1943, Brunk worked for eight months on a farm, close to Park View, which might have afforded him a draft deferment. His draft board, which included a number of Mennonites and Brethren, had no difficulty according him conscientious objector status. "I knew I couldn't take part in the fighting," Brunk recalled. "I felt pretty strongly about separation of church and state." The Mennonite tradition he was brought up in was strongly non-resistant. His Bible reading, as exemplified by the ideas contained in the Sermon on the Mount, also helped to shape his thinking about war and peace. Earlier, he had met Guy Hershberger of Goshen College, who spoke about war, peace, and non-resistance. Also, one of Brunk's uncles, Paul Bender, served as director of a CPS camp in Grotto, Virginia.[9]

Brunk's family markedly influenced him as well. As he later reflected,

> I was a man who had been raised by my mother to study the Bible and to believe that it meant what it said. I believed that the Sermon on the Mount was for now and not for some future dispensation. As such, then I could not take part in killing people. And therefore I signed up as a conscientious objector when I was drafted.

At the same time, Brunk believed that he had something to contribute to his nation, even in time of war. He later stated, "I felt I could take part in a national program" involving service. He was determined to do so, in part, because of abuse that came his way and that of other wartime opponents. This proved so in his hometown of Harrisonburg, despite its strong contingent of Mennonites. "They always called us yellowbellies and gave us a hard time," he declared.[10]

Three months following his eighteenth birthday, Brunk went to a CPS camp in Dennison, Iowa. There, he helped out on a soil conservation project that was involved with flood control. He also encountered in the person of foreman Harvey Weirich a veteran smokejumper who relayed detailed, instructive tales about smokejumping experiences. Brunk was already fascinated with planes and flying. As a youngster, his father had allowed Jim and one of his brothers to take a ride in an airplane, an "old biplane open-cockpit type." That had proven to be "quite a thrill to me," Brunk remembered.[11]

There was, admittedly, another reason why Brunk was drawn to the notion of becoming a smokejumper. Like many young conscientious objectors during World War II, he had heard disparaging talk about those who refused to fight. Thus, as he later related, "I thought that if I could get into the Smoke Jumpers there would be enough danger involved that people might realize that I was serious about my stand against war and was not just a 'yellow belly.'" Jim, who was younger than many of the CPS men, required his father's signature, which was attained notwithstanding real concerns on the elder Brunk's part.[12]

As matters turned, out, foreman Weirich influenced several of the young men at the Dennison camp to apply for the smokejumpers program. However, before Brunk's application went through, he was sent to California to help out during the fire season. He ended up in Camino, located above Placerville. But within a matter of days, while working in a dining room, Brunk spotted a list on a bulletin board. It contained the names of those whom the Forest Service was admitting into the smokejumper program. "My name was on the list but I had not been notified, so I was not sure what to do about it," Brunk recalled. In the meantime, Brunk was sent to a large station near Lake Tahoe to help maintain trails.[13]

His fourth day there, a ranger asked, "Is your name Brunk?" When Brunk replied, "Yes, Sir, it is," the ranger told him, "Get your gear packed, they are going to make a smokejumper out of you." Thoroughly thrilled, Brunk returned to the camp in Camino and then headed on to Missoula to undertake the training program for smokejumpers. For Brunk, that program proved memorable. As he related,

> I am sure that training will be long remembered by all of us who went through it. One day we would have fire-fighting training and physical conditioning and the next day jump training, so that on alternate days over a period of two weeks we were very quickly worked into better physical condition and trained to jump out of airplanes, while learning to fight forest fires as well.[14]

Fortunately for Brunk, some of the other smokejumpers, including Ad Carlsen, took him under their wing, treating him almost like a son. He encountered a wide range of philosophical differences, encountering men from the peace churches but also Methodists, Presbyterians, Jehovah's Witnesses, and Seventh-Day Adventists. All agreed on one thing only: they refused to take part in killing. On the other hand, his crew's squadleaders included a group of former Marines, who initially appeared to view the conscientious objectors with some distrust. The "rigorous" training included jumping from the tower, which proved to be jolting, particularly to Brunk's neck. The men also completed a series of daily calisthenics before breakfast and dinner, as well as spirited games of volleyball.[15]

Seven practice jumps were undertaken, affording the men the confidence they could take on the tasks likely awaiting them. None of his practice jumps presented any problems for Brunk. Before the actual fire season opened, Brunk went to Red Plume Lookout, where he assisted a veteran of the Royal Canadian Air Force who had served as a tail-gunner. That military veteran, who had survived a number of plane crashes, informed Brunk that he "would rather go in with a failing airplane that to jump out of it." Brunk's adviser sported a series of scars, an empty eye socket, and a series of skin grafts that went along with a batch of tattoos.[16]

Carrying spring water down a mountain path, Brunk spied the magnificent Rocky Mountains. At night, he read *Abundant Livings*, a book with daily devotional readings, by E. Stanley Jones. In addition, he followed the regular Bible reading program that his parents had encouraged. Turning to a series of writings that spoke of accepting the Holy Spirit within his life, Brunk "asked the Lord to do this and felt that prayer was answered." Within a short while, his mother wrote to him, indicating that she too "had been asking the Lord to send his Holy Spirit to empower me to live for Him." She had been assured that "He is in him."[17]

In addition to helping move Archie Keith out of harm's way, Brunk was involved in another pair of rescue operations during his smokejumping days. On one occasion, he helped to rescue Neilford Eller, whose back had been broken after his parachute failed to operate properly. Eller fell through the air, landing against a dead fall. A six-mile odyssey followed. The third rescue involved a search for Oliver Huset, who had banged into a tree, causing him to fall. Brunk helped to carry out Huset, who had suffered a concussion, throughout much of the night.[18]

Prior to his smokejumping days, Brunk had little experience tackling fires, other than the few days in California when he had learned "a little bit about making fire-lines." At the smokejumpers camp, he watched as trainers set fires. On one occasion, Earl Cooley was producing spot fires with his torch, before he realized that some of the CPS men were following behind, putting out those fires. This defeated the point of the exercise and upset Cooley.[19]

For Brunk personally, some of the toughest moments occurred when he joined to fight the Smith Mountain fire. That blaze actually raced across the fire line and scorched the crew's gear. The men battled the fire from about one o'clock in the afternoon until four the following morning, when they simply could continue no longer. After a bare two hours of sleep, however, they were back contending with the fire. Eventually, a group of Mexican workers was sent in to help out. Brunk's crew returned to their camp late that evening, but had to get up within an hour to head out to fight another fire. At that point, he encountered "the wildest crown fire I ever saw," Brunk related. Trees that were 75–80 feet tall suddenly exploded into flames, compelling the men to do the only thing they could: run away.[20]

Standing L–R: Ivan Holdeman, Norman Kauffman, Jim Brunk, Ned Arnett, Wesley Matson. *Sitting L–R:* Wayne Kurtz, Ray Funk, Don Unruh, Vic Peters, June 1945 (courtesy National Smokejumper Assn.).

Altogether, Brunk completed seven fire jumps, in addition to an equal number of practice runs. On his thirteenth jump, he sprained an ankle and had to ride a horse away from the site of the fire. "I could hardly sit nor stand for two weeks," he later remembered.[21]

In December 1945, Brunk's smokejumping unit was shut down, which saddened him because he was desirous of continuing with the Forest Service. He had been operating in the White Sulphur Springs region since late September. Brunk was transferred back to the CPS camp in Dennison, Iowa, but called on furlough and compensatory time to return home to Park View, Pennsylvania, for a ten-day visit during the Christmas season. He discovered that his mother had been afflicted with an acute case of myelocytic leukemia. Consequently, he sought and was granted permission to transfer to a CPS unit in Powellville, Maryland, an old CCC spot only six hours from his home. In Powellville, Brunk helped to dig drainage ditches for the Maryland Bureau of Reclamation Project.[22]

His new assignment included draining swamps in ice-cold water, which seemed more onerous than working in the 30 degrees below zero temperature he had encountered during a Montana winter. He also cut timber and dug ditches. But within about a month, Brunk, one of the few men at the camp with a high school diploma, was asked if he wanted to work in the office. For the next five months, Brunk worked there and then another opportunity for service arose that he could not pass up.[23]

Now, Brunk, along with a good number of CPS veterans, boarded a cattle ship operated by the Merchant Marines, which was bound for Eastern Europe to provide food relief. Their boat was the *Mt. Whitney* and it carried 1,500 head of horses. The date was June 20, 1946. Among those on board were Brunk's fellow smokejumpers, "Pete" and Norman Kauffman. On the continent, Brunk witnessed the terrible devastation that the war had wrought. He "could hardly believe how tremendously destructive people could be," if propelled by hate and war. The *Mt. Whitney* returned to the United States in July and Brunk received a temporary discharge.[24]

Plans were soon afoot to undertake another trip to war-torn Europe. Brunk and "Pete" Kauffman were slated to serve as foremen. However, the federal government did not appear amenable to the idea so Brunk, along with his friend "Pete" Kauffman, returned to Harrisonburg. Now, Brunk was treated differently than before his service in the smokejumpers. He, like Kauffman, was no longer labeled a "yellowbelly." Instead, "they thought we were crazy," because of the work that smokejumpers had conducted. One former tailgunner exclaimed to Brunk, "I wouldn't think of jumping out of an airplane."[25]

The two CPS men had arrived in Harrisonburg just as the academic year was about to begin at Eastern Mennonite College. Harry Brunk suggested Jim and his friend take G.E.D. tests, to enable them to enroll at the college. Possessing temporary discharges from the CPS, they did so and subsequently entered Eastern Mennonite College. The very day Brunk and "Pete" Kauffman registered at the college, they met up with a young woman whose family they had briefly resided with after departing from the *Mt. Whitney*. She informed them, "You fellas should have been in Newport News yesterday." When they inquired why, she responded, "They called up the crew for the *Mt. Whitney* and called your names to be the foremen of the crew." Although Brunk and "Pete" Kauffman had explicitly asked to be contacted if such an opportunity arose, no such information had been relayed to them.[26]

Brunk remained in school, taking pre-med courses. He also met Thelma Ketterman, who decided to withdraw from the college the following year so that she could "work for us." In July 1948, they were married and subsequently had four children. He remained at Eastern Mennonite College for the duration of his undergraduate studies. He did so despite being informed that no graduate of the college had ever been accepted into medical school. Brunk became the first, although a pair of classmates soon followed his lead. He attended the University of Virginia School of Medicine in Charlottesville, Virginia, where he remained for a rotating OB-GYN internship.[27]

In the midst of that internship, the United States became involved in the Korean War. Subsequently, Brunk became re-eligible for the draft and his draft board appeared determined to call him up. He was categorized as a "deferred registrant." When Brunk indicated that he had served for 27 months previously and had no desire to put in more time, he was told, "The further we could send you from here the happier we'd be." As a consequence, he received an assignment to the Blue Ridge Sanitorium in Charlottesville, where he remained for seven years, not just the two years required by the Selective Service.[28]

While working at the Blue Ridge Sanitorium, Brunk joined with two other physicians in the area to establish the Charlottesville Mennonite Church. This required approval from the Virginia Conference. Finally, Brunk decided to return to the University of Virginia for two years, after receiving a series of fellowships in cardiology, allergies, and pulmonary disease. That enabled him to become board certified in internal medicine. Afterward, he worked at the university's Student Health Center before moving into private practice. Brunk prayed, trying to receive guidance on where he should conduct that practice. He spoke with a pair of established physicians in Harrisonburg, a father-and-son team who happened to be distant relatives of his. The elder Dr. Wine, in fact, had delivered Brunk. As matters turned out, Brunk thought he received a message from God asking, "What more can I have the Wines do for you to prove to you that I want you in Harrisonburg at this time?" When he informed Thelma about the word he had received, she stated, "Well, we had better be about it then."[29]

The Brunks traveled widely, with Jim and his oldest son undertaking an "Out Spoken" tour in Europe, where they examined Anabaptist history. They rode bicycles in the Netherlands, western Germany, and Switzerland, seeking out locations referred to in the *Martyr's Mirror*, which were integral to developments pertaining to the Protestant Reformation. In 1984, Thelma and Jim carried out a similar odyssey before the Mennonite World Conference. They attended the 350th anniversary of the Oberammergau Passion Play.[30]

A host of other concerns drew Brunk's attention. He became involved with the Gideons International, a wing of the Mennonite Church. He served on the board of trustees at his undergraduate alma mater and also on the executive committee of Rockingham Memorial Hospital, where he briefly held the title of chief of staff. He was on the board of the National Ski Patrol, which resulted in his appointment as medical advisor of the Southern Appalachian area of the Eastern Region of the Ski Patrol.

CHAPTER 18

Montana's Native Son
DAVID V. KAUFFMAN

The summer of 1944 found David Vernon Kauffman in Bancroft, Iowa, where he was involved with the Farm Emergency Work program. Along with other CPS men, he helped farmers in the area, who were short of labor, pitch hay. But on hearing about the smokejumpers project, Kauffman determined to apply for it. He had some experience in battling forest fires, having served as a volunteer for the Forest Service. Like many others who applied for the program, Kauffman believed that "smokejumping had a certain glamour to it.... This was the elite of CPS, as far as I was concerned." In addition, Kauffman "thoroughly enjoyed the country" in Montana, where he was raised. Finally, this "was something I wanted to do more than anything else. I wanted to be a smokejumper. Partly because of the glamour, partly because of the fame that went with it, and partly because I liked that kind of work. I thought smokejumping would be great."[1]

He was also attracted to the program, having dealt with smokejumpers earlier. As Kauffman informed an interviewer several years later, "I knew the smokejumpers, they were just ... common ordinary fellows like you and I, except perhaps they had a little more pizazz about them. They liked the adventure a little more, they didn't mind doing that which was not necessarily totally safe and sane. The smokejumpers that I knew were just a real fine bunch of fellows.... They liked that kind of work."[2]

* * * * *

David Vernon Kauffman, who "grew up poor as a church mouse," was born at the family home on January 20, 1922, in Cresden, Montana, ten miles east of Kalispell. He was the eighth of 15 children born to Norman L.

and Anna G. Snyder Kauffman; both Norman and Anna were of Swiss and German ancestry. Both were "strong Mennonites." Their children, who grew up in a rural environment, were all assigned chores on the family farm. David helped to keep weeds out of the garden and went out to gather wood for the stove. He also milked cows, took care of the livestock, and drove horses, as soon as he was old enough.[3]

The Anabaptist church proved to be "the center of our social and religious life," Kauffman recalled. The family regularly attended both morning and evening services. Sunday was considered a day for leisure, although certain tasks still had to be attended to on the farm. But the children played ball or swam in potholes during the warmer months and skated or sledded

David Lauffman (courtesy David Kauffman).

when winter arrived; David for his part, had "plenty of playmates."[4]

Kauffman attended a one-room schoolhouse in Cactus Prairie, which was situated two miles from his home. A "tremendous" teacher, who managed to maintain order and pique interest in learning at the same time, guided Kauffman and 37 other kids. Kauffman, who shone academically, completed the eight-year regimen one year early in 1935. Because of hard economic times, attending high school, located 10 miles away, was out of the question. Not being able to continue his education was accepted as a way of life, Kauffman remembered. Instead, he returned to work on the family farm and "filled a man's place in the sawmill." When he received his full wage of one dollar, he passed it on to his mother so that she could purchase flour for the family.[5]

As he turned twenty-one, Kauffman suffered an acute case of tamarack poisoning that caused his entire body to peel. By the time he recovered, however, his position at the sawmill vanished. Feeling highly independent, he then decided to get a job away from Cresden. He acquired a position as a packer with the U.S. Forest Service, eventually receiving a nickname in the process: "Pete the Packer." Operating out of the Big Prairie Ranger Station in the Bob Marshall Wilderness, Kauffman found his work enjoyable: "It seemed almost as a continual vacation with pay." Kauffman was instructed to deliver supplies to side camps, lookout posts, and trail camps. This happened to be the summer of 1943, when the first batch of conscientious objectors arrived to begin training as smokejumpers. Kauffman met a number of the CPS men who were assigned to Big Prairie and found "their fellowship ... very enjoyable."[6]

The following spring, Kauffman was drafted. His parents, as good Mennonites, had counseled any number of conscientious objectors. His own attitude regarding war was clear: "In my heart, I knew it was wrong to take lives. War has never settled anything." Kauffman recalled the stance of the Mennonites, whose reading of the Bible led to their favoring of non-resistance. Jesus had purportedly indicated, "My Kingdom is not of this world, else would my servants fight?" Kauffman was opposed to participating in the military "in any way ... where the process of taking life is the main purpose." At the same time, he was not opposed "to working for the government doing work of national importance." Indeed, he was pleased that the American government "was very gracious" in allowing for conscientious objection. Consequently, he filed as a conscientious objector and ended up at the CPS camp in Downey, Idaho, where he helped out with a soil conservation project, serving for part of the time as a heavy equipment operator. Kauffman helped to construct a dam, packed it with rock, and "built a spillway faced with rock."[7]

The experience proved illuminating. It was, he noted, "my first real contact with people from all walks of life." To his surprise, he discovered "that every C.O. did not have the same convictions and feelings as I did." Thus, "it certainly was an opportunity to examine my own beliefs and ask myself why I did believe as I did." The CPS men possessed a wide range of religious backgrounds, with Kauffman encountering Mennonites, Methodists, Presbyterians, Quakers, members of the Disciples of Christ, and Jehovah's Witnesses. In his estimation, the relations of this vast array of men proved "excellent," notwithstanding occasional difficulties resulting from differences in personality. At various points, the men conducted "some real dandy theological discussions," Kauffman recalled.[8]

He was accepted in the smokejumping program and, in the spring of 1945, undertook the requisite training, which included seven practice jumps. He also conducted eight fire jumps and was fortunate to avoid any accidents. Like other smokejumpers, a variety of tasks was assigned to him. One involved sharpening axes and working on a crosscut saw at fire sites. "Because I'd worked in the woods, a lot of this came naturally," Kauffman acknowledged. The fact that he was "in good shape physically" also helped. During his training at Nine Mile, Kauffman and his crew were told, "Let's go for a hike, boys. We're going on a five-mile hike before supper." Approximately two miles from camp, the instructor, an ex–Marine, ordered them, "Ok, double-time!" At that point, only three or four of the CPS men, including Kauffman, had been able to keep pace with the military veteran. But at the end of the run, that same group was still running alongside him. "Being able physically to do that" made Kauffman feel good about himself.[9]

Other parts of the training were equally rigorous. Each morning, calisthenics were performed for at least a full hour before breakfast. They included several deep knee bends, running in place, and jumping jacks. One operation involved learning how to swing on a ladder and then how to move hand-to-hand. That was difficult for him because of damage suffered to the nerve in his right arm, the result of a misapplied blood pressure cuff when he had an operation on his appendix in late 1944. Nevertheless, Kauffman noted, "I got by ... because I could do all the other work and I could get by and I could do everything and I could go about three, four rungs sometimes on the ladder." In addition, he could wield a crosscut saw, a shovel, and a pulaski. The men also learned how to let themselves down from trees, get out of tangled chutes and climb to the ground. Much of the training revolved around how to fight fires. Again, as Kauffman remembered, "I had no problem with that because I knew what the score was before I ever hit smokejumping," in contrast to some of his compatriots who did not seem to know what a shovel was.[10]

Jumping from the tower, which saw the trainees, fully suited and harnessed, dropped as much as 30 feet before a large rope grabbed them, was "scary!," Kauffman recalled. Moreover, during training, they completed as many as ten jumps from the tower in a single morning. As Kauffman related, "You had a terrific sensation of falling off of that tower," something he never experienced on leaping from planes. Thus, jumping from the tower required "a lot of courage," sometimes necessitating several attempts before a man could step off. Kauffman, on the other hand, experienced no such difficulty. "I just blindly stepped off. [I] thought, 'Here goes, I guess the rope will hold me,'" he remembered.[11]

His first jump, the most difficult for Kauffman, saw him depart from an antiquated Ford Trimotor, which had slowed to approximately 75 miles an hour to let out the smokejumpers. Although Kauffman preferred to be the first man out of the plane, he was the second to jump. Later, he reflected about that initial adventure.

And the first jump was ... a little tough.... But once you get out ... you had no sense of falling. I always felt like ... the old plane took a jump away from me. Just went up in the air. Of course it didn't but ... you come out and you kind of face toward the tail and the old ... chute pops open and ... it's the greatest feeling in the world to be up there. Floating down, you look down here and you grab your guidelines and you ... start steering your chute around to wherever you want it. And if you have to slip it, why you learn how to slip a chute.[12]

Kauffman continued reflecting on what that last maneuver involved: "making it go faster forward" than the regular speed of five miles per hour.

To slip it, you would pull down your front risers. Get a hold of your front risers and pull them down so your forward speed was faster. So that you could if you were coming down and you were heading for a clearing or something, and you saw you weren't going to get there ... if you slipped your chute you went faster, or if you were into a wind, if you pulled down, you would go faster and you would drop a little faster. You would go forward a little faster, and you could hold it.

This was something one could only learn "up there coming down in the chute."[13]

After the first jump, Kauffman noted, "You knew what it was about, and then it wasn't hard to go out any more. You know, you got that feeling of security. You knew that chute was going to open." He grew to love jumping and, like many smokejumpers, proved highly competitive during the training jumps when the men tried to land on a certain spot. He even enjoyed hanging up in a tree, 125 feet or so above ground, before relying on a 100-foot rope to descend. Reflecting on that experience later, Kauffman admitted, "You're young, you're not necessarily foolish but you take chances you don't after you're older." More important, that particular knowledge proved helpful when he got hung up during a pair of fires and had to ease himself down to fires cropping up in heavily forested terrain. On the other hand, he never had to resort to his reserve chute.[14]

He served as a cook on a couple of fires, including one in Idaho where Kauffman and his crew of six mistakenly landed on Potlatch Timber. The foreman acknowledged that they were at the wrong fire site, but implored them, "Please stay and help because we need all the help we can get to contain this fire." Almost immediately, he asked, "Which one of you fellows can cook?" No response was forthcoming, not even from one fellow who had been trained as a cook. When Kauffman started to indicate that he would be willing to help out, the foreman suddenly blurted out, "You're it," and he began by making 12 dozen eggs and frying two hams for breakfast. Almost immediately after breakfast was done, Kauffman had to help clean up and then proceed to make lunches. This went on for several days, during which time he managed to grab only a few hours of sleep. By 2:30 A.M., he was up, beginning to prepare breakfast. Still, Kauffman discovered that he enjoyed the work. In fact, he indicated, "It was a terrific experience." On top of that, he accumulated eight or nine days of compensatory time for his six days' service as camp cook.[15]

His first fire jump took place at Meadow Creek in Idaho, where eight smokejumpers had been sent the night before. The squad leader had said, "Send 16 more jumpers ... and we'll corral this." He was told that 50 African American parachuters would be arriving, resulting in an argument about the need to deliver smokejumpers instead. In the meantime, the fire crowned and trapped the smokejumpers along the creek. Now, the squad leader asked who would volunteer to go help the men out and Kauffman was one of those who did. The creek proved wide and marshy, and the original group of firefighters was already departing.[16]

On another occasion, Kauffman's crew approached a fire raging on a mountain. The spotter detected some open space and said, "You better go for that." Kauffman was the first to jump, heading for a purportedly clear area that was actually filled with huge boulders. He got hung up in tall pines. Hiking back to the fire, the men worked past midnight, slept for a few hours, and ate K-rations on awakening. A Forest Service plane had dropped five-gallon water containers to help fight the fight but "that was no way to put it out." As matters turned out, that fire was not quelled until snow fell about two weeks later.[17]

Kauffman recalled one fire that had broken out in the national forest near Enterprise, Oregon. The smokejumpers "were coming in and landing very hard." One fellow, who was a former wrestler, oscillated, hitting the ground hard, resulting in paralysis from the waist down. The day was blistering, but the crew had to carry the injured man 11 miles down a river. Kauffman helped to find poles, cut and lace them to the side of a stretcher, shape short poles that would not collapse, and bind the poles together before half a dozen men could hold aloft their wounded compatriot. Once more, Kauffman found the work challenging but enjoyable.[18]

Some of the fires that he tackled proved to be largely "routine," or at least "routine for us," he later suggested. Another fire in the Bob Marshall Wilderness involved heavy timber and seemed easily manageable at first. As matters turned out, however, it took 12 working days to bring it under control. The crew had to build a fire line and knock down any hot-spots. At times, the men could not even take breaks for food or water, while at other points they were able to rest for a couple of hours and grab K-rations before returning to the task at hand. Again, Kauffman enjoyed this work, and was particularly happy that he and the smokejumpers could go tackle fires and then leave the mop-up for some other unit.[19]

His last fire jump occurred on August 15, 1945, shortly after the men received word of the dropping of the atomic bombs on Hiroshima and Nagasaki. "So we were happy" that the war was fast approaching its close, Kauffman recalled. He returned to Missoula but the fire season soon came to an end. His parents came and picked up both David and his brother Norman and drove them to Oregon, where his brother's wedding was being held near Eugene. Afterward, Kauffman moved over to a side camp at White Sulfur Springs in Montana, where he cruised timber and drove a crew truck. Through the smokejumpers, he had acquired a good deal of furlough time and was able to parlay that into a break from the CPS until January 1, 1946. His next assignment took him to Camino, California, the site of a large Forest Service camp. He did some logging around Lake Tahoe, which proved to be "another great experience."[20]

As Kauffman reflected on his smokejumping days, he believed that "for the most part ... I was respected." That was true when he dealt with soldiers: "I explained what I believed and why I believed ... I got nothing but respect. They might not agree with me, but I got a lot of respect." This was so, he reasoned, "because I knew why I believed what I believed and they respected me for it as a person." In addition, it also helped that his father had taught him "to put out a day's work for a day's pay." Consequently, Kauffman declared, "Whenever I had a job to do ... I did it to the best of my ability and as if I were getting paid for it.... You know, this was my personal philosophy, and I think this helped a great deal because they ... didn't think I was a goof off. They respected me for what I was, how I could work, and all of this."[21]

While in Camino, Kauffman heard about UNIRA's food relief program in Europe. Along with his younger brother Norman, a fellow smoke-jump veteran, Kauffman volunteered to head out on a cattle boat. The boat departed from Newport News outside Norfolk, Virginia, in July 1946. It contained the largest load of livestock that UNIRA ever shipped out: 1,500 head of horses. Once the ship arrived at the port in Danzig, Poland, it was docked there for five days. Kauffman was able to explore the little towns in the area. As he recalled, "I have never seen such devastation as I saw around Danzig." Shell holes could be spotted through industrial smokestacks. Kauffman was stunned by the destruction that he witnessed, although many churches appeared to have been spared. He was impressed by the evident willingness of the Polish people to rebuild. But he was taken aback when "packs of children" told the men who had come off the boat, "Come see my sister. She very good." Still, "the Polish people amazed me for they resolved to rebuild and endeavored to be a free people," Kauffman reported.[22]

When the boat arrived back in Norfolk, Kauffman prepared to depart, not knowing what he would do next, unlike his brother Norman who was planning to attend a small religious college in Kansas. David had considered the possibility of returning to Oregon to get a job logging. But a friend from the UNIRA boat, Jim Brunk, another former smokejumper who had worked as a timber cruiser at White Sulfur Springs, asked him, "Why don't you come up and meet my folks?" Packing $45 in his pocket, Kauffman went with Brunk to Harrisonburg, Virginia. As he later rationalized, "I was footloose and fancy free" and could easily accept the invitation, "little realizing how this would give a new direction to my life. I had no plans what to do next. I had several options, but going to college was not one of them." However, Brunk's mother convinced him otherwise, although Kauffman lacked the financial resources to return to school. His church was willing to cover tuition costs at Eastern Mennonite College, paying for every month he had served in CPS: 27 in all. Brunk's mother offered to provide room and board if Kauffman would cook and clean dishes from Monday through Saturday. Initially enrolling as a theology student, Kauffman soon switched to pre-med courses after obtaining a high school equivalency diploma. "I had always dreamed of being a doctor," he recalled. During his fourth year at Eastern Mennonite, Kauffman met Ruth Eberly, a registered nurse, whom he married in June 1950. The two eventually had four children.[23]

To help out with expenses, Kauffman drove an 18-wheel freight truck for about eight months. Eventually, he was accepted to the Hahnemann Medical School in Philadelphia, where he graduated in 1957. Wanting to return out West, Kauffman accepted a one-year internship — which paid $300 a month — at the large, privately owned Sacred Heart Hospital in Spokane, Washington. The medical staff was excellent: "There was nothing they couldn't teach you." As his internship neared an end, he was asked to stay on for a surgical residency. Subsequently, he and his growing family moved to Whitefish, Montana, where he established a general practice. For 29 years, he performed general surgery and obstetrics, made house calls, and ran an office. The work proved taxing but exhilarating. On many days, he saw up to 70 patients and conducted hospital rounds.[24]

The move to Whitefish proved a happy one in other ways as well. The Kauffmans eventually acquired 400 acres of land, where David could hunt elk and other game. Through a 30-mile drive, he could also return to the church he had grown up in. The Kauffmans attended there for about 14 years and then David was asked to speak at the Christian Church. After he did so on one occasion, the congregants kept requesting that he return again and again. For 14 years, he served as their minister, took a break for three and a half years, and then returned yet again. He particularly enjoyed holding wedding services, performing many in the park. "I enjoy it. If you can help people, why not do it?," Kauffman declared. For relaxation, Kauffman liked to ride horses, hunt, fish, and pack in the Bob Marshall Wilderness. He also farmed a little, mostly pitching hay. He logged a bit on his own property. Over the course of the past 15 years or so, he also sang in a barbershop chorus. In 1984, along with his wife, Ruth, Kauffman went on an Anabaptist Tour of Europe, which concluded with their attending the Mennonite World Conference in Strausburg, France.[25]

When interviewed at a reunion for CPS smokejumpers, Kauffman explained the forces that compelled him to act as he had.

> My personal conviction is that it is wrong to destroy life. If you look at the situation, at the history of wars, they never accomplish a great deal except to destroy life, to destroy the countryside. It meant something to me to do something more conscientious. You think of the term CO, and I don't see myself as an objector as much as someone who wants to help find a better way. Human life is sacred and so is helping other people.[26]

Beginning the ninth decade of his life, Kauffman was more than convinced about certain matters.

> Christianity still works for those who really believe in Christ. I have had great satisfaction in practicing medicine as a general practitioner. My philosophy and resolve is to help and treat whoever comes to me for help regardless of their ability to pay. This has paid off, not always financially, but in personal satisfaction and in the fact I believe this is what Christ taught.[27]

He also looked back fondly on his experience as a smokejumper.

> I am very thankful for what Civilian Public Service has done for me. The rewards especially as a smokejumper. I am happy and satisfied in spite of mistakes and errors made. Regardless of these, we endeavor to keep on doing the best we can with what we have.[28]

Denouement

In many regards, it had been a rousing success. At virtually no expense to the federal government, men from the Civilian Public Service had helped to keep alive the U.S. Forest Service's firefighting operations in the Pacific Northwest from 1943 to 1945. A highly dedicated crop of young men, physically fit and determined to prove something to neighbors, family members, and, yes, themselves, had battled fires and helped out with other projects initiated by the Forest Service. Like their age cohorts who went off to fight in the Black Forest of Germany, the deserts of North Africa, or the jungles of Indochina, the CPS smokejumpers served their nation in a determined fashion. Particularly during the extended months or even years when they did the bidding of the Forest Service, the CPS men engaged in, as they had hoped to, "work of national importance."

At the same time, they remained true to their own principles—many religiously based—and their general belief that one should not take up arms against one's fellow man. This was hardly an easy choice, as attested to by the fact that so many in the peace churches chose another path. After all, the Second World War did indeed appear to be a different kind of fight and a necessary one at that, with civilization itself seemingly at stake. But even in the midst of the deadliest and most important conflagration in human history, it was perhaps fitting that the world's leading democracy afforded some men an opportunity to hold onto biblical and other moral precepts of a non-violent cast. In the decades to follow, many of these same young men, now aging all the while, continued to give witness as they saw fit, offering alternative models of behavior that seemed so at odds with the violent nature of the era that swirled all about them.

Chapter Notes

Preface

1. Stephen J. Pyne, *Fire in America: A Cultural History of Wildland and Rural Fire* (Seattle: University of Washington Press, 1977), pp. 237–238.

Conscientious Objection

1. Peter Brock, *Pacifism in Europe to 1914* (Princeton, NJ: Princeton University Press, 1972), pp. 3–4.
2. *Ibid.*, pp. 25–58.
3. *Ibid.*, pp. 59–88.
4. Brock, *Pacifism in the United States: From the Colonial Era to the First World War* (Princeton, NJ: Princeton University Press, 1968), pp. 21–132.
5. Brock, *Freedom from War: Nonsectarian Pacifism, 1814–1915* (Toronto: University of Toronto Press, 1991), pp. 185–204.
6. Robert C. Cottrell, *Roger Nash Baldwin and the American Civil Liberties Union* (New York: Columbia University Press, 2001), pp. 60–102.
7. Albert N. Keim, *The CPS Story: An Illustrated History of Civilian Public Service* (Intercourse, PA: Good Books, 1990), p. 32.

Chapter 1

1. Norman Maclean, *Young Men and Fire* (Chicago: University of Chicago Press, 1993), pp. 214–215.
2. Earl Cooley, "Bull Session," Hungry Horse, Montana, July 16, 2002.
3. Various speakers, "Bull Session," Hungry Horse, Montana, July 16, 2002.
4. *Ibid.*
5. Bob Marshall, "Been There, Done That," Hungry Horse, Montana, July 16, 2002.

6. Norman Moody, "Been There, Done That;" Al Inglis, "Been There, Done That."
7. Lee Hebel, "Been There, Done That."
8. Dale Glandis, "Been There, Done That"; Joe Coffin, "Been There, Done That."

Chapter 2

1. Author's interview with Phil Stanley, July 26, 2001, Polson, Montana; Mark Matthews, "Trial by Fire," *Great Falls Tribune*, January 29, 1995, p. 1.
2. Author's interview with Stanley, July 26, 2001; Wallace "Pic" Littell, "NSA Member Profile: Philip B. Stanley"; Roxanne Farwell interview with Phil Stanley, Smokejumper Oral History Project, University of Montana, July 3, 1984, OH #133–99.
3. "CPS Provides Smoke Jumpers," *Smoke Jumper*, p. 30.
4. *Ibid.*
5. Author's interview with Stanley, July 26, 2001; Melvin Gingerich, *Service for Peace* (Akron, PA.: Mennonite Central Committee, 1949).
6. Author's interview with Stanley, July 26, 2001.
7. Stephen J. Pyne, *Fire in America: A Cultural History of Wildland and Rural Fire* (Seattle: University of Washington Press, 1997), pp. 227–229.
8. *Ibid.*, pp. 229–256; Stephen J. Pyne, *Year of the Fire: The Story of the Great Fires of 1910* (New York: Penguin, 2001).
9. Pyne, *Fire in America*, pp. 240–249.
10. *Ibid.*, pp. 250, pp. 255–256, 265–268, 439.
11. *Ibid.*, p. 275.
12. *Ibid.*, pp. 328–334; Maclean, *Young Men and Fire*, p. 20.
13. Pyne, *Fire in America*, pp. 341, 372.

14. *Ibid.*, pp. 372–373.
15. Author's interview with Stanley, July 26, 2001; Author's telephone interview with Stanley, April 8, 2003; Phil Stanley, "P. B. Stanley— Kiafeng to Missoula," *CPS Smokejumpers 1943 to 1946*, p. 1, Vol. I (Missoula, MT: Wenger, 1993).
16. Author's interview with Stanley, July 26, 2001; Author's telephone interview with Stanley, April 8, 2003; Stanley, "P. B. Stanley," p. 2.
17. Author's interview with Stanley, July 26, 2001; Stanley, "P. B. Stanley," p. 2.
18. Author's interview with Stanley, July 26, 2001; Author's telephone interview with Stanley, April 8, 2003; Stanley, "P. B. Stanley," p. 2; Farwell interview with Stanley.
19. Lawrence S. Wittner, *Rebels against War: The American Peace Movement, 1941–1960* (New York: Columbia University Press, 1969), p. 45.
20. Author's interview with Stanley, July 26, 2001; Stanley, "P. B. Stanley," p. 2; Farwell interview with Stanley.
21. Stanley, "P. B. Stanley," p. 3; Farwell interview with Stanley.
22. Author's interview with Stanley, July 26, 2001.
23. Farwell interview with Stanley.
24. *Ibid.*
25. *Ibid.*; Author's telephone interview with Stanley, April 8, 2003.
26. Farwell interview with Stanley; Stanley, "P. B. Stanley," p. 3; Stanley, "Phil Stanley-Missoula-1943, 1944, 1947," p. 62, in *Static Lines and Canopies: Stories from the Smokejumpers in Civilian Public Service Camp No. 103*, ed. Asa Mundell, (Beaverton, OR: Asa Mundell, 1993).
27. Stanley, "P. B. Stanley—Kiafeng to Missoula (Continued)," *CPS Smokejumpers 1943 to 1946*, Vol. I (Missoula, MT: Wenger, 1993), p. 1.
28. *Ibid.*, p. 2.
29. *Ibid*, pp. 2–3
30. *Ibid.*, p. 3.
31. Farwell interview with Stanley.
32. *Ibid.*; Author's telephone interview with Stanley, April 8, 2003.
33. Farwell interview with Stanley; Author's telephone interview with Stanley, April 8, 2003.
34. Stanley, "P. B. Stanley," pp. 3–4; Author's telephone interview with Stanley, April 8, 2003.
35. Stanley, "P. B. Stanley," p. 4; Author's interview with Stanley, July 26, 2001.

Chapter 3

1. Federal Writers' Project of the Work Projects Administration for the State of Montana, *Montana: A State Guide Book* (New York: Viking Press, 1939), pp. 172–173.
2. *Ibid.*
3. Author's interview with Roy Wenger, July 25, 2001, Missoula, Montana.
4. Author's interview with Roy Wenger, July 25, 2001; Roy E. Wenger, "All Decisions Have Their Consequences," *CPS Smokejumpers 1943 to 1946*, Vol. I, p. 1.
5. Author's interview with Wenger, July 25, 2001; Wenger, "All Decisions Have Their Consequences," p. 2.
6. Author's interview with Wenger, July 25, 2001.
7. Author's interview with Wenger, July 26, 2001; Wenger, "All Decisions Have Their Consequences," p. 2.
8. Author's interview with Wenger, July 26, 2001.
9. *Ibid.*
10. *Ibid.*; Wenger, "All Decisions Have Their Consequences," pp. 2–3.
11. Wenger, "All Decisions Have Their Consequences," p. 3; Charles Chatfield, *For Peace and Justice: Pacifism in America, 1914–1941* (Boston: Beacon Press, 1973), pp. 52–53.
12. Author's interview with Wenger, July 26, 2001.
13. Author's interview with Wenger, July 25, 2001.
14. *Ibid.*
15. *Ibid.*
16. *Ibid.*; Wenger, "All Decisions Have Their Consequences," p. 3.
17. Author's interview with Wenger, July 25, 2001.
18. *Ibid.*; Wenger, "All Decisions Have Their Consequences," p. 4.
19. Farwell interview with Roy Wenger, September 19, 1984, Smokejumpers Oral History Program, OH #133–113.
20. Author's interview with Wenger, July 25, 2001; Bill Wilson, "Into the Smoke to Put out Fires," p. 5, 1998, Roy Wenger Archives.
21. Wenger to Smoke Jumpers in the Field, July 5, 1943.
22. Farwell interview with Wenger; Matthews, "Trial by Fire," p. 4E; Wenger, "How I Happened to Become the First Director of the CPS Smokejumpers Camp," p. 1, *Static Line and Canopies*.
23. Farwell interview with Wenger; Wenger to Smoke Jumpers, August 3, 1945; Wenger to Smoke Jumpers, December 30, 1943.
24. Farwell interview with Wenger.
25. *Ibid.*
26. Author's interview with Wenger, July 25, 2001; Farwell interview with Wenger.
27. Author's interview with Wenger, July 25, 2001; Wenger, "All Decisions Have Their Consequences," pp. 4–5.
28. Author's interview with Wenger, July 25, 2001.
29. Author's interview with Susan Duffy, July 17, 2002, Hungry Horse.
30. *Ibid.*

31. Wenger, "...This Is Our Country," pp. 1–2, in *Smoke Jumper*.

32. Author's interview with Wenger, July 25, 2001; Wenger, "All Decisions Have Their Consequences," p. 5.

33. Wenger, "All Decisions Have Their Consequences," p. 5; Florence E. Wenger, "Teaching Was a Moving Experience," pp. 3–4, *CPS Smokejumpers 1943 to 1946*, Vol. I.

34. Wenger, "All Decisions Have Their Consequences," p. 6.

Chapter 4

1. Author's interview with Oliver Petty, July 16, 2002, Hungry Horse; Petty, "Oliver Petty: Smokejumper and Beekeeper," p. 3, *CPS Smokejumpers 1943 to 1946*, Vol. III (Missoula, MT: Wenger, 1995; Gregg Phifer interview with Oliver Petty, August 11, 1986, Smokejumpers Oral History Project, OH #163–30.

2. Petty, "Oliver Petty," p. 1

3. *Ibid.*

4. *Ibid.*, pp. 1–2.

5. *Ibid.*; Author's interview with Petty, July 16, 2002.

6. Author's interview with Petty, July 16, 2002.

7. *Ibid.*, p. 3.

8. Author's interview with Petty, July 16, 2002; Petty, "Oliver Petty," pp. 3–4.

9. Author's interview with Petty, July 16, 2002.

10. Petty, "Oliver Petty," p. 4; Author's interview with Petty, July 16, 2002.

11. Petty, "Oliver Petty," p. 4.

12. Author's interview with Petty, July 16, 2002; Petty, "Oliver Petty," p. 4; Phifer interview with Petty.

13. Author's interview with Petty, July 16, 2002.

14. Phifer interview with Petty; Petty, "Oliver Petty," p. 5.

15. Petty, "Oliver Petty," p. 5.

16. *Ibid.*, pp. 5–6; Phifer interview with Petty.

17. Petty, "Oliver Petty," p. 6; Phifer interview with Petty.

18. Phifer interview with Petty; Petty, "Oliver Petty," p. 6; Petty, "Oliver Petty—Three Forks Station—1945," in *Static Lines and Canopies*, p. 45.

19. Petty, "Oliver Petty," p. 7; Phifer interview with Petty.

20. Petty, "Oliver Petty," p. 7.

21. Phifer interview with Petty.

22. *Ibid.*

Chapter 5

1. Author's interview with Dick Flaharty, September 9, 2001, Yuba City, California; Dick Flaharty, "What Ever Happened to What's-His-Name?" *CPS Smokejumpers 1943 to 1946*, Vol. III, pp. 1–2.

2. Author's interview with Flaharty, September 9, 2001.

3. Charles Chatfield, *For Peace and Justice: Pacifism in America 1914–1941* (Boston: Beacon Press, 1973), pp. 125–129.

4. *Ibid.*

5. *Ibid.*

6. *Ibid.*; Flaharty, "What Ever Happened to What's-His-Name?" p. 1.

7. Author's interview with Flaharty, September 9, 2001; Flaharty, "What Ever Happened to What's-His-Name?" p. 2.

8. Flaharty, "What Ever Happened to What's His Name?" p. 3; Author's interview with Flaharty, September 9, 2001; Gregg Phifer interview with T. Richard Flaharty, August 11, 1986, Smokejumpers Oral History Program, OH #163–29.

9. Author's interview with Flaharty, September 9, 2001.

10. *Ibid.*

11. Author's interview with Flaharty, September 9, 2001; Flaharty, "What Ever Happened to What's-His-Name?" p. 3; Phifer interview with Flaharty.

12. Author's interview with Flaharty, September 9, 2001.

13. *Ibid.*

14. *Ibid.*; Flaharty, "What Ever Happened to What's-His-Name?" p. 3.

15. *Ibid.*

16. *Ibid.*, pp. 3–4.

17. *Ibid.*, p. 4; Author's interview with Flaharty, September 9, 2001.

18. Phifer interview with Flaharty; Author's interview with Flaharty, September 9, 2001.

19. *Ibid.*

20. Phifer interview with Flaharty; Author's interview with Flaharty, September 9, 2001.

21. Author's interview with Flaharty, September 9, 2001; Phifer interview with Flaharty.

22. Author's interview with Flaharty, September 9, 2001; Flaharty, "What Ever Happened to What's-His-Name?" p. 4.

23. Author's interview with Flaharty, September 9, 2001.

24. *Ibid.*; Flaharty, "What Ever Happened to What's-His-Name?" pp. 4–5; Flaharty, "Dick Flaharty—Potlatch, Idaho-1945," pp. 17–18, in *Static Line and Canopies*.

25. Flaharty, "What Ever Happened to What's-His-Name?" p. 5.

26. Gregg Phifer, "Why I Joined the Smoke Jumper Unit," in *Smoke Jumper*.

27. *Ibid.*, p. 6; Author's interview with Flaharty, September 9, 2001; Phifer interview with Flaharty.

28. Author's interview with Flaharty, September 9, 2001; Phifer interview with Flaharty.

29. Author's interview with Flaharty, September 9, 2001.

30. Phifer interview with Flaharty.

Chapter 6

1. Author's interview with Gregg Phifer, Hungry Horse, July 17, 2002.

2. Phifer, "Wahoo," p. 1.

3. *Ibid.*, pp. 1–2.

4. *Ibid.*, p. 2.

5. *Ibid.*, p. 1.

6. *Ibid.*, pp. 2–3.

7. *Ibid.*, p. 3.

8. *Ibid.*, p. 4.

9. Phifer, "From WHSS to COP to Iowa to FSU; A Stop at CPS 103," p. 1, in *CPS Smokejumpers 1943–1946*, Vol. III; Rosa Stone interview with Gregg Phifer, August 11, 1986, Smokejumpers Oral History Program, OH #163–21; Author's interview with Phifer, July 17, 2002.

10. Phifer, "Autobiographical Sketch," p. 1, May 1998.

11. Phifer, "From WHSS to COP to Iowa," p. 1; Phifer, "Autobiographical Sketch," p. 1.

12. Phifer, "Autobiographical Sketch," p. 1; Phifer, "From WHSS to COP to Iowa," p. 2.

13. Phifer, "Autobiographical Sketch," p. 1; Phifer, "From WHSS to COP to Iowa," p. 2.

14. Phifer, "Autobiographical Sketch," p. 1; Phifer, "From WHSS to COP to Iowa," pp. 1–2.

15. Phifer, "Autobiographical Sketch," p. 1; Phifer, "From WHSS to COP to Iowa," p. 2.

16. Phifer, "Autobiographical Sketch," p. 3; Phifer, "From WHSS to COP to Iowa," p. 2.

17. Phifer, "Autobiographical Sketch," pp. 3–4; Phifer, "From WHSS to COP to Iowa," p. 2; Interview with Phifer, July 17, 2002.

18. Phifer, "Autobiographical Sketch," p. 4; Phifer, "CPS 50 Years After," p. 2.

19. Phifer, "Autobiographical Sketch," pp. 4–5; Interview with Phifer, July 17, 2002; Phifer, "From WHSS to COP to Iowa," p. 3.

20. Phifer, "Autobiographical Sketch," p. 5; Phifer, "CPS 50 Years After," p. 2, *CPS Smokejumpers 1943 to 1946*, Vol. III; Phifer, "From WHSS to COP to Iowa," p. 3.

21. Phifer, "Autobiographical Sketch," p. 5; Interview with Phifer, July 17, 2002; Phifer, "CPS Communique #9," pp. 1–2; Phifer, "From WHSS to COP to Iowa," p. 3.

22. Interview with Phifer, July 17, 2002; Phifer, "CPS Communique #9," p. 2.

23. Phifer, "CPS Communique #9," pp. 6–7.

24. Phifer, "Autobiographical Sketch," p. 5; Interview with Phifer, July 17, 2002; Phifer, "From WHSS to COP to Iowa," p. 3.

25. Author's interview with Phifer, July 17, 2002; Phifer, "CPS Communique," p. 10.

26. Author's interview with Phifer, July 17, 2002; Phifer, "CPS Communique," p. 11; Phifer, "A Smokejumper's Seven Training Jumps," p. 1; Phifer, "From WHSS to COP to Iowa," p. 4; Phifer, "CPS 50 Years After," p. 3.

27. Phifer, "Autobiographical Sketch," p. 6; Phifer, "From WHSS to COP to Iowa," p. 4; Phifer, "CPS 50 Years After," p. 3.

28. Phifer, "A Smokejumper's Seven Training Jumps," p. 1–3.

29. *Ibid.*, pp. 1, 3.

30. Phifer, "Autobiographical Sketch," p. 6; Phifer, "From WHSS to COP to Iowa," p. 4; Phifer, "CPS 50 Years After," pp. 3–4.

31. Phifer, "Autobiographical Sketch," p. 6; Phifer, "CPS Communique 21," p. 4.

32. Phifer, "CPS Communique 21," p. 7; Phifer, "Autobiographical Sketch," p. 7; Phifer to Editor, *Smokejumper* 30 (January 2001): 11.

33. Phifer, "Autobiographical Sketch," p. 8; Phifer, "My Brush with History: CPS/USFS Smokejumpers," p. 3.

34. Phifer, "From WHSS to COP to Iowa," p. 5.

35. Phifer, "Autobiographical Sketch," p. 8.

36. *Ibid.*; Author's interview with Phifer, July 17, 2002; Phifer, "From WHSS to COP to Iowa," p. 5.

37. Phifer, "CPS Communique, August 1945," p. 1.

38. *Ibid.*, pp. 1–2.

39. *Ibid.*, p. 2.

40. *Ibid.*, pp. 2–3.

41. *Ibid.*

42. *Ibid.*, pp. 3–4.

43. Phifer, "Autobiographical Sketch," p. 9; Phifer, "From WHSS to COP to Iowa," p. 6.

44. Phifer, "Autobiographical Sketch," p. 9; Stone interview with Phifer.

45. Phifer, "Autobiographical Sketch," p. 9; Phifer, "From WHSS to COP to Iowa," p. 6; Interview with Phifer, July 17, 2002.

46. Author's interview with Phifer, July 17, 2002; Phifer, "Autobiographical Sketch," p. 10; Phifer, "From WHSS to COP to Iowa," p. 6.

Chapter 7

1. Clark C. Spence, *Montana: A History* (New York: Norton, 1978), pp. 161–162.

2. Author's interview with Earl Schmidt, July 17, 2002, Hungry Horse, Montana; Author's telephone interview with Schmidt, June 30, 2003; Schmidt, "Reminiscences," *CPS Smokejumpers 1943 to 1946*, Vol. I, p. 1.

3. Author's interview with Schmidt, July 17, 2002, Hungry Horse; Schmidt, "Reminiscences," p. 1.

4. Author's interview with Schmidt, July 17, 2002; Schmidt, "Reminiscences," p. 1.

5. Author's interview with Schmidt, July 17, 2002; Schmidt, "Reminiscences," p. 1; Greg Phifer interview with Earl Schmidt, Smokejumpers Oral History Program, OH #163–11.

6. Interview with Schmidt, July 17, 2002; Schmidt, "Reminiscences," p. 1.

7. Author's interview with Schmidt, July 17, 2002; Schmidt, "Reminiscences," p. 1; Phifer interview with Schmidt.

8. Author's interview with Schmidt, July 17, 2002; Schmidt, "Reminiscences," p. 1; Phifer interview with Schmidt.

9. Author's interview with Schmidt, July 17, 2002; Schmidt, "Reminiscences," p. 2.

10. Author's interview with Schmidt, July 17, 2002; Schmidt, "Reminiscences," p. 2; Phifer interview with Schmidt; Schmidt, "Sabe Creek Fire," July 22, 1945.

11. Author's interview with Schmidt, July 17, 2002; Schmidt, "Reminiscences," p. 2; Phifer interview with Schmidt.

12. Author's interview with Schmidt, July 17, 2002; Schmidt, "Reminiscences," p. 2; Phifer interview with Schmidt.

13. Schmidt, "Reminiscences," p. 3; Phifer interview with Schmidt.

Chapter 8

1. Lee Hebel, "Lee Hebel— Montana-Idaho Border —1945," *Static Lines and Canopies*, p. 21; Rosa Stone interview with Hebel, August 13, 1986, Smokejumpers Oral Project, OH #163–10.

2. Hebel, "Lee Hebel," p. 21.

3. *Ibid.*

4. *Ibid.*; Stone interview with Hebel.

5. Robert H. Craig, *Religion and Radical Politics: An Alternative Christian Tradition in the United States* (Philadelphia: Temple University Press, 1992), pp. 12–14; Donald K. Gorrell, *The Age of Social Responsibility: The Age of the Social Gospel in the Progressive Era, 1900–1920* (Macon, GA: Mercer University Press, 1988).

6. Ronald C. White Jr. and C. Howard Hopkins, *The Social Gospel: Religion and Reform in Changing America* (Philadelphia: Temple University Press, 1976), pp. 214–240.

7. Robert C. Cottrell, *The Social Gospel of E. Nicholas Comfort: Founder of the Oklahoma School of Religion* (Norman: University of Oklahoma, 1997), p. 31; White and Hopkins, *The Social Gospel*, pp. 167–171.

8. Gorrell, *The Age of Social Responsibility*, pp. 100–101.

9. C. Roland Marchand, *The American Peace Movement and Social Reform 1898–1918* (Princeton, NJ: Princeton University Press, 1972), pp. 375–376.

10. Chatfield, *For Peace and Justice*, pp. 179.

11. Author's interview with Hebel, Hungry Horse, July 17, 2002; Hebel, "By the Grace of God," *CPS Smokejumpers 1943 to 1946*, Vol. I, p. 1.

12. Hebel, "By the Grace of God," p. 1.

13. *Ibid.*, p. 2.

14. *Ibid.*, p. 1.

15. Author's interview with Hebel, July 17, 2002; Hebel, "By the Grace of God," p. 2.

16. Hebel, "By the Grace of God," p. 2; Author's interview with Hebel, July 17, 2002.

17. Author's interview with Hebel, July 17, 2002; Hebel, "By the Grace of God," p. 2.

18. Author's interview with Hebel, July 17, 2002.

19. Hebel, "By the Grace of God," p. 2; Author's interview with Hebel, July 17, 2002; Stone interview with Hebel.

20. Hebel, "By the Grace of God," p. 2; Author's interview with Hebel, July 17, 2002; Stone interview with Hebel.

21. Hebel, "By the Grace of God," pp. 2–3; Author's interview with Hebel, July 17, 2002; Stone interview with Hebel.

22. Stone interview with Hebel.

23. Hebel, "By the Grace of God," p. 3.

24. Author's interview with Hebel, July 17, 2002; Hebel, "By the Grace of God," p. 3.

25. Author's interview with Hebel, July 17, 2002.

26. Hebel, "By the Grace of God," p. 3; Stone interview with Hebel.

27. Stone interview with Hebel.

28. Author's interview with Hebel, July 17, 2002; Hebel, "By the Grace of God," p. 3; Stone interview with Hebel.

29. Author's interview with Hebel, July 17, 2002; Hebel, "By the Grace of God," p. 3.

30. Hebel, "By the Grace of God," p. 3–4.

31. *Ibid.*, p. 4.

32. Bill Wilson, "Into the Smoke to Put out Fires," p. 5.

Chapter 9

1. Author's interview with Alan Inglis, July 16, 2002; Inglis, "Alan Inglis," *CPS Smokejumpers 1943 to 1946*, Vol. II, p. 3; Inglis, "Alan Inglis— Missoula —1945," pp. 24–25, in *Static Lines and Canopies*.

2. Author's interview with Inglis, July 17, 2002; Inglis, "Alan Inglis," p. 4.

3. Inglis, "Alan Inglis," p. 4.

4. Author's interview with Inglis, July 17, 2002.

5. *Ibid.*

6. *Ibid.*

7. *Ibid.*

8. *Ibid.*; "Alan Inglis," p. 1.

9. "Alan Inglis," p. 1; Author's interview with Inglis, July 16, 2002.
10. "Alan Inglis," p. 1.
11. *Ibid.*, p. 2
12. *Ibid.*
13. *Ibid.*
14. *Ibid.*
15. *Ibid.*, pp. 2–3.
16. *Ibid.*, p. 3.
17. *Ibid.*
18. *Ibid.*
19. *Ibid.*, p. 5.
20. *Ibid.*
21. *Ibid.*
22. *Ibid.*, pp. 5–6.
23. *Ibid.*, p. 6.
24. *Ibid.*
25. *Ibid.*, p. 7.
26. *Ibid*; Author's interview with Inglis, July 16, 2002.
27. "Alan Inglis," p. 7.
28. *Ibid.*
29. *Ibid.*
30. *Ibid.*

Chapter 10

1. Author's interview with Wilmer Carlsen, July 17, 2002, Hungry Horse, Montana; Carlsen, "The ramblings of Wilmer Carlsen," *CPS Smokejumpers 1943 to 1946*, Vol. II (Missoula, MT: Wenger, 1993), p. 2.
2. Author's interview with Carlsen, July 17, 2002; Carlsen, "The ramblings of Wilmer Carlsen," p. 2.
3. Author's interview with Carlsen, July 17, 2002.
4. Author's interview with Carlsen, July 17, 2002; Carlsen, "The ramblings of Wilmer Carlsen," p. 1.
5. Author's interview with Carlsen, July 17, 2002; Carlsen, "The ramblings of Wilmer Carlsen," p. 1.
6. Author's interview with Carlsen, July 17, 2002; Carlsen, "The ramblings of Wilmer Carlsen," pp. 1–2.
7. Author's Interview with Carlsen, July 17, 2002; Carlsen, "The ramblings of Wilmer Carlsen," p. 2; Roxanne Farwell interview with Wilmer Carlsen, August 29, 1984, Smokejumpers Oral History Project, OH #133–13.
8. Author's interview with Carlsen, July 17, 2002; Carlsen, "The ramblings of Wilmer Carlsen," p. 2.
9. Farwell interview with Carlsen.
10. *Ibid.*; Author's interview with Carlsen, July 17, 2002; Carlsen, "The ramblings of Wilmer Carlsen," p. 2.
11. Author's interview with Carlsen, July 17, 2002; Carlsen, "The ramblings of Wilmer Carlsen," p. 3; Farwell interview with Carlsen.
12. Farwell interview with Carlsen.
13. Carlsen, "The ramblings of Wilmer Carlsen," p. 3; Interview with Carlsen, July 17, 2002; Carlsen, "Wilmer Carlsen—Nine Mile," p. 9, in *Static Lines and Canopies*.
14. Murray Braden, "...Fire on the Mountain," p. 1, in *Smoke Jumper*.
15. *Ibid.*
16. *Ibid.*
17. Farwell interview with Carlsen.
18. *Ibid.*
19. *Ibid.*
20. Carlsen, "The ramblings of Wilmer Carlsen," p. 4.

Chapter 11

1. Joe Coffin, "Review and Preview," *CPS Smokejumpers 1943 to 1946*, Vol. III, p. 3.
2. Author's interview with Joe and Audine Coffin, July 17, 2002; Rosa Stone interview with Joe and Audine Coffin, August 12, 1986, Smokejumpers Oral History Project, OH #163–19.
3. Author's interview with Joe and Audine Coffin, July 17, 2002; Stone interview with Joe and Audine Coffin.
4. Author's interview with Joe and Audine Coffin, July 17, 2002; Coffin, "Review and Preview, p. 1.
5. Coffin, "Review and Preview," p. 1.
6. *Ibid.*; Author's interview with Joe and Audine Coffin, July 17, 2002.
7. Coffin, "Review and Preview," p. 1.
8. *Ibid.*, p. 2.
9. *Ibid.*
10. *Ibid.*
11. Author's interview with Joe and Audine Coffin, July 17, 2002; Coffin, "Review and Preview," p. 2.
12. Author's interview with Joe and Audine Coffin, July 17, 2002; Coffin, "Review and Preview," p. 2.
13. Coffin, "Review and Preview," p. 2.
14. *Ibid.*, p. 3; Author's interview with Joe and Audine Coffin, July 17, 2002.
15. Author's interview with Joe and Audine Coffin, July 17, 2002; Stone interview with Joe and Audine Coffin.
16. Author's interview with Joe and Audine Coffin, July 17, 2002; Stone interview with Joe and Audine Coffin.
17. Author's interview with Joe and Audine Coffin, July 17, 2002.
18. *Ibid.*; Stone interview with Joe and Audine Coffin.
19. Author's interview with Joe and Audine Coffin, July 17, 2002; Stone interview with Joe and

Audine Coffin; Coffin, "Joe Coffin — Missoula —
1945," pp. 9–10, in *Static Lines and Canopies*.
　20. Author's interview with Joe and Audine
Coffin, July 17, 2002; Stone interview with Joe
and Audine Coffin; Coffin, "Review and Preview," p. 4.
　21. Stone interview with Joe and Audine
Coffin.
　22. *Ibid.*
　23. *Ibid.*
　24. Author's interview with Joe and Audine
Coffin, July 17, 2002; Joe Coffin, "Review and
Preview," p. 4.
　25. Coffin, "Review and Preview," p. 4.
　26. *Ibid.*
　27. *Ibid.*, pp. 4–5.
　28. Author's interview with Joe and Audine
Coffin, July 17, 2002.

Chapter 12

　1. Author's interview with George S. Leavitt, July 17, 2002, Hungry Horse.
　2. Kim Taylor interview with George S.
Leavitt, August 11, 1986, Smokejumpers Oral
History Project, OH #163–7; Author's interview
with Leavitt, July 17, 2002; Taylor interview
with Leavitt.
　3. Author's interview with Leavitt, July 17,
2002; Taylor interview with Leavitt.
　4. Author's interview with Leavitt, July 17,
2002, Leavitt, "Some Memories and Thoughts,"
CPS Smokejumpers 1943 to 1946, Vol. II, p. 1;
Taylor interview with Leavitt.
　5. Author's interview with Leavitt, July 17,
2002; Leavitt, "Some Memories and Thoughts,"
p. 1; Taylor interview with Leavitt.
　6. Author's interview with Leavitt, July 17,
2002.
　7. Leavitt, "Some Memories and
Thoughts," p. 2.
　8. Author's interview with Leavitt, July 17,
2002; Leavitt, "Some Memories and Thoughts,"
p. 3
　9. Author's interview with Leavitt, July 17,
2002.
　10. Author's interview with Leavitt, July 17,
2002; Leavitt, "Some Memories and Thoughts,"
p. 1; Taylor interview with Leavitt.
　11. Author's interview with Leavitt, July 17,
2002; Leavitt, "Some Memories and Thoughts,"
p. 3.
　12. Taylor interview with Leavitt.
　13. Author's interview with Leavitt, July 17,
2002; Taylor interview with Leavitt.
　14. Taylor interview with Leavitt.
　15. *Ibid.*
　16. *Ibid.*
　17. *Ibid.*
　18. *Ibid.*

　19. *Ibid.*
　20. Leavitt, "Some Memories and Thoughts,"
p. 1.
　21. Taylor interview with Leavitt.
　22. Author's interview with Leavitt, July 17,
2002.
　23. *Ibid.*
　24. *Ibid.*

Chapter 13

　1. Author's interview with Tedford Lewis,
October 22, 2002.
　2. *Ibid.*
　3. *Ibid.*; Roxanne Farwell interview with
Tedford Lewis, September 26, 1984, Smokejumpers Oral History Program, OH #133–59.
　4. Author's interview with Lewis, October
22, 2002.
　5. *Ibid.*
　6. *Ibid.*
　7. *Ibid.*
　8. *Ibid.*
　9. *Ibid.*
　10. *Ibid.*
　11. *Ibid.*
　12. *Ibid.*
　13. *Ibid.*
　14. *Ibid.*; Farwell interview with Lewis.
　15. Author's interview with Lewis, October
22, 2002.
　16. *Ibid.*
　17. Farwell interview with Lewis; Author's
interview with Lewis, September 26, 1984; Farwell interview with Lewis.
　18. Author's interview with Lewis, September 26, 1984.
　19. *Ibid.*; Roy Wenger, "Ted Lewis, a Day in
the Life of or the Saga of the Sagging Sill," p. 2,
CPS Smokejumpers 1943 to 1946, Vol. III.

Chapter 14

　1. Roy Piepenburg, "Roy Piepenburg —
Meadow Creek, Nez Perce —1945," *Static Lines
and Canopies*, p. 48.
　2. *Ibid.*; Author's interview with Piepenburg, July 18, 2002, Hungry Horse; Piepenburg,
"Recollections and Reflections," p. 3.
　3. Author's interview with Piepenburg, July
18, 2002, Hungry Horse; Piepenburg, "Recollections and Reflections," p. 3.
　4. Piepenburg, "Roy Piepenburg," p. 49.
　5. "Labor," in *Montana: A State Guide Book*,
compiled and written by the Federal Writers'
Project of the Works Projects Administration for
the State of Montana (New York: Viking Press,
1939), pp. 68–69; Melvyn Dubofsky, *We Shall Be
All: A History of the Industrial Workers of the
World* (New York: Quadrangle, 1969), p. 34.

6. Dubofsky, *We Shall Be All*, p. 41; Spence, *Montana*, pp. 99–100.

7. Spence, *Montana*, p. 101.

8. *Montana: A State Guide Book*, p., 75.

9. *Ibid.*, pp. 69–70; Dubofsky, *We Shall Be All*.

10. *Montana: A State Guide Book*, pp. 70–71.

11. Dubofsky, *We Shall Be All*, pp. 301–307.

12. Spence, *Montana*, p. 115; Dubofsky, *We Shall Be All*, pp. 366–369.

13. Dubofsky, *We Shall Be All*, pp. 391–392; *Montana: A State Guide Book*, p. 74; Spence, *Montana*, p. 124.

14. Spence, *Montana*, p. 124.

15. *Ibid.*, pp. 74–75.

16. *Ibid.*, p. 75; Spence, *Montana*, p. 125

17. *Montana: A State Guide Book*, pp. 75–76.

18. *Ibid.*, pp. 76–77.

19. Author's interview with Piepenburg, July 18, 2002.

20. *Ibid.*

21. *Ibid.*

22. *Ibid.*

23. Piepenburg, "Recollections and Reflections of a W.W. II CPS'er," p. 1, CPS Smokejumper 1943 to 1946, Vol. II.

24. Author's interview with Piepenburg, July 18, 2002.

25. Piepenburg, "Recollections and Reflections," p. 1.

26. *Ibid.*; Piepenburg, "Recollections and Reflections," p. 1.

27. Author's interview with Piepenburg, July 18, 2002; Piepenburg, "Recollections and Reflections, " pp. 1–2.

28. Piepenburg, "Recollections and Reflections," pp. 2–3.

29. Author's interview with Piepenburg, July 18, 2002; Piepenburg, "Recollections and Reflections," p. 2.

30. Piepenburg, "Recollections and Reflections," p. 2; Author's interview with Piepenburg, July 18, 2002.

31. Author's interview with Piepenburg, July 18, 2002; Piepenburg, "Recollections and Reflections," p. 3.

32. Author's interview with Piepenburg, July 18, 2002; Piepenburg, "Recollections and Reflections," p. 3.

33. Author's interview with Piepenburg, July 18, 2002; Piepenburg, "Recollections and Reflections," p. 3.

34. Author's interview with Piepenburg, July 18, 2002; Piepenburg, "Recollections and Reflections," p. 3.

35. Author's interview with Piepenburg, July 18, 2002; Piepenburg, "Recollections and Reflections," p. 4.

36. Piepenburg, "Recollections and Reflections," p. 4.

37. *Ibid.*

38. *Ibid.*

39. *Ibid.*

40. Author's interview with Piepenburg, July 18, 2002.

41. *Ibid.*

42. *Ibid.*

43. *Ibid.*; Piepenburg, "Recollections and Reflections," p. 5.

44. Piepenburg, "Recollections and Reflections," pp. 5–6.

45. *Ibid.*

Chapter 15

1. Author's interview with Norman Moody, Hungry Horse, Montana, July 17, 2002.

2. "Draft Objections Bring Year Term," *Lexington Leader*, January 17, 1949, p. 1.

3. *Ibid.*

4. *Ibid.*

5. "The Moody Case," *Lexington Leader*, n.d.

6. Author's interview with Moody, July 17, 2002.

7. *Ibid.*; Moody to Cottrell, July 27, 2002.

8. Author's interview with Moody, July 17, 2002.

9. *Ibid.*

10. *Ibid.*

11. *Ibid.*; Moody to Cottrell, July 27, 2002.

12. Nicholas Helburn, "...Hitting the Silk," *Smoke Jumper*.

13. *Ibid.*

14. *Ibid.*

15. *Ibid.*

16. Author's interview with Moody, July 17, 2002; Moody to Cottrell, July 27, 2002.

17. Moody to Cottrell, July 27, 2002; Author's interview with Moody, July 17, 2002.

18. Author's interview with Moody, July 17, 2002; Moody to Cottrell, July 27, 2002.

19. Author's interview with Moody, July 17, 2002.

20. *Ibid.*

21. *Ibid.*

22. *Ibid.*; Moody to Cottrell, July 27, 2002.

23. *Palm and Cycad Times* 6 (June 2002): 10.

Chapter 16

1. Robert Painter, "Witness of a Quaker Physician: The Life Story of Robert H. Painter, M.D.," *CPS Smokejumpers 1943 to 1946*, Vol. I, p. 3; Kim Taylor with Painter, August 12, 1986, Smokejumpers Oral History Program, OH #163–1.

2. Author's interview with Robert Painter, Hungry Horse, Montana, July 17, 2002; Painter, "Witness of a Quaker Physician," p. 1.

3. Author's interview with Painter, July 17,

2002; Painter, "Witness of a Quaker Physician," p. 1.

4. Author's interview with Painter, July 17, 2002; Painter, "Witness of a Quaker Physician," p. 1.

5. Painter, "Witness of a Quaker Physician," p. 2; Taylor with Painter; Author's interview with Painter, July 17, 2002.

6. Author's interview with Painter, July 17, 2002; Painter, "Witness of a Quaker Physician," p. 2; Taylor interview with Painter.

7. Author's interview with Painter, July 17, 2002; Painter, "Witness of a Quaker Physician," p. 2.

8. Author's interview with Painter, July 17, 2002; Painter, "Witness of a Quaker Physician," p. 2; Taylor interview with Painter.

9. Author's interview with Painter, July 17, 2002; Painter, "Witness of a Quaker Physician," pp. 2–3; Taylor interview with Painter.

10. Painter, George Item, and Bill Laughlin, "...Torture Chamber," in *Smoke Jumper*, p. 5.

11. Taylor interview with Painter; Item, and Laughlin, "...Torture Chamber."

12. Painter, Item, and Laughlin, "...Torture Chamber."

13. *Ibid.*

14. *Ibid.*; Taylor interview with Painter.

15. "Hit and Roll," in *Smoke Jumper*.

16. Painter, Item, and Laughlin, "...Torture Chamber"; "That First Parachute Jump," in *Smoke Jumper*, Painter, "Witness of a Quaker Physician," p. 3; Author's interview with Painter, July 17, 2002.

17. Taylor interview with Painter.

18. Painter, "Witness of a Quaker Physician," p. 3; Author's interview with Painter, July 17, 2002.

19. Author's interview with Painter, July 17, 2002; Taylor interview with Painter.

20. Painter, "Witness of a Quaker Physician," p. 3; Author's interview with Painter, July 17, 2002.

21. Painter, "Witness of a Quaker Physician," p. 3; Author's interview with Painter, July 17, 2002; Taylor interview with Painter.

22. Painter, "Witness of a Quaker Physician," p. 3.

23. Author's interview with Painter, July 17, 2002; Painter, "Witness of a Quaker Physician," pp. 3–4; Taylor interview with Painter.

24. Painter, "Witness of a Quaker Physician," p. 4.

25. Author's interview with Painter; July 17, 2002; Painter, "Witness of a Quaker Physician," pp. 4–5.

26. Taylor interview with Painter.

27. Author's interview with Painter, July 17, 2002; Painter, "Witness of a Quaker Physician," p. 5.

28. Wilson, "In the Smoke to Put out Fires," p. 15.

Chapter 17

1. James R. Brunk, "Some Information on My Life Experiences with Appropriate Emphasis on Smokejumping," p. 3, *CPS Smokejumpers 1943 to 1946*, Vol. I; Ted Lewis interview with James R. Brunk, August 11, 1986, Smokejumpers Oral History Project, OH #163–31; Brunk, "James R. Brunk, M.D.— Rescue Jumps—1944–45," *Static Lines and Canopies*, pp. 7–8.

2. Brunk, "Some Information," p. 1.

3. *Ibid.*; Lewis interview with Brunk.

4. Brunk, "Some Information," p. 1

5. Author's interview with Brunk, July 16, 2002; Brunk, "Some Information," p. 1.

6. Brunk, "Some Information," p. 1.

7. *Ibid.*

8. *Ibid.*

9. *Ibid.*, Author's interview with Brunk, July 16, 2002.

10. Lewis interview with Brunk; Author's interview with Brunk, July 16, 2002.

11. Author's interview with Brunk, July 16, 2002.

12. Brunk, "The Mennonite," p. 2; Author's interview with Brunk, July 16, 2002; Lewis interview with Brunk.

13. Brunk, "Some Information," p. 2.

14. *Ibid.*

15. Lewis interview with Brunk.

16. Brunk, "Some Information," p. 2.

17. *Ibid.*, pp. 2–3.

18. *Ibid.*, pp. 3–4.

19. Lewis interview with Brunk.

20. *Ibid.*

21. Author's interview with Brunk, July 16, 2002; Lewis interview with Brunk.

22. Author's interview with Brunk, July 16, 2002; Brunk, "Some Information," p. 4; Lewis interview with Brunk.

23. Author's interview with Brunk, July 16, 2002; Brunk, "Some Information," p. 4.

24. Brunk, "Some Information," p. 4; Author's interview with Brunk, July 16, 2002; Lewis interview with Brunk.

25. Author's inteview with Brunk, July 16, 2002; Brunk, "Some Information," p. 4.

26. Author's interview with Brunk, July 16, 2002; Brunk, "Some Information," p. 4.

27. Brunk, "Some Information," p. 5; Author's interview with Brunk, July 16, 2002.

28. Author's interview with Brunk, July 16, 2002; Brunk, "Some Information," p. 5.

29. Brunk, "Some Information," pp. 5–6.

30. *Ibid.*

Chapter 18

1. JN interview with David V. Kauffman, August 16, 1984, Smokejumpers Oral History Project, OH #133–54; Author's interview with Kauffman, July 18, 2002;

2. JN interview with Kauffman.

3. Author's interview with David Kauffman, July 18, 2002, Hungry Horse; JN interview with Kauffman; Kauffman, "Personal History of David V. Kauffman," *CPS Smokejumpers 1943 to 1946*, Vol. II, p. 1.

4. Kauffman, "Personal History of David V. Kauffman," p. 1.

5 *Ibid.*; Author's interview with Kauffman, July 18, 2002.

6. Kauffman, "Personal History of David V. Kauffman," p. 1; Author's interview with Kauffman, July 18, 2002; JN interview with Kauffman; Kauffman, "Dr. David Kauffman — Big Prairie — 1943," *Static Lines and Canopies*, p. 29.

7. Kauffman, "Personal History of David V. Kauffman," p. 1; Author's interview with Kauffman, July 18, 2002; JN interview with Kauffman.

8. Kauffman, "Personal History of David V. Kauffman," p. 1; JN interview with Kauffman.

9. JN interview with Kauffman; Author's interview with Kauffman, July 18, 2002.

10. JN interview with Kauffman.

11. *Ibid.*

12. *Ibid.*

13. *Ibid.*

14. *Ibid.*

15. Author's interview with Kauffman, July 18, 2002; JN interview with Kauffman.

16. Author's interview with Kauffman, July 18, 2002.

17. *Ibid.*

18. *Ibid.*

19. *Ibid.*

20. *Ibid.*

21. JN interview with Kauffman.

22. Author's interview with Kauffman, July 18, 2002; Kauffman, "Personal History of David V. Kauffman," p. 2.

23. Author's interview with Kauffman, July 18, 2002; Kauffman, "Personal History of David V. Kauffman," p. 2.

24. Author's interview with Kauffman, July 18, 2002; Kauffman, "Personal History of David V. Kauffman," p. 3.

25. Author's interview with Kauffman, July 18, 2002; Kauffman, "Personal History of David V. Kauffman," pp. 2–3.

26. Wilson, "In the Smoke to Put out Fires," p. 5.

27. *Ibid.*, pp. 3–4.

28. *Ibid.*, p. 4.

Bibliography

Braden, Murray. "...Fire on the Mountain." *Smoke Jumper.*

Brock, Peter. *Freedom from War: Nonsectarian Pacifism, 1814–1915.* Toronto: University of Toronto Press, 1991.

_____. *Pacifism in Europe to 1914.* Princeton, NJ: Princeton University Press, 1972.

_____. *Pacifism in the United States: From the Colonial Era to the First World War.* Princeton, NJ: Princeton University Press, 1968.

Brunk, James R. "James R. Brunk, M.D.— Rescue Jumps—1944–45." In *Static Lines and Canopies: Stories from the Smokejumpers in Civilian Public Service Camp No. 103*, ed. Asa Mundell. Beaverton, OR: Mundell, 1993.

_____. "Some Information on My Life Experiences with Appropriate Emphasis on Smokejumping." In *CPS Smokejumpers 1943 to 1946*, Vol. I. Ed. Roy E. Wenger. Missoula, MT: Wenger, 1993.

Carlsen, Wilmer. "The ramblings of Wilmer Carlsen." In *CPS Smokejumpers 1943 to 1946*, Vol. II. Ed. Roy E. Wenger. Missoula, MT: Wenger, 1993.

_____. "Wilmer Carlsen — Nine Mile." In *Static Lines and Canopies: Stories from the Smokejumpers in Civilian Public Service Camp No. 103*, ed. Asa Mundell. Beaverton, OR: Mundell, 1993.

Chatfield, Charles. *For Peace and Justice: Pacifism in America, 1914–1941.* Boston: Beacon Press, 1973.

Coffin, Joe. "Joe Coffin — Missoula — 1945." In *Static Lines and Canopies: Stories from the Smokejumpers in Civilian Public Service Camp No. 103*, ed. Asa Mundell. Beaverton, OR: Mundell, 1993.

_____. "Review and Preview." In *CPS Smokejumpers 1943 to 1946*, Vol. III. Ed. Roy E. Wenger. Missoula, MT: Wenger, 1995.

Cottrell, Robert C. *Roger Nash Baldwin and the American Civil Liberties Union.* Columbia University Press, 2001.

_____. *The Social Gospel of E. Nicholas Comfort: Founder of the Oklahoma School of Religion.* Norman: University of Oklahoma, 1997.

"CPS Provides Smoke Jumpers," *Smoke Jumper.*

CPS Smokejumpers 1943 to 1946. Volumes I-III. CPS Smokejumpers: Missoula.

Craig, Robert H. *Religion and Radical Politics: An Alternative Christian Tradition in the United States.* Philadelphia: Temple University Press, 1992.

"Draft Objections Bring Year Term." *Lexington Leader.* January 17, 1949.

Dubofsky, Melvyn. *We Shall Be All: A History of the Industrial Workers of the World.* New York: Quadrangle, 1969.

Federal Writers' Project of the Work Projects Administration for the State of Montana, *Montana: A State Guide Book*. New York: Viking Press, 1939.

Flaharty, Dick. "Dick Flaharty—Potlatch, Idaho-1945." In *Static Lines and Canopies: Stories from the Smokejumpers in Civilian Public Service Camp No. 103*, ed. Asa Mundell. Beaverton, OR: Mundell, 1993.

_____. "What Ever Happened to What's-His-Name?" In *CPS Smokejumpers 1943 to 1946*, Vol. III. Ed. Roy E. Wenger. Missoula, MT: Wenger, 1995.

Gingerich, Melvin. *Service for Peace*. Akron, PA.: Mennonite Central Committee, 1949.

Gorrell, Donald K. *The Age of Social Responsibility: The Age of the Social Gospel in the Progressive Era, 1900–1920*. Macon, GA: Mercer University Press, 1988.

Hebel, Lee. "By the Grace of God." In *CPS Smokejumpers 1943 to 1946*, Vol. I. Ed. Roy E. Wenger. Missoula, MT: Wenger, 1993.

_____. "Lee Hebel—Montana-Idaho Border—1945." In *Static Lines and Canopies: Stories from the Smokejumpers in Civilian Public Service Camp No. 103*, ed. Asa Mundell. Beaverton, OR: Mundell, 1993.

Helburn, Nicholas. "...Hitting the Silk." *Smoke Jumper*.

Inglis, Alan. "Alan Inglis." In *CPS Smokejumpers 1943 to 1946*, Vol. II. Ed. Roy E. Wenger. Missoula, MT: Wenger, 1993.

_____. "Alan Inglis—Missoula—1945." In *Static Lines and Canopies: Stories from the Smokejumpers in Civilian Public Service Camp No. 103*, ed. Asa Mundell. Beaverton, OR: Mundell, 1993.

Kauffman, David V. "Dr. David Kauffman—Big Prairie—1943." In *Static Lines and Canopies: Stories from the Smokejumpers in Civilian Public Service Camp No. 103*, ed. Asa Mundell. Beaverton, OR: Mundell, 1993.

Keim, Albert N. *The CPS Story: An Illustrated History of Civilian Public Service*. Intercourse, PA: Good Books, 1990.

_____. "Personal History of David V. Kauffman." *CPS Smokejumpers 1943 to 1946*. Volume II. "Labor." *Montana: A State Guide Book*. Compiled and written by the Federal Writers' Project of the Works Projects Administration for the State of Montana. New York: Viking Press, 1939.

Leavitt, George S. "Some Memories and Thoughts." In *CPS Smokejumpers 1943 to 1946*, Vol. II. Ed. Roy E. Wenger. Missoula, MT: Wenger, 1993.

Maclean, Norman. *Young Men and Fire*. Chicago: University of Chicago Press, 1993.

Matthews, Mark. "Trial by Fire," *Great Falls Tribune*. January 29, 1995.

Moody, Norman. Letter to author, July 27, 2002.

Painter, Robert. "Witness of a Quaker Physician: The Life Story of Robert H. Painter, M.D." In *CPS Smokejumpers 1943 to 1946*, Vol. I. Ed. Roy E. Wenger. Missoula, MT: Wenger, 1993.

_____, George Item, and Bill Laughlin. "...Torture Chamber." *Smoke Jumper*.

Palm and Cycad Times 6. June 2002.

Petty, Oliver. "Oliver Petty: Smokejumper and Beekeeper." In *CPS Smokejumpers 1943 to 1946*, Vol. III. Ed. Roy E. Wenger. Missoula, MT: Wenger, 1995.

_____. "Oliver Petty—Three Forks Station—1945." In *Static Lines and Canopies: Stories from the Smokejumpers in Civilian Public Service Camp No. 103*, ed. Asa Mundell. Beaverton, OR: Mundell, 1993.

Phifer, Greg. "Autobiographical Sketch." May 1998.

_____. "CPS Communique #9."

_____. "CPS Communique. August 1945.

_____. "CPS 50 Years After." In *CPS Smokejumpers 1943 to 1946*, Vol. III. Ed. Roy E. Wenger. Missoula, MT: Wenger, 1995.

_____. "From WHSS to COP to Iowa to FSU; A Stop at CPS 103." In *CPS Smokejumpers 1943 to 1946*, Vol. III. Ed. Roy E. Wenger. Missoula, MT: Wenger, 1995.

_____. "My Brush with History: CPS/USFS Smokejumpers."

_____. "A Smokejumper's Seven Training Jumps." Greg Phifer papers, Tallahassee, Florida.

_____. "Why I Joined the Smoke Jumper Unit." *Smoke Jumper.*

Phifer to Editor. *Smokejumper* 30. January 2001.

"Phil Stanley-Missoula-1943, 1944, 1947." *Static Lines and Canopies: Stories from the Smokejumpers in Civilian Public Service Camp No. 103*, ed. Asa Mundell. Beaverton, OR: Mundell, 1993.

Piepenburg, Roy. "Recollections and Reflections."

_____. "Roy Piepenburg — Meadow Creek, Nez Perce — 1945." In *Static Lines and Canopies: Stories from the Smokejumpers in Civilian Public Service Camp No. 103*, ed. Asa Mundell. Beaverton, OR: Mundell, 1993.

Pyne, Stephen J. *Fire in America: A Cultural History of Wildland and Rural Fire.* Seattle: University of Washington Press, 1997.

_____. *Year of the Fire: The Story of the Great Fires of 1910.* New York: Penguin, 2001.

Schmidt, Earl. "Reminiscences." In *CPS Smokejumpers 1943 to 1946*, Vol. I. Ed. Roy E. Wenger. Missoula, MT: Wenger, 1993.

_____. "Sabe Creek Fire, July 22, 1945." Earl Schmidt papers, Biglerville, Pennsylvania.

Smokejumper Oral History Project. University of Montana. 1984, 1986.

Spence, Clark C. Spence. *Montana: A History.* New York: Norton, 1978.

Stanley, Phil. "P. B. Stanley — Kiafeng to Missoula Continued." In *CPS Smokejumpers 1943 to 1946*, Vol. I. Ed. Roy E. Wenger. Missoula, MT: Wenger, 1993.

"That First Parachute Jump." *Smoke Jumper.*

Wenger, Florence E. "Teaching Was a Moving Experience." In *CPS Smokejumpers 1943 to 1946*, Vol. I. Ed. Roy E. Wenger. Missoula, MT: Wenger, 1993.

Wenger, Roy E. "All Decisions Have Their Consequences." In *CPS Smokejumpers 1943 to 1946*, Vol. I. Ed. Roy E. Wenger. Missoula, MT: Wenger, 1993.

_____. "How I Happened to Become the First Director of the CPS Smokejumpers Camp." In *Static Lines and Canopies: Stories from the Smokejumpers in Civilian Public Service Camp No. 103*, ed. Asa Mundell. Beaverton, OR: Mundell, 1993.

_____. "...This Is Our Country." *Smoke Jumper.*

_____. "Ted Lewis, a Day in the Life of or the Saga of the Sagging Sill." In *CPS Smokejumpers 1943 to 1946*, Vol. III. Ed. Roy E. Wenger. Missoula, MT: Wenger, 1995.

Wenger to Smoke Jumpers, July 5, 1943; August 3, 1945; December 30, 1943.

White, Ronald C. Jr., and C. Howard Hopkins, *The Social Gospel: Religion and Reform in Changing America.* Philadelphia: Temple University Press, 1976.

Wilson, Bill. "Into the Smoke to Put Out Fires." Roy Wenger Archives

Wittner, Lawrence S. *Rebels Against War: The American Peace Movement, 1941–1960.* New York: Columbia University Press, 1969.

Interviews by Author

Brunk, James R., July 16, 2002, Hungry Horse, Montana.

Carlsen, Wilmer, July 17, 2002, Hungry Horse, Montana.

Coffin, Audine, July 17, 2002, Hungry Horse, Montana.

Coffin, Joe, July 17, 2002, Hungry Horse, Montana.

Duffy, Susan, July 17, 2002, Hungry Horse, Montana.

Flaharty, Dick, September 9, 2001, Yuba City, California.

Hebel, Lee, July 17, 2002, Hungry Horse, Montana.

Inglis, Alan, July 16, 2002, Hungry Horse, Montana.
Kauffman, David V., July 18, 2002, Hungry Horse, Montana.
Leavitt, George S., July 17, 2002, Hungry Horse, Montana.
Lewis, Tedford, October 22, 2002.
Moody, Norman, July 17, 2002, Hungry Horse, Montana.
Painter, Robert H., July 17, 2002, Hungry Horse, Montana.
Petty, Oliver, July 16, 2002, Hungry Horse, Montana.
Phifer, Greg, July 17, 2002, Hungry Horse, Montana.
Piepenburg, Roy, July 18, 2002, Hungry Horse, Montana.
Schmidt, Earl, July 17, 2002, Hungry Horse, Montana.
_____, telephone interview, June 30, 2003.
Stanley, Phil, July 26, 2001, Polson, Montana.
_____, telephone interview, April 8, 2003.
Wenger, Roy, July 25, 2001, Missoula, Montana.
_____, July 26, 2001, Missoula, Montana.

Smokejumper Oral History Project Interviews, University of Montana

Farwell, Roxanne, with Wilmer Carlsen, August 29, 1984, Smokejumpers Oral History Project, OH #133–13.
_____, with Tedford Lewis, September 26, 1984, Smokejumpers Oral History Program, OH #133–59.
_____, with Phil Stanley, July 3, 1984, OH #133–99.
_____, with Roy Wenger, September 19, 1984, Smokejumpers Oral History Program, OH #133–113.
Lewis, Ted, with James R. Brunk, August 11, 1986, Smokejumpers Oral History Project, OH #163–31.
JN, with David B. Kauffman, August 16, 1984, Smokejumpers Oral History Project, OH #133–54.
Phifer, Gregg, with Oliver Petty, August 11, 1986, Smokejumpers Oral History Project, OH #163–30.
_____, with T. Richard Flaharty, August 11, 1986, Smokejumpers Oral History Program, OH #163–29.
_____, with Earl Schmidt, Smokejumpers Oral History Program, OH #163–11.
Stone, Rosa, with Joe and Audine Coffin, August 12, 1986, Smokejumpers Oral History Project, OH #163–19.
_____, with Lee Hebel, August 13, 1986, Smokejumpers Oral Project, OH #163–10.
_____, with Gregg Phifer, August 11, 1986, Smokejumpers Oral History Program, OH #163–21.Taylor, Kim, with George S. Leavitt, August 11, 1986, Smokejumpers Oral History Project, OH #163–7.
_____, with Robert Painter, August 12, 1986, Smokejumpers Oral History Program, OH #163–1.

Index